D0930027

PLACE IN RETURN BOX to remove this checkout from your record.
TO AVOID FINES return on or before date due.

DATE DUE	DATE DUE	DATE DUE

AS THE TWIG IS BENT . . .

AS THE TWIG IS BENT . . .

ESSAYS IN HONOUR OF FRITS VOS

EDITED BY

ERIKA DE POORTER

J.C. GIEBEN, PUBLISHER

AMSTERDAM 1990

This publication was made possible through the generous support of the
Isaac Alfred Ailion Foundation.

ISBN 90 5063 054 5 / Printed in The Netherlands

PREFACE

"As the twig is bent, so grows the tree."

This collection of articles on Japan, Korea and China is dedicated to Dr. Frits Vos, from 1958 to 1983 Professor of Japanese and Korean Language and Literature at Leiden University. They have been written by his disciples, who in publishing this book redeem a promise made long ago at the time of his retirement. Vos began his long career as a university teacher of Japanese in 1946, and from 1947 the teaching of Korean also was entrusted to him. With one exception, the writers of this book were his students in the sixties and early seventies, majoring in either Japanese, Korean or Chinese.

The imposing list of Vos's publications included in this volume testifies not only to his great productivity, which continues to the present day, but also to the diversity of his contributions to the study of Japan and Korea. His merits in the field of Korean studies, as the first professor of Korean in Western Europe, are well-known. As another indication of the variety of his interests and activities we may mention here his teaching of Ainu to interested students. In the broad range of his scholarly activities the influence of the old philological tradition of Oriental studies is clearly discernible. In this connection it may be illuminating to cite his own definition of the proper province of Japanese studies: "... I would like to preserve the term Japanology, but restrict its contents to the study of the language, literature and cultural history of Japan ... a study which will remain the indispensable base for a serious training in other disciplines related to Japan" ("Japanese Studies in the Netherlands", 1981, p. 66).

I think it is in these respects the diversity of subjects and the emphasis upon literary and cultural matters - that Vos has most strongly influenced the disciples who now follow in his footsteps at Leiden University and elsewhere. Perhaps in the old days, when students were still few in numbers and it was not so easy to visit the Far East, the personal influence of the teacher, the "Sensei", was greater than nowadays. Moreover, Frits Vos has always taken a personal interest in his students, those whose doctorates he supervised and those who became his junior colleagues in the growing staff of the Center for Japanese and Korean Studies. In any case the contributors are grateful to him for all that he has given them. They hope that these articles reflect the diversity of Japanese and Korean studies as they have developed under the influence and guidance of Frits Vos, so that the contents of this book may accord with its title.

March 1990   Erika de Poorter

CONTENTS

LIFE AND PUBLICATIONS OF FRITS VOS

Frits Vos was born on 6 November 1918 in Delft, the Netherlands. After attending a private primary school and the municipal grammar school (gymnasium) in his native city, he registered as a student of Chinese and Japanese at the University of Leiden in September 1937. There he obtained his B.A. (principal subject Chinese) on 24 June 1940. After the German occupying authorities had closed Leiden University, he obtained his M.A. on 10 October 1942 at the University of Utrecht (principal subject: Japanese, sub-subjects: Chinese philosophy and cultural anthropology). During the occupation period he was privately instructed in the Korean language by Dr. Johannes Rahder (the Leiden professor of Japanese, his teacher and predecessor) and Dr. Olaf Graf (a former Benedictine missionary at Wŏnsan).

From 1941 to 1943 he worked as assistant at the Sinological Institute, Leiden, and from 1943 to 1948 as assistant curator in the Japanese Department, National Museum of Ethnology, Leiden. On 1 March 1946 he was appointed lecturer in Japanese at the University of Leiden, the beginning of his long career as a university teacher.

After the outbreak of the Korean war, Vos went to Korea as captain for special services in the Netherlands Detachment of the United Nations forces, where he served from 1 October 1950 to 1 November 1951. The following six months (November 1951-April 1952) were spent in Japan on a UNESCO assignment. He assisted Dr. Jean Stoetzel (Bordeaux and Paris) who - in collaboration with a group of Japanese sociologists and the National Public Opinion Research Institute of Japan - made a study of the attitudes of youth in post-war Japan (see J. Stoetzel, *Jeunesse sans chrysanthème ni sabre: Études sur les attitudes de la jeunesse japonaise d'après guerre*, Paris, 1954). At the Indo-China and Korea Conference in Geneva Vos served as a Korea specialist in the Sixteen Nations Secretariat (April and May 1954).

On 12 July 1957 Vos took his doctor's degree at Leiden. His dissertation *A Study of the Ise-monogatari* gained him honours.

The next year (15 September 1958) he was appointed professor of Japanese and Korean studies.

He visited Japan and Korea many times in various capacities and lectured at universities there, as well as in Europe and the United States. A sabbatical year (1960-1961) was spent in Korea and Japan on a Rockefeller grant for the study of ancient Korean history and classical Japanese and Korean literature.

In the summer of 1963 he gave a series of lectures at the CIC (Committee on Institutional Cooperation) Far Eastern Language Institute, The University of Michigan, Ann Arbor.

On 30 November 1983 Vos retired, but as emeritus professor he remains active in the field of Japanese and Korean studies. He was visiting professor at Tōhoku University, Sendai (1983-1984) and at the National Institute of Japanese Literature (Kokubungaku Kenkyū Shiryōkan), Tōkyō (1985-1986).

During his distinguished career Vos has received may honours. In the Netherlands he was created Knight in the Order of the Netherlands Lion (Ridder in de Orde van de Nederlandse Leeuw, 1983). Japan awarded him the Order of the Sacred Treasure (*Zuihōshō*), 3rd class (1973) and the Order of the Rising Sun (*Kyokujitsushō*), 3rd class (1983), and Korea honoured him with the Order of Diplomatic Service Merits (*Sungnyejang*), 3rd class (1974). For his service in the Korean war he was given the Cross for Freedom and Justice (Kruis voor Vrijheid en Recht), the Korean War Medal and the United Nations Service Medal (1951). Moreover he shared the U.S. Presidential Unit Citation (twice) and the Korean Unit Citation (1951).

In 1984 he received the cultural prize of Ōsaka Prefecture (Yamagata Bantō Shō) and in 1985 he was created Permanent Visiting Professor of the Faculty of Letters, Tōhoku University, Sendai. Last but not least, Frits Vos is an honorary member of the Association for Korean Studies in Europe, the Netherlands Association for Japanese Studies and the European Association for Japanese Studies.

Books and articles

1. "Hendrick Hamel, Dutchman in Korea: From the Authentic Records of the Yi Dynasty", *The Voice of Korea* V, 108 (Washington D.C., 1948), pp. 1-3.

2. "Knighthood: Translation of the Chapter Shidō from Saitō Setsudō's *Shidō Yōron*", *Orientalia Neerlandica, A Volume of Oriental Studies*, Leiden, 1948, pp. 468-483.

3. "Enige Mededelingen over Japanse Zwaardstootplaten" (=Some remarks concerning Japanese *tsuba*), *Bulletin van de Vereeniging voor Japansche Grafiek en Kleinkunst* 2nd ser., 6,7,8 (Groningen, 1948), pp. 81-129.

4. "Een meesterwerk der Japanse filmindustrie: Rashomon" (=A masterpiece of the Japanese motion-picture industry: Rashomon), *De Groene Amsterdammer* (Amsterdam, 2 May 1953), pp. 9, 11.

5. "Kim Yusin, Persönlichkeit und Mythos: Ein Beitrag zur Kenntnis der altkoreanischen Geschichte", *Oriens Extremus* I, 1 (Wiesbaden, 1954), pp. 29-70 and II, 2 (Wiesbaden, 1955), pp. 210-236.

6. "De betrekkingen tussen China en Korea in het perspectief der geschiedenis" (=The relations between China and Korea in historical perspective), *Internationale Spectator* IX, 15 (The Hague, 1955), pp. 491-508.

7. "Yoshida en Hatoyama: Enige aspecten van de ontwikkelingen in het na-oorlogse Japan" (=Yoshida and Hatoyama: some aspects of the developments in post-war Japan), *Internationale Spectator* IX, 19 (The Hague, 1955), pp. 615-632.

8. *A Study of the Ise-monogatari with the Text according to the Den-Teika-hippon and an Annotated Translation*, 2 vols., The Hague, 1957.

9. "Letteratura coreana", *Le Civiltà dell'Oriente* II (Roma, 1957), pp. 1025-1042.

10. "Religioni e filosofia della Corea", *Le Civiltà dell' Oriente* III (Roma, 1958), pp. 1081-1099.

11. *Volken van Eén Stam? Enige Beschouwingen over de Problemen van een Koreaans-Japanse Cultuur- en Taalverwantschap* (= Peoples of common descent? Some observations concerning cultural and linguistic ties between Korea and Japan), The Hague, 1959.

12. "De 'Hollandse Wetenschap' in Japan" (= "Dutch science" in Japan), *350 Jaar Nederland-Japan*, Rotterdam, 1959, pp. 30-40.

13. "Iets over Nederlandse woorden in het Japans" (= Some remarks on Dutch words in Japanese), *ibidem*, pp. 40-42.

14. "Yŏn'am Pak Chiwŏn und sein Hŏ-saeng chŏn", *Koreanica: Festschrift Professor Dr. Andre Eckardt zum 75. Geburtstag*, Baden-Baden, 1960, pp. 35-57.

15. "Wolkendroom en Lentegeur: Een Beschouwing over het Karakter van de Traditionele Koreaanse Roman" (= Cloud Dream and Spring Fragrance: a study of the characteristics of the traditional Korean novel), *Forum der Letteren* I, 2 (Leiden, 1960), pp. 121-133.

16. "Han'guk kungminsŏng-ŭi p'yohyŏn-ŭrosŏ-ŭi sijo" (= The *sijo* as an expression of the Korean national character), *Hyŏndae munhak* VII, 1 (Seoul, 1961), pp. 273-283.

17. "De recente politieke ontwikkelingen in Zuid-Korea" (= Recent political developments in South Korea), *Internationale Spectator* XV, 21 (The Hague, 1961), pp. 577-594.

18. "Oriental Studies in the Netherlands", *The Korean Research Center Seminars Series* I (Seoul, 1962), pp. 110-132.

19. "Historical Survey of Korean Language Studies", *Papers of the CIC Far Eastern Language Institute*, Ann Arbor: The University of Michigan, 1963, pp. 11-21.

20. "Korean Writing: the Hyang'ga", *ibidem*, pp. 23-28.

21. "Korean Writing: Idu and Han'gŭl", *ibidem*, pp. 29-34.

22. "History of the Korean Language", *ibidem*, pp. 35-44.

23. "Korean Language and Culture", *ibidem*, pp. 127-136.

24. "The Yangban-jeon and Some Reflections on the Fate of Korea", *Tongbang Hakchi* VII (Seoul, 1963), pp. 175-199.

25. "Living through Art and the Art of Living", *Felix Tikotin zum siebzigsten Geburtstag*, Basel, 1963, pp. 1-3.

26. "Dutch Influences on the Japanese Language (with an Appendix on Dutch Words in Korean)", *Lingua* XII, 4 (Amsterdam, 1963), pp. 341-388.

27. (In collaboration with E. Zürcher:) *Spel zonder snaren: Enige beschouwingen over Zen* (= Music without strings: some observations concerning Zen), Deventer, 1964.

28. "De 'derde macht' in Japan: het politiek Boeddhisme van de Sōka-gakkai" (= The "third power" in Japan: political Buddhism of Sōka-gakkai), *Internationale Spectator* XVIII, 17 (The Hague/Brussels, 1964), pp. 459-476.

29. "In Japan leeft het oude naast het nieuwe voort" (= In Japan old and new exist side by side), *De Kern, Elseviers Maandblad* XXXIV, 10 (Amsterdam/Brussels, 1964), pp. 20-30.

30. "Het Bal" (= The ball; Dutch translation of Akutagawa Ryūnosuke's *Butōkai*), *ibidem*, pp. 39-45.

31. "Droomkarper" (= Dream-carp; Dutch translation of Ueda Akinari's *Muō no rigyo*, adapted by J. Besançon), *Yang* II,2 (Ghent/Utrecht, 1964), pp. 3-9.

32. "Een ontmoeting in de nacht" (= A meeting in the night) and "De wraak van de slang" (= The snake's revenge) (Dutch translations of a Chinese and a Korean tale, adapted by J. Besançon), *Manifest* V, 3 (Eindhoven, 1964).

33. "Koreaanse Literatuur" (= Korean literature), *Moderne Encyclopedie der Wereldliteratuur* IV, Ghent, 1966, pp. 497-506.

34. "Het Boeddhisme in Japan" (= Buddhism in Japan), *Rondom het Woord* VIII, 4 (Hilversum, 1966), pp. 225-233.

35. "Shinto, de 'weg der goden' in Japan" (= Shinto, the "way of the gods" in Japan), *Correspondentieblad de Christelijke Onderwijzer* XIII (The Hague, 1967), 34, pp. 957-958; 35, pp. 990-991; 38, pp. 1076-1078; 40, pp. 1136-1138.

36. "Rotterdam and the earliest Dutch-Japanese relations", *Rotterdam-Europoort-Delta* (Rotterdam, 1969), pp. 9-10.

37. "La letteratura coreana", *Storia della Letteratura d'Oriente* IV, Milano, 1969, pp. 759-830.

38. Translations of Korean poetry in M. Muccioli, *La letteratura giapponese/la letteratura coreana*, Milano, 1969 and R. Beviglia & A. Tamburello, *Antologia delle letterature coreana e giapponese*, Milano, 1970.

39. "Japan in heden en verleden" (= Japan, in past and present), *Intermediair* VI, I (Amsterdam, 1970), pp. 1-5, 57-65.

40. "De Ontwikkelingsgang der Japanse Cultuur" (= The development of Japanese culture), *Spiegel Historiael* V, 3 (Bussum, 1970), pp. 131-137.

41. "Het 'Ik' en de 'Weg' in Japan" (= The "I" and the "Way" in Japan), *ibidem*, pp. 144-150.

42. "Taal, schrift en letterkunde van Japan" (= Language, writing and literature of Japan), *Intermediair* VI, 22 (Amsterdam, 1970).

43. "Nippon Ontwaakt" (= Nippon awakes), *Bericht van de Tweede Wereldoorlog* II, 25 (Amsterdam, 1970), pp. 677-678.

44. "De Japanse Politiek in Azië" (= Japanese policy in Asia), *ibidem*, pp. 679-682.

45. "De Opkomst van het Supernationalisme" (=The rise of supernationalism), *ibidem*, pp. 683-686.

46. Twelve translations of Korean, Japanese and Chinese tales of mystery adapted by Jacques Besançon in *De wraak van de slang en andere oude verhalen uit Korea, Japan en China* (=The snake's revenge and other old tales from Korea, Japan and China), Laren (Nh.), 1970.

47. "Taal, schrift en letterkunde van Korea" (=Language, writing and literature of Korea), *Intermediair* VII, 14 (Amsterdam, 1971).

48. "Forgotten Foibles: Love and the Dutch at Dejima (1641-1854)", *Asien Tradition und Fortschritt: Festschrift für Horst Hammitzsch zu seinem 60. Geburtstag*, Wiesbaden, 1971, pp. 614-633.

49. "De Binnenlandse Situatie in Japan in 1944: Het Jaar van de Slechte Rammenas" (=The interior situation of Japan in 1944: the year of the bad black radish), *Bericht van de Tweede Wereldoorlog* LXXI, 5 (Amsterdam, 1971), pp. 1985-1987.

50. "The Rôle of Women in Tokugawa Classicism", *Acta Orientalia Neerlandica*, Leiden, 1971, pp. 206-213.

51. "De Jaren 1960-1970" (=The years 1960-1970), a chapter added to Richard Storry, *Japan: de opkomst van een wereldmacht*, Utrecht/Antwerpen, 1971 (the Dutch translation of *A History of Modern Japan*), pp. 257-267.

52. "Van beschermgod tot souvenir: de Changseung in Korea" (=From tutelary deity to souvenir: the *changsŭng* in Korea), *Verre Naasten Naderbij* V, 2 (The Hague, 1971), pp. 33-44.

53. "Japan tegen het Einde van de Oorlog: Nederlaag in Zicht" (=Japan by the end of the war: defeat in sight), *Bericht van de Tweede Wereldoorlog* XCIV, 6 (Amsterdam, 1971), pp. 2611-2614.

54. "De problemen rond Okinawa in historisch perspectief"
     (= The problems around Okinawa in historical perspective),
     Civis Mundi X, 11/12 (The Hague, 1971), pp. 458-467.

55. "De Amerikaanse Democratiseringspolitiek in Japan" (= The
     American democratization policy in Japan), *Onze jaren 45-
     70* 21 (Amsterdam, 1972), pp. 643-646.

56. "Zen en het Westen" (= Zen and the West), *Toekomst van
     de religie: religie van de toekomst?*, Nijmegen, 1972, pp.
     122-133.

57. "Yaesu kara porudā made" (= From Jan Joosten to polder),
     Bungei shunjū L, 11 (Tōkyō, 1972), pp. 82-84.

58. "De traditionele vormen van dramatische kunst in Korea"
     (= Traditional forms of the dramatic arts in Korea), *Forum
     der Letteren* XIII, 4 (Leiden, 1972), pp. 9-31.

59. "De Verlichting in Zen: het ontdekken van de eigen Boed-
     dha-natuur" (= Enlightenment in Zen: the discovery of one's
     own Buddha-nature), *Oosterse filosofie*, Amsterdam/Brussels,
     1973, pp. 52-65.

60. "A Distance of Thirteen Thousand Miles: The Dutch
     Through Japanese Eyes", *Delta: A Review of Arts Life and
     Thought in the Netherlands* XVI, 2 (Amsterdam, 1973), pp.
     29-46.

61. "Maatschappij als spinneweb: Het naoorlogse cultuurpatroon
     van Japan" (= Society as a cobweb: cultural patterns in
     post-war Japan), *Onze jaren 45-70* 85 (Amsterdam, 1973),
     pp. 2712-2714.

62. "Zengakoeren Banzai: De Studentenrevoltes in Japan" (= Zen-
     gakuren Banzai: student revolts in Japan), *Onze jaren 45-
     70* 98 (Amsterdam, 1973), pp. 3126-3129.

63. "De Ainu: De geschiedenis van een volk zonder geschiede-
     nis" (= The Ainu: history of a people without history), *Han-
     delingen van het tweeëndertigste Nederlands Filologencon-
     gres*, Amsterdam, 1974, pp. 306-308.

64. "Oranda ni okeru Kankokugaku kenkyū" (= Korean Studies in the Netherlands), *The Han* IV, 10 (Tōkyō, 1975), pp. 55-63.

65. "El Zen y occidente" (= Zen and the West), *El futuro de la religion*, Salamanca, 1975, pp. 151-168.

66. "De mystiek van het Zen" (= Mysticism in Zen), *Over Mystiek*, Groningen, 1975, pp. 7-18.

67. "Master Eibokken on Korea and the Korean Language: Supplementary Remarks to Hamel's Narrative", *Transactions of the Korea Branch of the Royal Asiatic Society* L (Seoul, 1975), pp. 7-42.

68. "Japanese and Korean Studies Past and Present", *Higher Education and Research in the Netherlands, Nuffic Bulletin* 19, 4 (The Hague, 1975), pp. 8-12 (simultaneously published in Spanish under the title "El estudio del Japones y el Coreano: Antano y Ahora").

69. Myth-making in the Democratic People's Republic of Korea", *Asian Perspectives* 2 (The Hague, 1976), pp. 8-15.

70. "The Dutch through Japanese Eyes", *Introducing Japan: History, Way of life, Creative world, Seen and heard, Food and wine*, Kent, 1976, pp. 34-37.

71. "HUNG Ying-ming", *Dictionary of Ming Biography 1368-1644* I, New York and London, 1976, pp. 678-679.

72. "Hollanders als curiosa" (= The Dutch as rarities), in J. van Tooren, *Senryū - De waterwilgen: Vierhonderdnegentig senryū-gedichten*, Amsterdam, 1976, pp. 131-136.

73. "Wakker Nippon: De geschiedenis van Japan vanaf de Russisch-Japanse oorlog tot 1918" (= Vigilant Japan: the history of Japan from the Russo-Japanese war to 1918), *14-18 de eerste wereldoorlog* (Amsterdam, 1976), pp. 846-850.

74. "Japan in beweging: De ontwikkelingen in Japan in 1918 en de eerste helft van 1919" (= Japan in movement: the devel-

opments in Japan in 1918 and the first half of 1919), *14-18 de eerste wereldoorlog* (Amsterdam, 1976), pp. 1777-1780.

75. "Taal- en letterkunde in Japan" (= Language and literature in Japan), *Prana* 7 (Deventer, 1977), pp. 4-16.

76. "350 Jaar Nederland-Korea" (= 350 years of Dutch-Korean contacts), *Gids voor Korea*, Seoul, 1977, pp. 147-162.

77. *Die Religionen Koreas*, Stuttgart/Berlin/Köln/Mainz, 1977.

78. "Onze voorouders in Japan: Handel, wetenschap en liefde" (= Our ancestors in Japan: trade, science and love), *De Gids* 141, 4/5 (Amsterdam, 1978), pp. 215-226.

79. "De Japanse taal" (= The Japanese language), *ibidem*, pp. 261-268.

80. "De Ainu: de geschiedenis van een volk zonder geschiedenis" (= The Ainu: history of a people without history), *ibidem*, pp. 332-341.

81. *Liefde rond, liefde vierkant: Bloemlezing uit de sijo-pöezie* (= Love round, love square: anthology of *sijo* poetry), Amsterdam, 1978 (*De Oosterse Bibliotheek* 7).

82. "Het Ontdekken van de Eigen Boeddha-natuur: De Plotselinge Verlichting in Zen" (= The discovery of one's own Buddha-nature: the sudden enlightenment in Zen), *Concilium* XIV, 6: *Boeddhisme en Christendom* (Amersfoort, 1978), pp. 35-44 (simultaneously published in French, Spanish, Italian, Portuguese and German under the titles: "L'homme et la découverte de sa nature de Bouddha: l'illumination soudaine dans le Zen", "La iluminación subita en el Zen", "La scoperta della propria natura Buddha: la repentina illuminazione nello Zen", "A Descoberta da Verdadeira Natureza de Buda: A Súbita Iluminação no Zen", "Die Entdeckung der eigenen Buddha-Natur: Die plötzliche Erleuchtung im Zen").

83. "Dutch Words in Kimono: Dutch Influences on the Japanese Language", *Philipp Franz von Siebold: A Contribution to*

the Study of the Historical Relations between Japan and the Netherlands, Leiden, 1978, pp. 41-50.

84. "Yŏksa-wa chŏnt'ongsog-ŭi Kim Yusin" (= Kim Yusin in history and tradition), *Minjoksa-ŭi inyŏm (Kŭ chŏngt'ong-gwa hyangbang): chesamch'a t'ongil munje kukche haksul hoeŭirok*, Seoul, 1978, pp. 79-103.

85. "De Japanse en Koreaanse verhaaltraditie" (= Traditional narration in Japan and Korea), *Volksverhalen: sprookjes, fabels, mythen, sagen, legenden en gezongen vertellingen* II, Utrecht: Rijksuniversiteit, 1978, pp. 46-64.

86. "Korea van de oudste tijd tot heden" (= Korea from prehistory until the present), *Universele Wereldgeschiedenis* XI, The Hague/Hasselt, 1978, pp. 117-142.

87. "Japan sedert 1941" (= Japan since 1941), *Universele Wereldgeschiedenis* XI, The Hague/Hasselt, 1978, pp. 143-161.

88. "Japan in Transition: some additional observations", *Japan in Transition: some views on the impact of the Meiji Restoration on the modernization of Japan* II, Leiden, 1979, pp. 33-38.

89. "The Role of Shintō as an Acting and Reacting Factor in the Process of Accelerated Social Change During the Meiji Era", *ibidem*, pp. 39-52.

90. "Tung-fang Shuo, Buffoon and Immortal, in Japan and Korea", *Oriens Extremus* XXVI, 1/2 (Wiesbaden, 1979), pp. 189-203.

91. "Le Ts'ai-ken t'an (Ch'aegŭndam) en Corée", *Mélanges de coréanologie offerts à M. Charles Haguenauer*, Paris, 1979, pp. 89-99.

92. *Van keurslijfjes en keesjes, bosschieters en lijfschutten: onze voorouders in Japan en Korea en het begin der Japanse en Koreaanse studiën in Nederland* (= Our ancestors in Japan and Korea and the beginning of Japanese and Dutch studies in the Netherlands), Leiden, 1980.

93. "Doeff, Tablada, Couchoud en andere Westerse Haijin" (=Doeff, Tablada, Couchoud and other western *haijin*), *Over Haiku Gesproken*, Utrecht, 1980, pp. 9-18.

94. "Korean Studies in the Netherlands: Past and Present", *Papers of the 1st International Conference on Korean Studies*, Söngnam: The Academy of Korean Studies, 1980, pp. 115-138.

95. "Japanse Literatuur" (=Japanese literature), *Moderne Encyclopedie van de Wereldliteratuur* IV, Haarlem/Antwerpen, 1980, pp. 374-382.

96. "Japanese Studies in The Netherlands", *Modern Relations between Japan and The Netherlands*, Leiden, 1981, pp. 52-67.

97. "Schoonheidservaring in de Japanse en Koreaanse poëzie" (=The aesthetic sense in Japanese and Korean poetry), *Vuursteen* I, 2 (Schiedam, 1981), pp. 15-23.

98. "Een stout meisje en een lief meisje in the Heian-literatuur" (=A naughty girl and a sweet girl in Heian literature), *Women in Japanese Literature*, Leiden, 1981, pp. 7-26.

99. "Tales of the Extraordinary: An Inquiry into the Contents, Nature and Authorship of the *Sui chŏn*", *Korean Studies* V (Honolulu, 1981), pp. 1-25.

100. "The Princess from Ayodhyā: Indian Names and Sanskrit Words in the *Samguk yusa*", *Papers Presented at the 6th Annual Conference of AKSE, held in Seoul, Korea, August 2-5, 1982*, Seoul, 1982, pp. 169-182 and 429-438 (Korean text).

101. "Koreaanse Literatuur" (=Korean literature), *Moderne Encyclopedie van de Wereldliteratuur* IV, Haarlem/Antwerpen, 1982, pp. 497-506.

102. "The Study of Korean Literature in Europe", *Korea Journal* XXII, 10 (Seoul, 1982), pp. 42-51.

103. "Inleiding tot de *kyōka*, de 'gekke' tanka" (= Introduction to *kyōka*, the "funny" tanka), *Vuursteen* II, 4 (Leuven, 1982), pp. 17-27.

104. "A Meeting between Dutchmen and Koreans in 1828", *Korea Journal* XXIII, 1 (Seoul, 1983), pp. 4-12.

105. "Les relations historiques entre le Japon et les Pays-Bas", *Septentrion: Revue de la culture néerlandaise* XII, 2 (Rekkem/Raamsdonkveer, 1983), pp. 24-31.

106. "Het dagelijks leven der Nederlanders op Deshima" (= Daily life of the Dutch on Deshima), *Vier Eeuwen Nederland-Japan*, Lochem, 1983, pp. 19-25.

107. "De Nederlandse taal in Japan" (= The Dutch language in Japan), *ibidem*, pp. 57-64.

108. *Met de neus op de rand: speurend naar de* p *in* ōgi (= With the nose on the rim: in search of the *p* in *ōgi*), Leiden, 1983.

109. "Nichiran no yoake wa kōshite..." (= The dawn of the relations between Japan and the Netherlands was as follows...), *Windmill* (*KLM Oranda Kōkū kinaishi*), Tōkyō, 1983, no. 7, pp. 8-9; no. 8, pp. 8-9; no. 9, pp. 10-11.

110. Six articles in the Kodansha Encyclopedia of Japan (Tōkyō, 1983: a. "Ariwara no Narihira" (I, pp. 85b-86a); b. "Ise monogatari" (III, pp. 337a-b); c. "Netherlands and Japan, Modern Period" (V, pp. 362b-363a); d. "Saikontan" (VI, p. 371a); e. "Siebold, Philipp Franz von" (VII, pp. 192b-193a); f. "Western learning" (VIII, pp. 241a-243a).

111. "*Meishin hōkan* ni tsuite" (= The *Ming-hsin pao-chien*), *Tōhoku Daigaku Nihon bunka kenkyūjo kenkyū hōkoku* 21 (Sendai, 1985), pp. 1-15.

112. "A 400-Year Relationship: The Netherlands and Japan", *Look Japan* 348 (Tōkyō, 1985), pp. 22-23, 26.

113. "Roman to shite no *Ochikubo monogatari*" (= The *Ochikubo monogatari* as a novel), *Kokusai Nihon bungaku kenkyū shūkai kaigiroku* 9 (Tōkyō: Kokubungaku kenkyū shiryōkan, 1985), pp. 70-88.

114. "Van kok tot polder: Nederlandse woorden in kimono" (= From kok to polder: Dutch words in kimono), *Onze Taal* LIV, 5 (Amsterdam, 1985), pp. 50-52.

115. "Nihongaku to watakushi" (= Japanology and I) in Arisaka Takamichi (ed.), *Nihon yōgakushi no kenkyū* VII, Ōsaka: Sōgensha, 1985, pp. 3-15. Republished in *Yamagata Bantō-shō no kiseki*, compiled by the Osaka Prefectural Government, Ōsaka, 1989, pp. 111-132.

116. "Seiyō no haijin" (= Haiku poets of the West), *Nihon yōgakushi no kenkyū* VII, Ōsaka: Sōgensha, 1985, pp. 17-26.

117. "*Yūsenkutsu* to *Sai Chien den*" (= *Yu hsien-k'u* and *Ch'oe Ch'iwŏn chŏn*), *Chōsen gakuhō* CXIX/CXX (Tenri, 1986), pp. 569-580.

118. "Les relations historiques entre la Corée et les Pays-Bas", *Septentrion: Revue de la culture néerlandaise* XV, 2 (Rekkem/Raamsdonkveer, 1986), pp. 29-36.

119. "Oranda ni okeru Nihon bungaku kenkyū to honyaku ni tsuite" (= The study and translation of Japanese literature in the Netherlands), *Kokubungaku kenkyū shiryōkan hō* 27 (Tōkyō, 1986), pp. 1-4.

120. "Haiku: dichtkunst in harmonie met het eindige" (= Haiku: poetry in harmony with the finite), *Preludium: Concertgebouwnieuws* (Amsterdam, March 1987), pp. 2-6.

121. "Wakon Yōsai - Japanese spirit and Western achievement", *Meiji: Japanese art in transition*, The Hague, 1987, pp. 11-20.

122. "Japanese Loan Words in Ainu", *Rocznik Orientalistyczny* XLVI, 5 (Warsaw, 1987), pp. 171-182.

123. "*Ochikubo monogatari* no goi: Toku ni Kango, ninshō dai-meishi, iwayuru ninshō daimeishi wo megutte" (= The vocab-ulary of the *Ochikubo monogatari*: particularly the Chinese words, the personal pronouns and so-called personal pro-nouns), *Kokubungaku kenkyū shiryōkan kiyō* XIII (Tōkyō, 1987), 1-22.

124. "Japanse Historiografie" (= Japanese historiography), *Tussen traditie en wetenschap: Geschiedbeoefening in niet-westerse culturen*, Nijmegen, 1987, pp. 37-66.

125. "Koreaanse Historiografie" (= Korean historiography), *ibidem*, pp. 77-101.

126. *Als dauw op alsembladeren: Het levensverhaal van een Japanse vrouw uit de elfde eeuw* (= Like dew on mugwort leaves: the life-story of an 11th century Japanese woman; Dutch translation of the *Sarashina nikki*), Amsterdam, 1988.

127. "Shīboruto zatsuwa" (= Some remarks on Ph. Fr. von Sie-bold), *Siebold Kenkyū: Bulletin of the Von Siebold Society of Hosei University* 5 (Tōkyō, March 1988), pp. 1-11.

128. "Chūgoku sennin no gaiyū - Nihon to Chōsen bungaku ni okeru Tōbō Saku" (= The peregrinations of a Chinese immortal - Tung-fang Shuo in Japanese and Korean litera-ture), *Nihon Tōhoku Daigaku Nihon bunka kenkyūjo hōkoku*, special issue (Sendai, 1988), pp. 47-58.

129. "Latent Dutch, a Precious Treasure and Master Lonely Cloud", *Papers of the 5th International Conference on Korean Studies* I, Sŏngnam, 1988, pp. 20-34.

130. "Die Mythologie der Koreaner", *Wörterbuch der Mythologie*, Stuttgart, 1988, pp. 389-435.

131. "Mihatenu yume - An unfinished dream: Japanese studies until 1940", *Leiden Oriental Connections 1850-1940*, Lei-den/New York/København/Köln, 1989, pp. 354-377.

132. "Yōroppa no Tōyō gogaku kotohajime" (= The beginnings of Far Eastern language studies in Europe), *Nihon Tōhoku*

Daigaku Nihon bunka kenkyūjo kenkyū hōkoku XXV (Sendai, 1989), pp. 1-18.

133. *Doppo Kunikida: De fatalist en andere verhalen* (= The fatalist and other stories; Dutch translation of stories by Kunikida Doppo), Amsterdam, 1989. Reprinted from this book were: "Lentevogel" (= Spring bird) in *Avenue* XXIV, 10 (Amsterdam, 1989), pp. 161-167, and "Jongensverdriet" (= A boy's sorrows) in *Knippenbergs Krant* 1989, no. 10 (Amsterdam), pp. 27-30.

134. "Waarom honden niet spreken: De Ainu en hun letterkunde" (= Why dogs do not talk: the Ainu and their literature), *Kunst & cultuur* (Brussels, November 1989), pp. 6-11.

135. "De kok, de hors d'oeuvre en een hele halve zondag: Nederlandse en Franse leenwoorden in het Japans", *Oranda: De Nederlanden in Japan (1600-1868)*, Brussels, 1989, pp. 51-68. Simultaneously published in French under the title "Le chef coq, le hors-d'oeuvre et un 'demi-dimanche entier'", *Oranda: Les Pays-Bas au Japon*, Brussels, 1989, pp. 51-69.

136. "A Chinese book in Korean disguise: some problems concerning the *Myŏngsim pogam*", *Twenty Papers on Korean Studies offered to Prof. W.E. Skillend*, *Cahiers d'études coréennes* 5 (Paris, 1989), pp. 327-350.

137. "Portuguese loan words in Japanese", *Bruno Lewin zu Ehren: Festschrift aus Anlass seines 65. Geburtstages* I, Bochum, 1989, pp. 369-401.

138. "Korea: I. Religionsgeschichtlich" (= Concise history of Korean religion), *Theologische Realenzyklopädie* XIX, 3/4 (Berlin/ New York, 1990), pp. 610-615.

Book reviews

1. Mirok Li, *Der Yalu Fliesst: Eine Jugend in Korea* in *The Voice of Korea* VI, 137 (Washington D.C., 1949), pp. 2-3.

2. Charles Haguenauer, *Morphologie du japonais moderne, I, Généralités: Mots invariables*, Paris, 1951 in *T'oung Pao* XLII (Leiden, 1954), pp. 341-344.

3. Peter Hartmann, *Einige Grundzüge des japanischen Sprachbaues. Gezeigt an den Ausdrücken für das Sehen*, Heidelberg, 1952 in *Orientalistische Literaturzeitung* 49 (Berlin/Leipzig, 1954), pp. 461-464.

4. John W. Hall, *Japanese History: A Guide to Japanese Reference and Research Materials*, Ann Arbor: University of Michigan Press, 1954 in *T'oung Pao* XLIII (Leiden, 1955), pp. 402-403.

5. Herschel Webb, *An Introduction to Japan*, New York, 1955, *ibidem*, pp. 403-404.

6. Johannes Laures, *Takayama Ukon und die Anfänge der Kirche in Japan*, Münster, 1954, *ibidem*, pp. 404-406.

7. J.L. Pierson, *The Manyôsú, Translated and Annotated, Book VIII*, Leiden, 1954, *ibidem*, pp. 406-408.

8. *Korean Studies Guide* by B.H. Hazard et al., Berkeley and Los Angeles, 1954, *ibidem*, pp. 408-431.

9. *A Selected List of Books and Articles on Japan in English, French and German, Revised and Enlarged*, Cambridge (Mass.), 1954 in *T'oung Pao* XLIV (Leiden, 1956), pp. 296-298.

10. Joan V. Underwood, *Concise English-Korean Dictionary Romanized*, Vermont/Tōkyō, 1954 in *Lingua* V (Amsterdam, 1956), pp. 306-307.

11. G.J. Ramstedt, *Studies in Korean Etymology* II, edited by Penti Aalto (*Mémoires de la Société Finno-Ougrienne* XCV,

2), Helsinki, 1953 in *Lingua* VI (Amsterdam, 1956), pp. 108-109.

12. L. Broom and John I. Kitsuse, *The Managed Casualty: The Japanese-American Family in World War II*, Berkeley, 1956; Chitoshi Yanaga, *Japanese People and Politics*, New York, 1956 in *The Sociological Review* New Series, V, 1 (Keele, Staffordshire, 1957), pp. 154-156.

13. Charles Haguenauer, *Origines de la civilisation japonaise: Introduction à l'étude de la préhistoire du Japon*, Paris, 1956 in *T'oung Pao* XLVI (Leiden, 1958), pp. 452-456.

14. Henry van Straelen, *The Religion of Divine Wisdom: Japan's Most Powerful Religious Movement*, Kyōto, 1957, *ibidem*, pp. 457-462.

15. *Sino-Japonica. Festschrift André Wedemeyer zum 80. Geburtstag*, Leipzig, 1956 in *Orientalistische Literaturzeitung* 54 (Berlin/Leipzig, 1959), pp. 418-424.

16. Kazuo Kawai, *Japan's American Interlude*, Chicago: The University of Chicago Press, 1960 in *T'oung Pao* XLVIII (Leiden, 1961), pp. 480-482.

17. Peter H. Lee, *Kranich am Meer: Koreanische Gedichte*, München, 1959 and Peter H. Lee, *Studies in the Saenaennorae: Old Korean Poetry*, Roma, 1959, *ibidem*, pp. 482-487.

18. F.J. Junker, *Ki-san. Alte koreanische Bilder, Landschaften und Volksleben*, Leipzig, 1958 in *Oriens* XVII (Leiden, 1964), pp. 280-281.

19. "Rechter op Snijtafel: Historische Fouten bij Bertus Aafjes" (= A judge on the dissecting table: Historical Errors in Bertus Aafjes' Ōoka series), *Algemeen Dagblad* 1 May 1971.

20. "Bergamini's boek over Hirohito is geïnspireerd door haat" (= Bergamini's book on Hirohito is inspired by hatred: review of David Bergamini, *Japan's Imperial Conspiracy*, London, 1971), *Trouw* 11 December 1971.

21. Kim Dong-uk, *History of Korean Literature*, transl. by Leon Hurvitz, Tōkyō, 1980 in *Korea Journal* XX, 1 (Seoul, 1982), pp. 70-71.

22. J. van Tooren, *Tanka: het lied van Japan*, Amsterdam, 1983 in *Vuursteen* III, 3 (Bilthoven/Overijse, 1983), pp. 110-115.

23. Noriko de Vroomen en Leo de Ridder, *De zomermaan en andere Japanse kettingverzen uit de school van Matsuo Bashō*, Amsterdam, 1984 in *Vuursteen* V, 2 (Leuven, 1985), pp. 72-79.

24. Hung Ying-ming, *The Roots of Wisdom: Saikontan*, transl. by William Scott Wilson, Tōkyō, New York & San Francisco, 1985 in *Journal of Asian Studies* XLV, 3 (Ann Arbor, Mich., 1986), pp. 600-602.

25. Eberhard Friese, *Philipp Franz von Siebold als früher Exponent der Ostasienwissenschaften. Ein Beitrag zur Orientalismusdiskussion und zur Geschichte der europäisch-japanischen Begegnung (Berliner Beiträge zur sozial- und wirtschaftswissenschaftlichen Japan-Forschung* XV), Bochum, 1983 in *Siebold Kenkyū: Bulletin of the Von Siebold Society of Hosei University* 5 (Tōkyō, March 1988), pp. 52-55.

26. Grant K. Goodman, *Japan: The Dutch Experience*, London and Dover, New Hampshire, 1986 in *The International History Review* X, 2 (Burnaby, British Columbia, May 1988), pp. 45-46.

(Current to 31 March 1990)

AN ASPECT OF SOWŎL'S OWN POETRY REFLECTED IN HIS TRANSLATIONS FROM THE CHINESE

J.C. Bleijerveld

To say that Sowŏl Kim Chŏngsik (1902-1934) is probably one of Korea's most popular poets[1] is not exactly displaying reckless daring. Since about 1950, alongside of a continuous stream of anthologies of varying quality, an ever growing number of studies on Sowŏl has been published.[2] Still it was nearly fifty years after the poet's death before Sowŏl's published and unpublished poetry appeared in an exhaustive collection together with variant readings.[3] Among the 269 pieces there are 16 translations of Chinese poems, four of which not published during his life.

It is of course nearly impossible to provide a completely satisfying explanation for Sowŏl's lasting popularity, but in many studies a consensus of opinion on important elements of his poetry seems often to have been found. Everyone stresses the traditional side of Sowŏl; Cho Yŏnhyŏn may be speaking for all the others when he writes about the traditional form of his poems with their regular metre and often 3/4 or 5/7 syllables alternation, and about their traditional contents with Nature, longing and being separated from the loved one. His poems are defined as ballads and folk-song and may be compared with *kasa* from the Yi dynasty, and *kayo* from the Koryŏ.[4] Sowŏl through his traditionalism is for Cho interesting because of his opposition against an excessive Westernization *in poeticis* during the '20s. A kind of "Korean feeling" he finds in his poems is a result of the traditionalism - and may well be a factor in his popularity - and finally and indirectly he mentions the absence of a "masculine tone" in Sowŏl's poetry caused by his preference for themes as parting, longing and sadness: traditionally feminine themes.[5]

This last aspect - meant in the title of this article - is more fully expressed by others.[6] Kim Yangsu sees feminine associations in Sowŏl's use of such words as "beloved", "sadness", "waiting", "lonesome" and "missing" and contends that he wrote his poems on a basis of feminine feeling. "In Sowŏl's poetry is no masculinity; even when written from a masculine viewpoint the feeling is feminine", he writes literally, and he sees the "I" in Sowŏl's poems as alone in an empty house, deserted, unable to sleep, and with a tearsoaked pillow: his poetic world is indeed lonely "without (my) lord, (in) the empty mountains".[7]

Two more reasons, other than the one connected with his traditionalism, for Sowŏl to choose a feminine *persona* (*yŏsŏnghwaja*) are given by Kim Chuno: in a society where male superiority is thought normal, the expression of feeling *überhaupt* can be done best through a woman; how Sowŏl came to discover this feminine outlet he explains by Sowŏl's early loss of his father,[8] so that from his earliest childhood on he must have begun to identify himself emotionally with the dominating female characters in the household.[9] Later, femininity may have been engendered as a reaction upon and also been used as a weapon in the fight against fascism as the expression of extreme masculinism during the period of Japanese annexation.[10]

Looking at the highlights of his poetry from here in the light of this "femininity" (*yŏsŏngjui* or *yŏsŏngch'wihyang*) it is not surprising to see why *Chindallae-kkot* and *Sanyuhwa* are generally considered the most famous of his poems: together they show the aspect of woman deserted, being left alone in an empty world.

Although it is probably wise to attach only a relative importance to the fact, the following chronologically arranged list of Sowŏl's translations from the Chinese[11] does show three periods: one with publication dates around the time when his collection *Chindallae-kkot*[12] appeared, one published just before his death, and the last posthumously.

Following the list I will try to give a short interpretation of each poem, in connection with the feminine aspect.

Poet's name:	Chinese title and approximate translation:	Korean transl. published in:
1. Pai Chü-i (772-846)	*Han-shih yeh wang-yin* "With Cold Food-Day outside the city looking and sighing"	*Tonga ilbo*; 1925.2.2

2.	Meng Hao-jan (689-740)	*Ch'un-hsiao* "Spring dawn"	*Tonga ilbo*; 1925.4.13
3.	Li Pai (701-762)	*Niao yeh-t'i* "Crows cawing at night"	*Chosŏn mundan*; 14; 1926.3
4.	Tu Fu (712-770)	*Ch'un-wang* "Spring view"	*Chosŏn mundan*; 14; 1926.3
5.	Li Ho (791-817)	*Su-hsiao-hsiao ko* "Su-hsiao-hsiao's song"	*Chosŏn mundan*; 14; 1926.3
6.	Tu Mu (803-852)	*P'o Ch'in Huai* "Mooring along in the Ch'in Huai"	*Chosŏn mundan*; 14; 1926.3
7.	Liu Ts'ai-ch'un (T'ang poetess)	*Lo-kung ch'ü* "Lo-kung's song"	*Samch'ŏlli*; 53; 1934.8
8.	Wang Wei (699-761)	*Sung Yuan Erh shih An-hsi* "Sending off Yuan Erh to An-hsi"	*Samch'ŏlli*; 53; 1934.8
9.	Anonymous	*I-chou ko* "Song of the I-region"	*Samch'ŏlli*; 53; 1934.8
10.	Anonymous	(The same, II)	*Samch'ŏlli*; 53; 1934.8
11.	Ts'ui Hao (d. 754)	*Ch'ang-kanhsing* "Ch'ang-kanjourney"	*Samch'ŏlli*; 53; 1934.8
12.	Ts'ui Hao (d. 754)	(The same, II)	*Samch'ŏlli*; 53; 1934.8
13.	Liu Ch'ang-ch'ing (1st half 8th c.)	*Wu t'i* "Without title"	*Chogwang*; 48; 1939.10
14.	Wang Wei	*Sung-pieh* "Seeing off"	

15. Wang Wei   *Chu li kuan*
                      "Bamboo-grove"

16. Wang Chi-huan   *Teng Kuan-ch'üeh-lou*
    (8th c.)   "Ascending Kuan-ch'üeh tower"

For practical reasons it is unfortunately impossible ˉto provide the original Chinese texts; the interested reader will not have much difficulty in finding these. All of them are in the *Ch'üan T'ang-shih* ("Complete T'ang Poems").

Connecting "femininity" with certain words expressing sadness, parting and longing as we have seen before is done by Korean critics, it is easy to see what can have attracted Sowŏl in the first poem. The elements are there: the visit to the grave on Cold Food-Day, the wailing, the impossibility of communication beyond the grave - which is called the definite place of separation between life and death - and the rain, traditionally connected with this day. Among Sowŏl's own poems we find several with comparable subjects: *Kŭmjandi*, *Mudŏm*, and *Ch'ohon*.

In Meng Hao-jan's *chüeh-chü* probably the important words are "last night"; it has been argued that in Sowŏl's poetry world the irreparable has happened, the "beloved" has gone, even the parting is over and the separation a fact for good, just as in this poem the blossoms of yesterday are fallen. The theme reminds of Sowŏl's *Puhŏngsae* where he mixes about the same ingredients.

The voice of the woman-persona is clear in Li Pai's "Crows cawing at night". This symbolizes the being separated from her loved one, and "her tears fall like rain" because "she is alone in her empty room". The rain-like falling tears are by the way in contrast with Sowŏl's *Chindallae-kkot* when the "I" says not to cry even though dying.

Tu Fu's poem of course is definitely a man's viewpoint, and the "I", though alone, is *away* from home and not deserted *at* home; in short the opposite of the essentials we have seen as characteristic of Sowŏl's poetry.

The song of Su Hsiao-hsiao, is an old folk-song in which a courtesan tries to make a courtier to keep his promise. Two other T'ang-poets besides Li Ho elaborated on the theme, that contains the well-known feminine elements. Sowŏl's translation in its turn has been translated[13] by David McCann.

In Tu Mu's poem reference is made to the sad ending of Yang Kuei-fei, emperor Hsüan-tsung's favourite concubine who deserted her and so caused her death. This may well be the reason why the poem attracted Sowŏl's attention, especially so because of the explicit mention in the poem of innocent girls, whom a similar unhappiness may await.

Also connected with the Ch'in-huai River is Liu Ts'ai-ch'un's poem in which a woman accuses the river to have taken her husband away, leaving her behind, deserted.

Although the tone in Wang Wei's sending-off poems (nos. 8 and 14) is of course masculine, Sowŏl may have been attracted by the aspect of someone who in spite of being left behind, tries to let the other go with all the best wishes, which after all is the theme of *Chindallae-kkot*.

In both the anonymous I-chou songs a woman speaks: in the first she asks the moon to shine into the barracks for the soldiers faraway who will not come home this year or next; in the second she asks the orioles not to sing and so disturb her dream of going to the border (where the soldiers are). In both cases again a woman deserted by her loved one in the army.

The next poems by Ts'ui Hao form a dialogue between a woman and a man and are in a way uncharacteristic for Sowŏl: not only is the man spoken to physically present but he even answers. Maybe it is the nuance of regret in the statement, they are both from the same place but have never known each other, that attracted Sowŏl.

I found it impossible to discover a feminine aspect in the last four poems without farfetched interpretations. Maybe it is meaningful to note that these (and only these) four poems were not published during Sowŏl's life.

I have tried to show that just as in many of Sowŏl's poems a feminine note, latent or clear, may be heard, so we may suppose he heard a similar note in the Chinese poems he translated. The theory of the presence of a feminine aspect in his own poetry as advocated by many Korean scholars may be strengthened by considering that more than half of his translated poems contain that same aspect.

NOTES

1. That is, South Korea. In the fifties an anthology and a study have been published in North Korea, but nowadays Sowŏl's popularity there seems to have disappeared.
2. See the very exhaustive bibliography of 170 items between 1929 and 1981, in Kim Chinguk (ed.), *Wŏnbon Sowŏl chŏnjip*, 2 vols., Seoul: Hongsŏngsa, 1982 (*Hongsŏng sinsŏ* 60-61), pp. 1039-1048.
3. *Wŏnbon Sowŏl chŏnjip*. Cf. note 2.
4. Specifically *Kasiri* and *Chindallaekkot* have been compared.
5. Cho Yŏnhyŏn, *Han'guk hyŏndae munhak sa*, Seoul: Sŏngmungak, 1969 (original ed. 1959), pp. 437-449.
6. Only after having finished writing this, in January 1984, an article by Yi Kyuho, entitled: "Sowŏr-ŭi Hansi pŏnyŏk-ko" (in Kim Yongjik et al., *Hanguk hyŏndaesisa yŏngu*, Seoul: Iljisa, Dec. 1983, pp. 121-144) in which he develops a similar idea, came to my attention.
7. Kim Yangsu, "Kim Sowŏl-lon kaksŏ", *Hyŏndae munhak* VI, 12 (No. 72, 1960), pp. 39-48. "Without my love, in the empty mountains" (*Muju kongsan*) is the title of one of the sections of Sowŏl's collection *Chindallaekkot*.
8. When Sowŏl was about three years old his father was beaten up by a gang of railroad labourers and received permanent mental injury; his function to communicate well with people never came back.
9. Especially with his aunt who came to the house after her marriage. She was only twelve years older than Sowŏl and loved to tell him stories.
10. Kim Chunó, "Sowŏl sijŏng-gwa wŏnch'ojŏk ingan: Sowŏr-ŭi kamjŏng yangsingnon", in Kim Yŏlgye et al. (ed.), *Kim Sowŏl yŏn'gu*, Seoul: Saemunsa, 1982, pp. II 34-II 47.
11. *Wŏnbon Sowŏl chŏnjip* II.
12. His (only) collection of poetry was published in 1925. A photomechanical reprint in the 1970's.
13. David R. McCann (ed.), *Black Crane: an anthology of Korean literature*, Ithaca (N.Y.), 1977 (*Cornell University East Asia papers* 14), p. 61.

DOCTOR AT SEA: CHOU MEI-YEH'S VOYAGE
TO THE WEST (1710-1711)

Leonard Blussé

In recent historiography an image of the Dutch East India Company (VOC) has emerged which the directors of this monopolistic trading company would hardly have recognized: the Company as an active intermediary in the *rapprochement* between Western and Eastern culture. The profound effect of the presence of the VOC factory at Nagasaki is often cited in support of this thesis. Located on the island of Deshima the trading factory not only functioned throughout the Tokugawa period as a detached outpost of Dutch trading interests in the Far East, it also offered the Japanese the opportunity to look abroad: *sakoku no mado*, "the window of the closed country". Yet, when the Amsterdam burgomaster Nicolaes Witsen (1641-1717) - a boardmember of the VOC as well as a prominent patron of the world of learning - was asked by a correspondent whether the affairs of the Company contributed to the progress of Western learning about the Orient, he answered with a sigh: "No sir, it is money, not learning that our people are seeking over there, which is indeed a pity!"[1]

Is the wider implication of this ironic remark that the transfer of scientific knowledge and the export of Dutch books to Tokugawa Japan should merely be seen as a Dutch investment in the curiosity of the Japanese in the outside world? This would amount to a slap in the face for such famous pre-Enlightenment and Enlightenment Japanophiles as François Caron, Johannes Camphuys, Andreas Cleyer, Engelbert Kaempfer, Carl Thunberg, Isaac Titsingh or Hendrik Doeff, to name but a few. Let me put it this way: in Japan, as elsewhere, the VOC trading network played a crucial role as a go-between, in spite of its mercantile character. The true agents in this cultural traffic, however, were the individual Company servants. They acted either on their own initiative or received encouragement or support from a Maecenas inside the Company management such as Nicolaes Witsen. Individually Company servants served as (letter-)carriers of essential bits and pieces of information, thus enabling European armchair-scholars to add new pieces to the jigsaw-puzzle out of which an image of Oriental civilization gradually emerged.[2] The Board of Directors never formulated policies aimed at furthering the advancement of Western learning about the Orient. On the contrary, all correspondence with the East was severely censored for fear of espionage by foreign competition.

Yet, in spite of the official VOC policy of banning information about its enterprises abroad, some fundamental research by individual "fieldworkers" among its personnel was preserved and published during or shortly after their lifetime. Georg Everhard Rumphius' studies of Ambonese flora and fauna were copied by Governor-General Joannes Camphuijs and sent to the Dutch Republic, where they were eventually published with a subsidy from the Company; Van Rheede tot Drakenstein (1636-1691) saw the twelve volumes of the *Hortus Malabaricus* into print and several prominent people in and outside the Republic saw to it that Kaempfer's studies on Persia, Siam and Japan were printed before and after his death.[3] Unfortunately, much precious material was lost as well. Witsen helplessly witnessed the confiscation of part of the information sent to him from Asia upon arrival in Amsterdam and the loss of precious information concerning Ceylon due to sheer negligence: "all these data get stifled. As far as I know nobody even spares them a glance. Papers lie scattered in boxes and are forgotten..."[4]

Is it purely accidental that the individual fieldworkers I have just mentioned were all contemporaries of each other? If closer research were to be carried out on the fluctuation of Western interest in Asia during the 17th and 18th centuries, then the period 1670-1700 would certainly be designated as a peak. Several explanations may be advanced for this. First of all there was the *Zeitgeist*, the intellectual temper of the period. As has often been pointed out, around the second half of the seventeenth century the spirit of Europe was changing from theology to science, from superstition to scholarship, from biblical history to world history. Knowledge was spread in literary circles through correspondence, scientific journals and books. Learned societies were founded, libraries established. In addition to and in conjunction with this general phenomenon several factors facilitated the implementation of scientific discovery in Asia. In the third quarter of the 17th century the VOC reached its widest sphere of action as an intra-Asian trading corporation and entered into a phase of consolidation in Asia, thus providing better conditions for local research. There also was an influx of a different kind of personnel: after the Treaty of Westphalia (1648), which brought the Thirty Years War in Germany to an end, a relatively large aggregate of German adventurers entered the Company's service. It was mainly from this group that the naturalists emerged who devoted themselves wholeheartedly to the study of Asia's languages and culture, flora and fauna. Finally, there was the extraordinary influence of the learned Nicolaes Witsen as a patron of scholarly research in the Indies. These four factors, Europe's spirit of scientific discovery, the Company's increasingly peaceful co-operation with, and adaptation to Asian society, the abundance of enthusiastic fieldworkers, and the presence of a "sounding board" in Europe contributed to the formation of a chain of cultural transmission.

One cultural *terra incognita* which was gradually charted during the Ancien Régime was the Chinese Empire. China appealed to the imagination of European scholarship because of its antiquity, its vast size and its well organized bureaucracy. The slow pace at which the secrets of the Middle Kingdom were disclosed was not only the result of its difficult script and the closed circuit of its political system, but also its geographical remoteness. Only a small number of Roman Catholic missionaries were tolerated in China on a permanent basis by the court, and it was mainly through their "lettres édifiantes et curieuses" to the French king that the European world of learning was informed about China.[5]

VOC servants also made a modest contribution to the European discovery of Chinese civilization. Johan Nieuhoff's *Embassy to the Grand Tartar Cham, Emperour of China*, a detailed description of the first Dutch embassy to China (1655-1657), appeared in print in Amsterdam in 1665 with the famous publisher of ethnographic works, Jacob van Meurs. Two years later Van Meurs also published *China Illustrata* by the Jesuit Athanasius Kircher (1601-1680) in which Chinese culture is portrayed as a derivative of Egypt.[6] Nieuhoff, an adventurer and artist, had been added to the suite of the Dutch ambassadors at the suggestion of Cornelis Witsen (Nicolaes' father) in order to sketch sights of interest along the route from Canton to Peking.[7] The hundred and fifty-odd pictures which resulted from this voyage provided the European reader with a glimpse of

China's interior for the first time. Nieuhoff's book became an instant bestseller. Within a few years translations into French, English, German and Latin followed. A second volume, covering the second and third embassies to China, was edited by Olfert Dapper five years later. Together with Van Braam Houckgeest's account of his visit to the court of Ch'ien Lung (1795), these travel stories basically represent the VOC's main contribution to the cultural and scientific discovery of China during the Ancien Régime.[8]

In this essay I should like to focus on one almost forgotten case of transfer of knowledge about China. It is a snapshot (anno 1710) of several ideas or issues then in progress in the learned discourse about China: the search for keys to the Chinese script and Chinese medicine (*Clavis China et Clavis Medica*), the antiquity of Chinese culture and more specifically the enigmas surrounding the *Monumentum Sinicum*, a recently discovered stèle, which according to the Jesuits served as a proof of the long history of the Christian faith in China. What the tale, however, does illustrate in detail is the progress by which the transfer of knowledge occurred and the crucial role played by intellectual friendships and correspondence in this information process. The withdrawal of one correspondent at a critical moment proved fatal to the continuation of all further research.

The *Kai-Pa li-tai shih-chi*, the Chinese chronicle of Batavia, which was probably codified in its present form at the beginning of the nineteenth century, mentions a Chinese citizen of Batavia who visited the Dutch Republic in the closing years of the seventeenth century.[9] The short entry about this adventurous traveller in the chronicle is unique, revealing and - let us face it - a bit disappointing at the same time. Unique because here we are dealing with the testimony of one of the few literate sons of Han who visited the Western Barbarian regions in the seventeenth and eighteenth centuries;[10] revealing because the tale contains a number of desultory remarks representative of colonial society; and disappointing because the traveller seems neither to have enjoyed the trip nor does he provide us with any visual impressions at all. Did the Kalverstraat in Amsterdam excite his enthusiasm in the same way as the shopping alleys in Nanjing excited Nieuhoff? Was the Amsterdam town hall also in his eyes the eighth wonder of the world? But before making any further comments let us first listen to what the *Kai-Pa li-tai shih-chi* has to tell us.

> In 1681 of the Dutch calendar Governor-General Rijklof van Goens fell ill and retired from office... At the time there was a Chinese physician named Chou Mei-yeh (Minnan dialect: Tsiú Bi-ya). Van Goens knew him well and put great trust in his abilities. He went to see the Council of the Indies and said: "I should like to take along Chou Mei-yeh on the way home in order to cure my illness". The Council granted his request. Thereupon Van Goens and the physician left aboard a Company vessel on November 25th of the same year. After he arrived in patria, Van Goens ordered the physician to live in a house, and posted a guard outside the door. He was provided with all drinks, food, clothing and appliances he needed, but was not permitted to leave the house and amuse himself. He stayed one year in Holland (sic!). In the sixth month of 1682 a Company vessel arrived in Batavia, carrying the letter which formally appointed Van Goens' successor, Cornelis Jansz. Speelman, Governor-General. Chou Mei-yeh came home on the same ship. He went to congratulate Speelman who met with his Council.
>
> By Order in Council the Indies administration awarded Chou Mei-yeh with the privilege of using a large *payong* (parasol) and permitted him to go in and out of Batavia castle - even though he was not involved in *mi-cha-la* (Malay *bicara*, palavers), i.e. the administration! - whenever he felt like doing so.
>
> Only when the Governor-General or another high-ranking official fell ill, were Chou Mei-yeh's services called upon. Thus he received the title "Number One Eminent Physician".[11]

In 1840 a Dutch translation of the Chinese chronicle was published which slightly differs from the above account. According to this version the authorities of The Netherlands "had presented Tjoe-bi-tia a hat and a stick adding some words of encouragement" after he had cured many distinguished people. According to this apocryphal text the doctor availed himself well of the stick:

When Tjoe-bi-tia arrived in Batavia the Dutch burghers
did not know that the government of Holland had bestowed a hat and a stick on him. One day, when he got into
an argument with a Dutchman, Tjoe-bi-tia beat him with
the stick. As soon as the victim saw that this stick was a
"royal" present he no longer dared to insult Tjoe-bi-tia.
In the year 1685 the eminent physician died".[12]

Despite its brevity, the general purport of the story is clear. A
meritorious Chinese doctor accompanied a sick retired Governor-
General to Holland to look after him during the voyage. The
visitor was not very taken with his new surroundings. His hosts
provided him with food in abundance - a gesture pleasing to any
Chinese - but it was virtually impossible for him to get a breath
of fresh air or do some sightseeing. Upon his return in Batavia,
in addition to the hat and stick received in Holland, the physician was presented with even more tokens of honour. He was
allowed to use the payong, and the gates of Batavia castle,
which remained barred to other Asians, were opened for him.
Apart from Chou Mei-yeh only the Captain, or headman, of the
Chinese was assigned the latter privilege, but this, of course,
was part and parcel of the administration of the Chinese
population group. Hats, sticks and other paraphernalia were
traditionally handed out by the colonial administration to the
headmen of local communities.

What else is known about this Chinese visitor to the Dutch
Republic? Do contemporary Dutch sources perhaps also refer to
him and his visit? At a time when the *Chinoiserie* craze seized
Europe, the visit of an authentic Chinese physician to the Low
Countries will surely not have passed unnoticed.

Fortunately, the early eighteenth century colonial historian
François Valentijn comes to our help in this case. In his six
volume treasure trove *Oud en Nieuw Oost-Indiën*, reverend
Valentijn draws from daily life the customs and manners of the
Chinese population group of Batavia and does not fail to men-
tion that, also in his time (1686-1713), the Chinese had dif-
ficulty in pronouncing the Dutch r. "Yet I have known two
Chinese" he asserts, "who not only pronounced this letter very
clearly and forcefully, but even spoke Dutch as well as a
Dutchman". One of these two, a certain "Vaderlandse Willem"
(William the Patriot) had "visited many towns in Holland, and
had also visited London in England where he had the honour to

converse for some time with King William III".[13] The question of whether the memorable meeting yielded this Chinese his curious name must remain unanswered, as nothing else is known about him. In any case, it is clear from the account that this sight-seer did not lead such as isolated an existence in Europe as Chou Mei-yeh. Furthermore, the dates - stadtholder William III was not proclaimed King of England until 1689 - would not seem to tally with those of the Chinese chronicle of Batavia. But anybody who has read the Chinese chronicle critically will not be much impressed by the latter argument. For however chrono-logical the *Kai-Pa li-tai shih-chi* advertises itself to be, this local history is not at all accurate in dating events. As the second Chinese who could pronounce the Dutch r "zeer net en krachtig", Valentijn mentions "the physician Tsiewbitja, who left (Batavia) for Holland in 1709 with Mr. Joan van Hoorn". Without the slightest doubt we are dealing here with one and the same person, even though the dates do not coincide. Before I shall try to formulate answers to the questions about the identity of Chou Mei-yeh and the circumstances under which he sailed to the Dutch Republic, let us first acquaint ourselves with Joan van Hoorn, in whose retinue he made his voyage to the West.

Governor-General Joan van Hoorn (1653-1711) cuts an inter-esting historical figure - especially if we consider him in the light of the theme of the "transfer of knowledge".[14] Van Hoorn was known for his love for Asia - he spent most of his life in the tropics - and he corresponded with many learned persons in and outside the Indies, thereby making his own contribution to the advancement of Oriental learning. He was born at Amster-dam on November 16, 1653, the eldest son of Pieter van Hoorn and Sara Bessels, both scions of well-established families. In early 1663 the Van Hoorn household, which had been enlarged in the meantime by four more children, left for the Indies. Three years later Pieter van Hoorn, extraordinary councillor of the Indies, was appointed by order in Council (*de dato* June 6, 1666) ambassador to the Chinese court in Peking. His twelve-and-a-half year old son, Joan, was allowed to accompany him with the rank of junior assistant. The embassy itself yielded the VOC little profit in terms of trade but the travel account, edited by Olfert Dapper and published by Van Meurs in 1670, received nearly as much response in learned circles as Nieuhoff's book had five years earlier. Less well-known is the Ode to Confucius which Pieter van Hoorn published himself at Batavia: "*Eenige Voornaeme eygenschappen van de ware Deugdt, Voorsichtigheydt, Wijsheydt en Volmaecktheydt, Getrocken uyt den Chineschen Confucius en op rijm gebracht*".[15] This attempt at introducing the teachings of Master Kung to Dutch readership was not composed entirely by the author's own efforts. During his sojourn at Fuchou Van Hoorn had met two Dutch-speaking missionaries, Father François De Rougemont and Father Philippe Couplet, respectively natives of Maastricht and Mechelen, who were in the process of putting together *Confucius Sinarum Philosophus*, a translation of the Analects or *Lun-yü*.[16] They undoubtedly provided the subject matter for this doggerel in praise of the Chinese sage.

Joan van Hoorn quickly mounted the ladder of success in the service of the VOC: junior assistant in 1665; assistant in 1671; junior merchant in 1673; merchant and first clerk at the secretarial department (*generale secretarie*) in 1676. On August 11, 1682, the breakthrough occurred: he was appointed extraordinary-councillor of the Indies through the personal intervention of Governor-General Speelman, and thus joined the administrative elite in the Indies. In the following years Van Hoorn occupied numerous management positions in Batavia and its immediate vicinity, such as President of the Orphanage Board (*Weesmeesters*), President of the Polder Board (*Heemraden*) and Commissioner of the Native Population (*Gecommitteerde over den inlander*). Thereupon followed the appointment to Director-General on September 1691, a position which opened up the road to the highest office. Even though he steadfastly showed a lack of interest in the supreme function, he finally gave in to pressure from his fellow-councillors and served as Governor-General from 1704 until 1709.

Joan van Hoorn was a recognized authority on Javanese society at a time when the VOC was normalizing its ties with the Central Javanese kingdom of Mataram. While serving as *gecommitteerde over den inlander* he had shown himself committed to further the welfare of "common man Kromo" in the Ommelanden. The personal archivalia of Van Hoorn, which are kept at the Royal Institute of Anthropology (Leiden) and the National Archives (The Hague), do indeed bear testimony to this lively interest in native society.[17] To put it in his own words: "I have made great efforts ever since General Speelman was in office to become acquainted with native affairs and learn how to deal with them".[18] Van Hoorn belonged to a select company of high officials who in this particular period - the last two decades of the seventeenth century - shared a common interest in indigenous society. Major Isaac de Saint Martin, collector of Javanese manuscripts; Governor-General Camphuys, historian of the foundation of Batavia in 1619 and patron of learned men such as Kaempfer and Rumphius; Anthoni Hurdt, the Director-General who was until his death in 1688 Witsen's main correspondent on Asian affairs and himself a serious student of the languages of the Archipelago - all these formidable men belonged to the inner circle of Joan van Hoorn's friends.

Only after Van Hoorn had passed away, was it realized how crucial his help to others had been. In 1715 Witsen, for instance, complained about the intellectual backwardness of Van Hoorn's successors: "our East Indian councillors often start out as sailors and soldiers and do not know anything about scholarship or European learning; Malay and Portuguese are the languages to which they apply themselves".[19] On another occasion he lamented: "nowadays among those in command at Batavia there are no amateurs of botany or the cultivation of new crops, like Mr. Van Hoorn in the past".[20] Here Nicolaes Witsen was referring to the successful experiments he and his distant cousin, Van Hoorn, had carried out around the turn of the century. On his own estate Van Hoorn planted coffee seedlings, imported from Mocha at Witsen's instigation. The later introduction of the coffee cultivation in Java was the direct result of this initiative.

Less well known and documented is the interest both correspondents shared for the Chinese Empire. Witsen's curiosity was mainly of a scientific nature and was a logical offshoot of his famous researches on Tartary.[21] Initially he had pursued a correspondence with Dutch missionaries in China, but after their death or repatriation he addressed himself to Joan van Hoorn in Batavia. "Pray forgive me for vexing you so often with my queries and curious requests. They refresh me while I am toiling in the service of our fatherland" is the characteristic opening sentence of a letter in which Witsen broached the question of the origin of the Australian aboriginals. "Do these people by any chance originate from populous China?" he wondered. It was a mere guess "considering that the Chinese are white and the *Zuidlanders* black, this does not seem to tally, or these people must have changed colour over time".[22] On another occasion he sent Van Hoorn a mirror excavated in Siberia with the request that its inscription be deciphered by local Chinese.[23] Van Hoorn would hardly handle questions on widely diverging matters like these himself, but he wisely sought out persons with the necessary expertise and let them provide the answers. It was not only that he did not have spare time to do so, he also seems to have lacked the intellectual curiosity and zeal to study academic subjects.

Van Hoorn was first and foremost a man of practical interests. He purchased and opened up virgin territory in the Ommelanden of Batavia, introduced new crops and collaborated closely with the local Chinese in promoting both that community's and his own mercantile interests. By gradually expanding the property his father had left him, Van Hoorn became the largest landowner in Batavia. According to François Valentijn, the Governor-General thus became the richest man in the Indies.[24] In his private business Van Hoorn of course received a little help from his friends and this explains his great affection towards the Chinese in Batavia.

For Joan van Hoorn China was not a far-away empire with a mysterious, elusive culture. He knew China and its inhabitants from personal experience: he had visited the country in his youth, as we have seen, and his contacts with the Chinese of Batavia were intimate as well as "businesslike". He received Chinese visitors daily in his residence: tax-farmers, sugar-mill operators on his own plantations, merchants from Amoy, with whom he conducted his affairs, and venerable personalities such as his personal physician, Thebitsia. It was even rumoured that the Governor-General showed these visitors preferential treatment to the detriment of his own countrymen. As Valentijn put it: "it bothered some people that they had to wait for quite some time outside at the steps or in front of His Excellency's domicile, while this or that Chinese was ushered in before them".[25]

A familiar figure among the stream of Chinese visitors was the aged physician, Chou Mei-yeh, Tjoe-bi-tia or Thebitsia as he is commonly called in Dutch sources. From the Dutch archival data and the *Kai-Pa li-tai shih-chi* we know that the Chinese doctor also served as *boedelmeester* (estate administrator) for the inheritances of the Chinese inhabitants of Batavia - a combination of functions which would seem a bit paradoxical. Let us conclude that Thebitsia was appointed *boedelmeester* on account of the confidence he enjoyed in the Chinese community. Thebitsia was also an entrepreneur. By Resolution of Governor-General and Council, d.d. 21-10-1709, he and the headman of the Balinese in Batavia were granted a plot of land in hereditary tenure, which Thebitsia had already leased from the Government two years earlier in order to start a sugar plantation and operate a mill on it.[26]

These titbits of information reveal that the Chinese doctor was a local dignitary, standing high in the personal favour of the administration and of the Governor-General. How he became personally acquainted with Van Hoorn is related in the Latin correspondence between Nicolaes Witsen and his scholarly friend, Gijsbert Cuper (1644-1716), the burgomaster of the town of Deventer.

A certain Mr. Mesquita - "Mesquita Judaeus, sed ultra Judaeum sapiens!" Cuper specifies, as if to emphasize the dependability of his source - had heard from Van Hoorn himself how Thebitsia had diagnosed the Governor-General's second wife's illness upon having been called to her bedside. After having silently palpated the patient's right arm for an hour or so he disclosed the true character of her illness. Because Van Hoorn had urged him to tell the unvarnished truth, the physician explained to the Vice-Roy that his wife had only three more days to live. Three days later she did indeed die. This correct, though depressing, diagnosis gained Thebitsia the respect of the Governor-General.[27] He was enlisted as physician to Van Hoorn, who suffered himself from chronic tightness of the chest and, as the years passed by Thebitsia became the help and and mainstay of the family.

When in 1708 Governor-General Van Hoorn notified the Gentlemen Seventeen in the Netherlands that he wished to retire from office on account of his failing health, the directors of the Company expressed themselves willing to comply with his wishes, on condition that he return to patria with his family. It was feared in Holland that with his extensive landed property in Batavia and his close relations with his successor Abraham van Riebeeck (the father of Joan van Hoorn's third wife, Joanna Maria) the Governor-General would continue to exercise substantial influence even after having stepped down. The formation of a strong, locally embedded landed élite at Batavia was a thorn in the flesh of the Gentlemen in Amsterdam, who found it increasingly difficult to impose their will on the administration overseas.[28]

When the decision of the Gentlemen Seventeen was made known in Batavia it caused an upsurge of anxiety among the Chinese community. Thirty-one elderly Chinese addressed a petition to Governor-General Van Hoorn pointing out "that they had arrived from China as young men and that they had consequently already lived thirty, nay! most of them forty years in town". They had all come to know the Governor-General as a person "with a gentle disposition, who had often preserved them, their relatives and dependants from disaster, had supported them, and had helped those who had met with adversity". The thirty-one signatories were alarmed at the prospect of losing their influential friend and therefore humbly suggested that he postpone his departure and remain in their midst for a few more years. Among the signatures was Thebitsia's.[29]

However Van Hoorn was not to be dissuaded from his purpose. His health left much to be desired, and he hoped that the change of air might do him some good. His extensive landed properties were offered for sale and preparations were made for departure. By the end of October 1709 Van Hoorn was ready to board the Patria fleet, but fearing possible medical complications at sea, he asked the Batavian authorities to grant permission to "Thoebittia, who had already looked after him for many years" to accompany him and his family on the voyage home.[30] The request was granted straight away.

On October 31st, Mr. and Mrs. Van Hoorn, their daughter, Pieternel, and the Chinese physician went aboard the flagship the *Sandenburg*. The first leg of the voyage to the Cape of Good Hope passed off smoothly. Van Hoorn's letter book shows that he contemplated the "46 years spent in Java and Batavia" and tried to arrange some historical data concerning Batavia in what leisure time he had during the voyage while also serving as Admiral of the fleet.[31] But once the anchors had been cast in Table Bay the entire family was soon absorbed by local events. Van Hoorn was taken aback by the mood of Cape society and concluded that harmony was as much absent in the Cape administration as in that of Batavia: "a wind which anywhere in the Indies seems to blow stronger than the southeastern trade wind".[32] Joanna Maria van Riebeeck met faithful servants who had known her father and her grandfather (Joan van Riebeeck, the founder of the Cape Colony), and "our dear Pieternelleke was as little amused by the Cape flies as by the Hottentots".[33]

As for Thebitsia, he mediated for four exiled Chinese convicts from Batavia, who appealed for mercy and begged to return home.[34]

Van Hoorn informed his friends in Batavia that the sea air had done wonders for his health. He not only felt better but he also had been diagnosed as such by Thebitsia "who his advanced age notwithstanding comports himself well too, and proves himself to be a good sailor, so that I congratulate myself on having brought him along... I do hope he will find opportunity in the days to come to teach my wife how to take a patient's pulse".[35]

This last remark ushers us *in medias res*. Did the Chinese physician pass on his knowledge of Chinese-style diagnosis to Joanna van Hoorn? After the departure from the Cape lessons did indeed commence. Van Hoorn's wife eagerly took down notes on the instruction she received on the ship's deck. Among her posthumous papers are two drawings of the left and right hands, indicating on which spots the function of the liver, the kidneys, heart and lungs can be checked. These fine drawings were probably copied out by Van Hoorn's personal secretary Jacob Heyrmans.[36] They tally with the illustrations in the Latin translation by the Jesuit, Michael Boym, and the Batavian physician, Andreas Cleyer of the Chinese medical treatise *Mo ching* by Wang Shu-ho (265-317).[37] Thebitsia's prescriptions for several illnesses that can be diagnosed by palpation are rather peculiar. Not having ready access to Boym and Cleyer's *Clavis Medica*, I do not know whether the same prescriptions also figure in that book but all Chinese drugs are here indicated with romanized Chinese names. These Chinese herbs either were not available in Europe or still awaited further determination and classification. It is consequently rather doubtful whether Joanna was ever able to put into practice what she had picked up during the lessons.[38]

As we know from his notes and his log-book, Van Hoorn also had some instructive conversations with his physician about various aspects of Chinese civilization. The foundation for these conversations was laid during the courtesy visit of the English skipper, Harrison, who had joined the VOC convoy with his own squadron of five ships upon leaving Cape Town for Europe.

> "The time has come", the Walrus said,
> "to talk of many things:
> Of shoes - and ships - and sealing - wax,
> Of cabbages - and kings..."

Picture for yourself the Patria fleet on the sunny afternoon of April 20th close to the Equator somewhere on the high seas of the Atlantic.[39] The fleet has reached the Doldrums, the sails hang listlessly from the yards, flapping against the rigging as the ships slowly roll in the rippleless swell of the mid-Atlantic. The English commander orders the boat lowered and is rowed over to the nearby Dutch flagship to pay a courtesy visit. A moment later the *Sandenburg*'s poop deck is crowded with Van Hoorn, his Chinese physician, the English visitors and some of the ship's officers. Captain Harrison, on the way back from Canton to his native land, ventures to inform his host about recent commercial developments in Canton; a matter of great interest for the Dutch because since 1689 the VOC has stopped sending its own vessels to China and is now depending solely on the shipping link provided by the Chinese junks sailing annually to and from Batavia on the rhythm of the monsoons. Harrison foresees a worsening in the trading climate for the Europeans in China. Since his first visit (he had visited China in 1705 and 1709) political tension has been mounting steadily. The K'ang Hsi emperor shows signs of senility, and rumours about an imminent succession struggle at the court hold little promise for a stable political future. Van Hoorn nods approvingly and tells his visitor that Thebitsia could not agree more and "has forewarned him of the same already two years ago". The discussion of court affairs then inevitably turns to the vicissitudes of the Jesuits at the court and the rites controversy they are involved in. Will they be able to hold their own against the jealous infighting of the other Roman Catholic orders? Dutch gin, claret brought by the visitors and, possibly, even wine from the recently planted vineyards at the Cape loosen tongues and soon the somewhat formal exchange turns to a bantering about more exotic matters, such as the miraculous effects of the ginseng root in restoring the vital functions of the body. Such is the "inherent strength or heat of this root", Harrison asserts, that in early spring at night "tiny lights" can be observed above the fields where ginseng grows. Then, as the sun sinks behind the horizon, the English commander bids farewell and is rowed back by a merry crew of sailors. Presently dusk envelops the fleet, the lanterns of the ships in their turn becoming like dancing will-o-the-whisps themselves above the vast ocean.

> "The night is fine", the Walrus said
> "Do you admire the view?"

If we pass in review the topics discussed during that afternoon, it becomes clear what issues governed the discourse about China: the emergent direct European trade at Canton, the Portuguese at Macao, the missionaries who entered China via Macao and kept Europe enlightened by way of their *lettres édifiantes et curieuses* about the Chinese court, and, finally, the fabulous effects of Chinese medicine. Although the presence of Thebitsia certainly will have stimulated the discussions, it should be pointed out that ginseng had already figured for several decades as a topic in European learned discourse about China: even Athanasius Kircher mentioned the root's miraculous powers in his *China Illustrata* but cautioned: "Contra vim mortis non sit medicamen in hortis".[40]

Harrison's short visit did not fail to stir up interest. In the days that followed Van Hoorn drew up a list of questions for his physician about "the Antiquity and the Religions of China", and wanted to hear more about the Portuguese presence in China. Thebitsia first dwelt on the history and organization of the *san chiao*, the three religions or "sects" as he called them: Confucianism, Taoism and Buddhism. "The creed of the Portuguese and European fathers", which was now also being propagated in China, he singled out as the newest religious sect. He turned to the principles of the Yang and Yin and the five capital virtues: *fidelitas, prudentia, urbanitas, justitia,* and *pietas* whose author was "den Chineesen leermeester Confutius".[41] He rounded off this exposé with a few words devoted to the hierarchical relations within the family. These remarks must have had a familiar ring in Van Hoorn's ears, for his father's Ode to the Great Sage had also dealt with these matters. Finally Thebitsia touched on Chinese chronology, a matter of great concern at the time, as the Christian world for the first time discovered a civilization which could boast of an antiquity vastly more ancient than the biblical world. Thebitsia drew up an extensive chronological list of the reigns of all the Chinese emperors, starting with "Pan-kou-sie" (Pan Ku) and ending with Conghi

(K'ang Hsi) and indeed left the audience of the Sandenburg amazed with his great knowledge of the past.[42] In hindsight all this labourious noting down in romanization of the strange names of exotic emperors - Van Hoorn will have had his doubts about the longevity of some of the emperors - was quite needless. Almost fifteen years earlier, in 1696, in Berlin Christian Mentzel had published his *Kurtze chinesische Chronologia oder Zeit-Register, aller chinesischen Käyser* on basis of data procured from Father Couplet, and what Thebitsia had to tell about Confucianism's basic tenets was already quite well known in learned circles in Europe at the time. Van Hoorn, not aware of this, studiously noted down the words of the Chinese physician and we can only hope that this intellectual effort will have banished boredom during the long voyage.

Upon arriving at the Texel roads (17 July 1710) Van Hoorn immediately notified his friend Witsen in Amsterdam that he had brought along the venerable Chinese physician from Batavia. It is well known that travellers returning from far-away regions need an exotic pet to show off. In the past the ordinary sailor produced a monkey or parrot as a token of his exploits, Columbus brought a few Indians, Joan van Hoorn a Chinese physician. Unfortunately - or should we say fortunately? - Witsen was ill and confined to his bed. He could not meet Van Hoorn and his company on the quay but had to await their arrival at his own house. In letters to his faithful correspondent Gijsbert Cuper, we find an occasional reference to Thebitsia. "I felt nauseous when (the Chinese doctor) first visited me. He took my pulse, without asking anything, sank into deep thought for quite some time and finally made a fully correct diagnosis. But, in the end, I did not dare to swallow any of his drugs!" Witsen added drawings of both the left and the right arm, indicating which spots the Chinese physician palpated to diagnose the patient's illness.[43]

Van Hoorn kept the "rather curious questions" Witsen posed at arm's length, and delegated his secretary, Heyrmans, to lend a helping hand in providing the answers. He soon recognized that his distant cousin, notwithstanding his influential position in the city and state government, was a somewhat awkward *Einzelgänger*. Though Witsen's personal *motto* was *Candide et Fortiter*, Van Hoorn believed it should be *ego sum solo*.[44] He probably meant *solus*. Not only Witsen met Thebitsia, "several other gentlemen (also) showed much courtesy to the Chinese

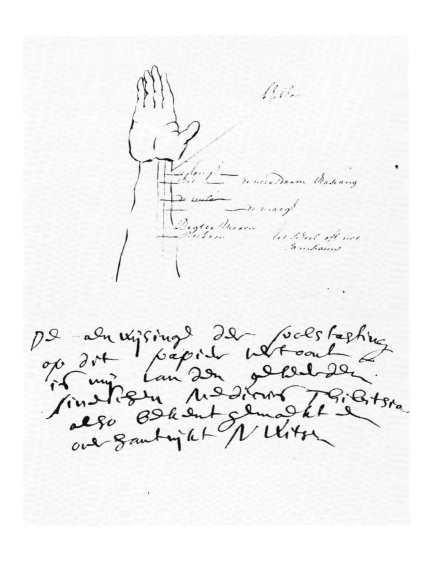

Drawing of the right arm with N. Witsen's subscription: "De aenwijsinge der polstasting op dit papier vertoont is mij van den geleerden sineeschen medicus Thibitsia also bekent gemaekt en overhantrijkt. N. Witsen". (Amsterdam University Library, N. Witsen collection)

doctor". Yet, all this entertaining did not conceal the bare fact that Thebitsia's mission was fulfilled - he had safely escorted his patient to the Netherlands - and now all he wished for was to return as soon as possible. Whether he also felt restricted in his movement (as the Chinese chronicle suggests) or whether he simply feared the coming of winter, we do not know. By order in Council of September 29, 1710, the Gentlemen XVII allowed Thebitsia to return to Batavia on the autumn fleet.[45] The idea of the impending separation from their family friend "our old doctor Thebitsia, who has provided us with so much friendship and service" depressed the Van Hoorn couple but they acceded to his wishes. In a letter to Governor-General Van Riebeeck they wrote that "they would feel much obliged if he (the Governor-General) would extend as much favour (to Thebitsia) as fairness would permit".[46]

After the bird had flown - Thebitsia stayed only six weeks in Amsterdam - Witsen felt remorse that he had not seized upon the occasion to pose more questions; or rather to follow up initial questions with more profound ones. He had, for instance, briefly touched upon the authenticity of the inscriptions of the *Monumentum Sinicum*, the Nestorian stone slab which had been excavated at Sian-fu (North China) in 1625. Athanasius Kircher had published the entire Chinese text of this stèle dating from 781 in the *China Illustrata* (1667), adducing it as a proof of the long history of Christianity in China. The Calvinist Witsen, who held this claim to be yet another proof of popish propaganda, had therefore asked Thebitsia what his opinion of the text was, and noted down his reply. The Chinese doctor acknowledged that the inscription contained *moralia* or moral teachings, but it was not quite clear to him whether these touched upon the Christian religion or not.

Witsen now sincerely regretted that he had failed to ask Thebitsia for a complete translation of the inscription: "That Chinese gentleman could read or write anything in Chinese; if he had stayed longer, I could have learned more from him", he wrote shortly after his departure in a letter to Cuper.[47] The latter could only echo what Witsen had just written: "It is indeed a terrible pity, that this man did not stay with you for a longer time, so that we might have heard the whole history of the *Monumentum Sinicum*. No greater service could have been rendered to the general public, and to the history of the church in particular, if Your Lordship had but obtained a translation from this learned Chinese or from another one of that ilk".[48] A few months later Witsen received a courtesy letter from Thebitsia saying that he had reached Cape Town safely.[49] Two years later he received another one.[50] That was about the last sign of life he was to receive from the physician. The complete translation of the Nestorian inscription never reached him.

Cuper and Witsen tried to make the best of it and now hoped to turn to Joan van Hoorn with further questions about China, but unfortunately Van Hoorn's malady surfaced again that same winter. Before the retired Governor-General could move into the house of the Amsterdam merchant Josephus Deutz, which he had purchased for the then gigantic sum of 73,000 guilders, he passed away on 22nd February 1711.[51]

What remains of the scholarly correspondence between Witsen and Cuper shows that their dilettante discussion of Chinese affairs died a natural death because of the lack of information from the Indies. In the years that followed Witsen used his influence to purchase Chinese books in Batavia for an Italian correspondent.[52] Cuper regained some of his former enthusiasm when he heard from Mathurin Veyssière de Lacroze, the librarian of the Elector of Brandenburg, that he was looking for a key for deciphering Egyptian hieroglyphs and Chinese characters with the help of the Coptic language. His excitement was soon tempered by Witsen's disbelieving reply.[53]

Thebitsia emerged one more time in the Witsen-Cuper correspondence, when Cuper brought up Isaac Vossius' rather fantastic calculations of the population of China. The sceptic Witsen first dismissed Vossius' imaginative flights with a few well-chosen words: "I used to know Vossius well; apart from his knowledge of Latin and of Roman scholarship, he was very inexperienced and ushered a lot of falsehoods into print. I told him so when I met him twenty-five years ago in England".[54] But then, as if to temper his earlier stern comment, he returned in a later letter to the issue and added "In China there are a lot of people. The Chinese, to whom I spoke, told me that he noticed no crowds, not even at The Hague or in Amsterdam where the eye encounters the most people. In Peking he said people were squeezed to death at the city gate almost every day".[55]

Several conversation pieces have been dealt with in passing in this anecdotal story about an adventurous Chinese physician: the antiquity of Chinese civilization and its chronology, the search for a key to decipher the Chinese character script, China's enormous population, Chinese medicine and its methods of diagnosis, Chinese drugs such as the ginseng root and its miraculous curative powers. Here I need not expatiate further about these topics which roughly constituted the talk of early eighteenth century European armchair Sinology; others have done so elsewhere.

Yet there remains one question: What became of Thebitsia after his return home? Apart from the apocryphal anecdote about the physician's quarrel with the Dutch burgher in Batavia, we know nothing about his further career. Let us give our imagination free rein, reconstructing the situation in which that clash may have occurred. The old doctor proudly struts out of the gate of Batavia castle, a slave holding the payong following in his wake. Upon seeing his path obstructed a Dutch visitor tauntingly jibes: "Pray, Thebitsia, what sutra brought from the West justifies thy haughty demeanour?"

The answer was... a stick.

NOTES

1. J.F. Gebhard, *Het leven van mr. Nicolaas Cornelisz Witsen (1641-1717)*, Utrecht, 1881, p. 341. A collection of Witsen's letters to the Deventer burgomaster Gijsbert Cuper has been published as an appendix to Gebhard's bibliography.

2. A fine description of such a network, spreading from the fieldworkers in Asia via Holland to scholars like Leibniz in Hanover or Lacroze in Berlin, is given by Marion Peters in her recent study "Nicolaes Witsen and Gijsbert Cuper: two seventeenth century Dutch burgomasters and their Gordian Knot", *Lias* 16, 1 (1989), pp. 111-150.

3. For a recent study on Van Rheede see the biography by J. Heniger, *Hendrik Adriaen van Reede tot Drakenstein (1636-1691) and Hortus Malabaricus*, Rotterdam/Boston, 1986.

4. Gebhard, *Het leven van N. Witsen*, p. 370.

5. The emergence of Chinese studies in Europe is surveyed by D.E. Mungello, *Curious Land, Jesuit Accommodation and the Origins of Sinology*, Hawaii University Press, 1989 and Knud Lundbaek, *T.S. Bayer (1694-1738), Pioneer Sinologist*, London: Curzon Press, 1986 (*Scandinavian Institute of Asian Studies Monograph Series* 54). Lundbaek gives a partial

translation of the preface to Bayer's *Museum Sinicum*, which constitutes a history of European proto-sinology written by a participant-observer.

6. The Dutch version appeared in 1665, the English translation by John Ogilby in 1669.

7. The original travelogue with water-colour drawings was discovered by the author in the Bibliothèque Nationale (Paris). See L. Blussé, R. Falkenburg, *Johan Nieuhofs Beelden van een China reis 1655-1657*, Middelburg, 1987. Recently Amoy University press also published a Chinese translation: Pao Lo-shih, Chuang Kuo-t'u, *Ho-shih chu-fang Chung-kuo chih yen-chiu*, Hsiamen, 1989.

8. A.E. van Braam Houckgeest, *Voyage de l'ambassade de la Compagnie des Indes orientales hollandaises, vers l'empereur de la Chine, dans les années 1794 et 1795*, 2 vols., Philadelphia, 1798. Olfert Dapper, *Het Gedenkwaerdig Bedrijf der Nederlandsche Oost-Indische Maetschappije, op de Kuste en in het Keizerrijk van Taising of Sina*, Amsterdam, 1670.

9. Hsü Yün-chiao (ed.), "Kai-Pa li-tai shih-chi" ("A Chronicle of Batavia"), *Nan-yang Hsüeh-pao* 9, 1 (1953), pp. 1-64.

10. Visits to Europe by other Chinese travellers have been described by Theodore Foss, "The European Sojourn of Philippe Couplet and Michael Shen Fu-tsung (1683-1692)" in Marcel van Nieuwenborgh (ed.), *Philippe Couplet (1623-93), the Man who Brought China to Europe*, Leuven, 1990?. For the "Record of Personal Observations" by Fan Shou-i who accompanied the Jesuit missionary Francesco Provana to Europe and lived there from 1710-1720, see Fang Hao, *Chung-kuo Hsi-t'ung shih* ("History of Sino-Western Relations"), 2 vols., Taipei, 1983, pp. 855-862. Jonathan D. Spence's superb study *The Question of Hu* describes in vivid detail the ordeal of Hu Juo-wang who in 1721 accompanied Father Jean-François Foucquet to France. Hu spent most of his time in France locked up in a lunatic asylum until he was finally released by the French authorities and sent back to China in 1726.

11. "Kai-Pa li-tai shih-chi", p. 33.

12. P. Mijer en W.R. van Hoëvell, "Chronologische geschiedenis van Batavia, geschreven door een Chinees", *Tijdschrift voor Neerland's Indië* III, 2 (1840), pp. 33-34.

13. F. Valentijn, *Oud en Nieuw Oost-Indiën*, 8 vols., Dordrecht,

1724-1726, IV-1, p. 254.

14. For biographical data about Joan van Hoorn see F.W. Stapel, *De Gouverneurs-Generaal van Nederlandsch-Indië in beeld en woord*, The Hague, 1941, pp. 38-39, and F. de Haan, *Priangan, De Preanger-Regentschappen onder het Nederlandsch Bestuur tot 1811*, 4 vols., Batavia, 1910-1912, I, Personalia, pp. 1-15.

15. Of this booklet published by "Joannes van den Eede, Boeck-verkooper, en Boeckdrucker der Ed. Compagnie: Wonende in de Prince-straet, in de Batavische Mercurius, 1675" only one copy is left, now treasured in the Museum Pusat, Jakarta.

16. *Confucius Sinarum philosophus sive scientia Sinensis latine exposita* was published in Paris in 1687. The title page mentions the following authors: Frs. Intorcetta, Herdtrich, Rougemont and Couplet.

17. The Van Hoorn-Van Riebeeck collection in the Algemeen Rijksarchief (ARA, National Archives) at The Hague runs to 65 invoice numbers covering about 1,25 running metres. The other part of the Van Hoorn-Van Riebeeck manuscript collection can be consulted at the KITLV (Koninklijk Instituut voor Taal-, Land- en Volkenkunde, Royal Institute of Anthropology), Leiden.

18. F. de Haan, *Priangan* I, p. 9.

20. Gebhard, *Het Leven van N. Witsen*, p. 457.

21. *Ibidem*, p. 461.

21. Nicolaes Witsen, *Noord en Oost Tartarijen*, Amsterdam, 1692 and 1705.

22. KITLV, H 335b, letter N. Witsen to J. van Hoorn, d.d. 23-12-1706.

23. When nobody in Batavia was able to read the antique seal-script, Van Hoorn sent the mirror to China to have it deciphered over there. See Gebhard, *Het Leven van N. Witsen*, p. 308.

24. Valentijn, *Oud en Nieuw Oost-Indiën* IV, p. 338.

25. *Ibidem* IV, p. 336.

26. ARA, VOC 725, "Resolutie Gouverneur-Generaal en Raden" d.d. 21-10-1709, f. 643.

27. Never shy of name-dropping, Cuper adds that this same source "adseret mihi salutem ab illustri Leibnitzio". Amsterdam University Library, manuscript coll., B f 63, 1 verso-2 verso.

28. See F. de Haan, *Priangan* I, p. 12.
29. KITLV, H 316. Request supplianten Goudienko c.s. Batavia 1709. Thebitsia signs here, Chou Mei-kuan.
30. Resolutie G.G. en Raden 1-10-1709, see F. de Haan, *Priangan* I, p. 12.
31. See letter-book J. van Hoorn and his wife J.M. van Riebeeck to G.G. A. van Riebeeck 31-10-1709 until 2-2-1711. ARA, Van Hoorn-Van Riebeeck coll., no. 19. "Op het schip Sandenburg... in de *kajuit*", the G.G., his wife, daughter, two slave girls, and one Dutch and one moorish boy... "in de hutte" the Chinese doctor.
32. ARA, Van Hoorn-Van Riebeeck coll., no. 19, f. 45.
33. *Ibidem*, f. 25 verso.
34. *Ibidem*, letter to Isaak Persijn, 22-1.1710, f. 43.
35. *Ibidem*, f. 42.
36. About Heyrmans, see F. de Haan, *Priangan* I, pp. 25-26.
37. Michael Boym, *Clavis Medica ad Chinarum Doctrinam De Pulsibus*, Nürnberg, 1686. See also Hartmut Walravens, *China illustrata, Das europäische Chinaverständnis im Spiegel des 16. bis 18. Jahrhunderts*, Wolfenbüttel, 1987.
38. "Memorie der Recepten door doctor Thebitia op sijn wedervertrek naar Batavia aan mijn huijsvrouw opgegeven". KITLV, H 269.
39. KITLV, H 375, Travel-diary J. van Hoorn, Monday 21 April 1710, f. 179.
40. A. Kircher, *China Illustrata*, p. 178.
41. KITLV, H 269. "Eenige aanteekeningen uijt de mont van den Chinees doctor Thebitia".
42. KITLV, H 269. "Naamen en Tijtreeckening der keysers van China in den tijt door den Chinees doctor Thebitia aan mij opgegeven uijt sijn Chineese geschriften in't schip Sandenburgh den 27 april 1710".
43. Gebhard, *Het leven van N. Witsen*, pp. 333-336. Upon having studied the drawings Cuper answered that instead of talking about the "pulse theory of Chinese medicine", one should speak of the "palpation of the arms". Amsterdam University Library, Be 51 a, b. f. 150. Letter 16-12-1710.
44. ARA, Van Hoorn-Van Riebeeck coll., no. 19, f. 155. Letter 30-9-1710 to Abraham van Riebeeck.
45. ARA, VOC 115. Resolutie Heren XVII 29-9-1710.
46. ARA, Van Hoorn-Van Riebeeck coll., no. 19, f. 155 verso. Letter 30-9-1710.

47. Gebhard, *Het leven van N. Witsen*, p. 332. Letter of 5-12-1710.

48. Amsterdam University Library, Be 51 a, b. f. 150 verso. Letter 16-12-1710. The debate about the stèle continued for almost two hundred years until Henri Havret, in 1895, at long last proved the authenticity of the Nestorian monument. See D. Mungello, *Curious Land*, pp. 164-171 and Henri Havret, "La stèle chrétienne de Si-ngan-fou", *Variétés Sinologiques* nos. 7, 12, 20, T'ou-sè-wè, 1895-1902.

49. Gebhard, *Het leven van N. Witsen*, p. 345.

50. *Ibidem*, p. 367.

51. ARA, aanwinsten 1897, no. LIV-2 "copy-boeck van Oost-Indische brieven 1695-1730". Letters 15-5-1711 and 25-5-1711.

52. Witsen promised Cuper that he would order Chinese books in Batavia (Gebhard, *Leven van N. Witsen*, p. 341). Many years ago, he claimed, he had also assisted the German orientalist Andreas Müller (1630-1694) in the purchase of Chinese books for the Electoral Library in Berlin. (Gebhard, *Leven van N. Witsen*, p. 362). This is confirmed by Bayer, who saw the books. See Lundbaek, *T.S. Bayer*, p. 66.

53. Amsterdam University Library, Be 61. Cuper's letter of 19-8-1712. De Lacroze wrote: "je cherche une clef universelle de tous ces caractères tant Egyptiens, que chinois. Je n'oserois vous dire ce que j'ai trouvé. J'ai en vérité fait des découvertes, dont je m'étonne moi même, mais je n'en publierai rien, que mon système ne soit tout fait...". For Witsen's reply see Gebhard, *Het leven van N. Witsen*, p. 343.

54. Gebhard, *Het leven van N. Witsen*, p. 373. Letter of 8-2-1714.

55. *Ibidem*, p. 431. Letter of 6-4-1715.

THE MONK AND THE MYTH:
JIGEN-DAISHI AT COURT

W.J. Boot

One of the most intriguing and enigmatic characters at the court of Tokugawa Ieyasu (1542-1616), and at the court of his son Hidetada (1579-1632) and grandson Iemitsu (1604-1651), was the Tendai monk Tenkai (died 1643), posthumously named Jigen-daishi. As Tsuji Zennosuke rightly remarks, the most interesting fact of Tenkai's career is that he restricted himself to religious matters. He did not owe his position to his knowledge of laws or precedents, nor did he let himself be usefully employed in drawing up law codes or in drafting foreign correspondence. He did not even concern himself with the overall aspects of the reorganization of the Buddhist church that the *bakufu* carried out in the first few decades of the seventeenth century. These matters he left to Konchiin Sūden (1569-1633). What occupied Tenkai was the restoration of the Tendai sect under his supreme direction.[1] The grand temple complexes in Nikkō (Tōshōgū and Hōrinji) and at Ueno (Kan'eiji and Tōshōgū) which he erected were (and partly still are) a continuing testimony to his success.

As far as the fortunes of the Tendai sect were concerned Tenkai was thus a pivotal figure. Yet the studies that have been made of his life and actions are few, and very unsatisfactory. We have one full length, but very uncritical, biography by Sudō Kōki[2], and we have the chapter Tsuji Zennosuke devotes to him in his *Nihon Bukkyō shi*[3]. The remainder is but a few articles which have appeared in journals or collective works.[4]

In contrast to the neglect Tenkai has suffered in the modern period, in the Edo period he was a well-known figure about whom much was written. The *Jigen-daishi zenshū*[5] contains four full-fledged biographies of Tenkai, apart from many shorter entries and references culled from other works. The biographies are, in chronological order, the *Tōei-kaisan Jigen-daishi denki*, completed in Keian 3 (1650)[6] and the *Bu-shū Tōei-kaisan Jigen-daishi den*, completed in Manji 2 (1659)[7], both in Chinese. Next we have the *Tōei-kaisan Jigen-daishi engi*, written by Inkai (1611- ?) and completed in Enpō 7 (1679)[8], in Japanese, and lastly the voluminous *Jigen-daishi go-nenpu*, completed in Tenpō 13 (1842).[9] Apart from these one very short but original chronological record, the *Jigen-daishi ryakki*, should be mentioned.[10] Thus four biographies of Tenkai were written in the seventeenth century, within forty years after his death in Kan'ei 20 (1643). The fifth one, the *Jigen-daishi go-nenpu*, was evidently compiled in view of the second centenary of Tenkai's death. All writers were connected with the Tendai sect; four of them had known Tenkai personally.

If only for reasons of space, a full biography of Tenkai cannot be attempted here. For the purposes of this article I will concentrate on the last years of the Keichō era, i.e. the period during which Tenkai first met Ieyasu and rose in his favour, thus laying the foundation for his future greatness as the executor of Ieyasu's will and founder of the Tōshōgū in Nikkō. Tenkai's later career is a sequel to what happened in these few decisive years. His early years, on the other hand, are shrouded in mystery, and Tenkai left them that way intentionally, refusing to give even his date of birth or particulars of his descent.[11] These years are a happy playground for his biographers, but the hagiographic stories and anecdotes they relate must be used with caution. As I will proceed to show in this article, exceedingly few of them can be substantiated from independent sources.

As a foil to the rest of the article I will first summarize the necrology of Tenkai that appears in the *Tokugawa jikki* under the date of his demise[12], since this is, after all, the official account of the *bakufu* and should contain what he was remembered for officially.

Tenkai, it says here, belonged to the Miura, a branch of the Ashina, and was born in Takada, Aizu-gun, in Mutsu. He was a bright child, shunned meat and devoutly believed in Buddhism. At the age of eleven he was tonsured and ordained by the priest Benyō of the Inari-dō in Wakamatsu, and exerted himself in the study of the esoteric doctrines of the Tendai sect. During the Tenbun and Kōji eras (1532-1558), from his fourteenth year onwards, he traveled to the "famous mountains and sacred places", studied under various famous monks and erudites, visited Hieizan and obtained all secrets and "seals of mind" of the Tendai sect. He stayed some time with Takeda Shingen (1521-1584) in Kōyō, and then, on the invitation of Ashina Moritaka

(1561-1584), he returned to his native country where he stayed in the Inari-dō. In Tenshō 17 (1589) Moritaka's heir Ashina Morishige (1575-1631) was attacked by Date Masamune (1567-1636). Morishige, betrayed by his vassals, had to flee with his family, but Tenkai, "though only a monk," dispersed a large enemy army and helped him escape. After the siege of Odawara (1590) Morishige received a new fief from Toyotomi Hideyoshi (1536-1598) in Edosaki (Hitachi). Here he invited Tenkai and had him restore the Fudōin. Thereafter Tenkai was successively abbot of several temples in the Kantō, and then went to the Enryakuji and resided in the Nankōbō of the Eastern Pagoda.

In Keichō 13 (1608) he was summoned by Ieyasu to Sunpu, who asked his advice and also had Tenkai occasionally assemble the monks of his sect in order to hold disputations on points of Buddhist doctrine. In his moments of leisure Tenkai revealed to Ieyasu the secret doctrines of his sect and spoke to him of the *Sannō ichijitsu shintō*, which seemed especially to interest Ieyasu. "Since then he was always in Ieyasu's proximity and all his proposals were accepted." The burial of Ieyasu on the Kunōzan, his removal to Nikkō and the divine name given him posthumously by the emperor were all Tenkai's doing.

Ex-Emperor Go-Yōzei placed particular trust in him. That Tenkai was appointed Great High Priest (*dai-sōjō*) was due to his support. He was also the one who gave Tenkai the name of Bishamondō[13].

Tenkai founded the temple in Nikkō and the Tōeizan (Kan'eiji) in Ueno, which together with Hieizan were the three centres of the Tendai sect during the Edo period. Under the *shōgun* Hidetada (1579-1632) and Iemitsu (1604-1651) he was treated very well, as became someone who had been so highly valued by Ieyasu. When Tenkai fell ill, the *rōjū* and other important officials came to visit him, *bakufu* physicians "appeared in droves and discussed ways to heal him," and even the *shōgun* himself visited him in his temple quarters and with his own hands gave him a hot potion to drink.

His age is not known, the *Jikki* concludes, but since at the time he was entertained by Takeda Shingen he must have been in his thirties or forties, he must have been over a hundred years old when he died. In the twelfth month of Shōhō 4 (1647) he was given the *gō* Jigen-daishi by the emperor, on the request of his foremost disciple Kōkai.[14]

Early history

It is not possible to substantiate Tsuji Zennosuke's claim that
Tenkai "lived in" (i.e. was the abbot of) the Kitain in Kawagoe
as early as Tenshō 16 (1588), or even as early as Keichō 4
(1599), as is claimed in Tenkai's biographies.[15] It is a pity, for
one of the two major miracles of Tenkai's early years took
place in this temple. The *Denki* places it in Keichō 5, in the
early morning of the thirteenth day of the twelfth month (17-1-
1601). A circumstantial dating, and a circumstantial account:

> Tenkai had ambition and continuously worshipped [the
> Bodhisattva] Kokūzō (S. Ākāśagarbha or Gaganagarbha). In
> the second year that he lived there, from the night of the
> twelfth day of the twelfth month onward, he performed
> the ritual exquisitely, cleansed in body and mind. At
> daybreak on the thirteenth, the appointed hour, he wanted
> to pay homage to the bright stars. At this moment from
> the pond in front of the temple a ball of miraculous light
> suddenly flew forth and disappeared to the east. It had a
> subtle, wondrous colour. It was a rare, auspicious omen.
> Others asked him, saying: "What does this mean?" He
> answered: "When a dragon moans clouds issue forth, when
> a tiger sighs the wind rises. The tiger is the virtue of
> fire, the dragon the virtue of water. Clouds bring forth
> water, wind engenders fire. This is the invariable logic [of
> nature]. The state of the heart is in complete accord with
> the ultimate reality of all phenomena. A good man will
> have good dreams and see all kinds of good sights, a bad
> man will have bad dreams and see all kinds of bad sights.
> The fiery wagon rumbles [to the house of the sinner to
> take him to hell] and [over the house of the just] purple
> clouds hang down, [so] the same applies again, [also in
> regard to the question] whether one dies a good death or
> a bad one. Why then should it be cause for amazement
> that I, Tenkai, saw this rare, miraculous light?"[16]

As the monks of the Kitain were not at a loss to point out, the
same miracle, a bright star rising from the pond and climbing
towards heaven, occurred when the founder of the temple,
Sonkai, first came to live there; actually, this had been the
origin of the name of the temple: *Seiyasan* or Star-field Moun-

tain.[17] It was thus a very appropriate miracle, and according to the *Denki* Tenkai did not fail to mention it to Ieyasu in Keichō 17 (1612), when Ieyasu was about to give the temple to him.[18] To the miracle, however, the same applies as to the date of Tenkai's first stay in the Kitain: no external sources exist that substantiate it. Even within the charmed circle of Tenkai's biographies support is slight. The *Denki* and the *Den* describe it, the *Ryakki* mentions it, but in the *Engi* both the later reference and a description of the miracle itself are lacking.[19]

The first time Tenkai emerges from the *clair-obscur* of myth into the harsh light of history is in connection with the Fudōin that we found mentioned in the *Tokugawa jikki*. Here we do have independent records that link Tenkai to the temple. These are three letters addressed to one Imakōji, a *bōkan* (i.e. a senior servant of a *monzeki*) of the Myōhōin, and the colophon of a book, dated Keichō 2/3/1. One of the letters is signed "Tenkai Fudōin Fūshi", one is signed "Fudōin Tenkai" and the colophon is signed very circumstantially as "Jō-shū Edosaki Fudōin hōin dai-kashō Zuifū" ("the Great Priest Following-The-Wind, Seal of the Law, of the Fudōin in Edosaki in the Province of Hitachi"), figuring both the name "Fudōin" and the character "fū" ("wind"), and thus providing a putative date for the letters.[20]

The letters, written between the twenty-fourth and the twenty-seventh of a tenth month (no year is specified), offer a number of problems for interpretation and translation; I cannot say that I have solved them all. It is clear, however, that the letters all concern the "Rengein-hōryū", i.e. (probably) the Renge-ryū, one of the many "Schools" within the Tendai sect.[21] Of this Renge-ryū it is said that "it is the School of the *ue-sama*". In view of Imakōji's function, this "*ue-sama*" will have been the *monzeki* of the Myōhōin, Prince Jōin (1548-1621)[22], who as an imperial prince certainly rated this form of address. This supposition is borne out by the fact that the Renge-ryū is contrasted with the Sanmai-ryū, another Tendai School, and the *ue-sama* with the *monzeki* of the Shōren'in, which is another of the three major *monzeki* temples of the Tendai sect.

Next two priests are introduced, referred to as Hōninbō and Hannyain, who have already approached the Myōhōin in connection with the Renge-ryū. Apparently they are to some extent Tenkai's subordinates, for Tenkai offers his excuses for a sudden visit they paid to Imakōji. The point of the exercise seems to be that Tenkai and his associates want to organize those Tendai temples in East Japan that belong to the Renge-ryū under the aegis and protection of the Myōhōin, in the same way as those of the Sanmai-ryū depend from the Shōren'in. As the letter carefully specifies, this would mean that all appointments to monastic functions and ranks would go through the Myōhōin. Tenkai is, in fact, requesting the protection of the Myōhōin to carve out his own little empire in the Kantō.

In order to be able to head these temples of the Renge-ryū in East Japan, however, Tenkai needs to be "baptized" into the Renge-ryū, i.e. undergo the ritual of initiation into the secrets of the School (the so-called *dengyō kanjō*). He is so anxious for this initiation that he does not insist on the full ritual: the *ue-sama* need not come to Hieizan, where Tenkai seems to be staying; Tenkai is willing "to come down" and if the ceremony is celebrated in a simple way in the *monzeki*'s palace, in secret, it would be more than sufficient.

Finally he broaches the delicate matter of compensating the *monzeki* for his pains. "Since the troubles", he confesses, "temple domains have dwindled and we have suffered enormous losses," but nevertheless he will be able to offer two pieces of gold, "country weight" (*inakame*, i.e. heavier that the gold coins circulating in the capital region).

Apart from the signature Fudōin there is some internal evidence that points to the last decade of the sixteenth century as the period in which the letters most probably were written. This is (1) the reference to "the troubles" - "*rango*" is used twice[23] - and (2) the phrase "Since I am responsible for the temples of the *naifu* and the Satake" (*warera mo Naifu Satake no jike o ai-kakae-sōrō no aida*.)[24] In this context "troubles", I think, refers to the unsettling effects of the fall of the Hōjō in 1590, when Ieyasu and other *daimyō* moved into the Kantō and everything was changed around. "*Naifu*" is a term commonly used to the 1590's, but not later, in reference to Ieyasu, and the Satake were most in evidence in this part of the world between 1590, when Hideyoshi enfeoffed Satake Yoshinobu (1570-1633) and his brother (and Tenkai's patron) Ashina Morishige in Hitachi, and 1602, when Ieyasu transferred both to Akita.

Tenkai's attempt to be initiated into the "*Rengein-hōryū*" seems to have failed. At least, the Renge-ryū is specifically named as one of the schools of which he did not receive the baptism.[25]

According to the biographies, Tenkai's next stage, after the Kitain and the Fudōin, was the Sōkōji, one of the most ancient Tendai temples in the Kantō.[26] It was originally located in Ōta (Naganuma, Haga-gōri, Shimotsuke). For some reason, however, the monks of this temple had fallen foul of their lord Tagaya Shigetsune (1558-1618) and they had left the temple in Tenshō 18 (1590).[27] Whatever the reason may have been for abandoning the temple, under the direction of Ryōben, who led the exodus, the Sōkōji was rebuilt as the Shin-Sōkōji in Kugeta (Haga-gōri). In this enterprise Ryōben was helped by a local potentate, Mizunoya Masamura (1521-1596), also known as Banryū-nyūdō.[28] Once Tenkai had joined the temple, on Ryōben's insistence, his qualities, too, were recognized by the Mizunoya. Banryū's brother, adoptive son and successor, Katsutoshi (?1541-1606)[29], presented him with an income (*shiryō*) of 200 *koku*.

The original site, however, had also been resettled, by a monk named Nōkai. In 1600 he had finally prevailed upon Tagaya Shigetsune to order the original Sōkōji to be restored in Naganuma, but in this fatal year Shigetsune joined the wrong side and his fief was taken away from him by Ieyasu in 1601. It was Tenkai who at long last, in Keichō 9/10/18, returned the Sōkōji to Naganuma. The name of the Shin-Sōkōji in Kugeta was changed to Zensuiji, and Ryōben remained there to nurse his old age.[30] Needless to say, under Tenkai's direction the Sōkōji became a major centre of study and learning.

Hardly anything of the above can be substantiated by independent evidence. Even the year in which Tenkai first came to the Sōkōji is not clear. With the exception of the *Sōkōji rekidai shi*, which gives Keichō 9[31], all bibliographies assert that it was in Keichō 8 (1603). The *Denki* even gives the amazingly precise date of Keichō 8/11/2.[32] No independent evidence exists to confirm either of these dates.

The earliest evidence linking Tenkai to the Sōkōji is a number of letters that he signed in the second month of Keichō 10 (1605). These letters, in which he appoints one "Ken'yū of the Shikan'in" to the offices of *gon-daisōzu*, *gon-risshi*, and *hōin*, are preserved in the Sōkōji. Since the Shikan'in was a part of the Sōkōji[33], we may assume that Tenkai was living there at the time and had a position exalted enough to allow him to appoint other monks "according to the imperial decree".[34] This tallies with the few other items of independent evidence we have that link Tenkai to the Sōkōji. These are Tenkai's *chigyō-chō* of the Sōkōji for the year Keichō 13[35], an undated letter addressed to an undecipherable addressee, and an undated poem *cum* introduction addressed to one Benkai. If the temple described in the introduction refers to the Sōkōji, it was an excellent temple indeed: "Established by the vows of emperors, restored by Yoritomo, the crown of all monasteries East of the Pass. Who does not delight in knowledge cannot live there. As no other animal lives in the lion's den, so it is with scholars."[36]

A sojourn on Hieizan

Tenkai, however, was destined for higher things than struggling rural monasteries. He had a role to play on a grander scale, and the one who would give him this role was Tokugawa Ieyasu. The most circumstantial account of the events leading up to the first meeting of Ieyasu and Tenkai is given in the *Tōei-kaisan Jigen-daishi engi*:

> In the year Keichō 12 a quarrel arose among the monks of Hieizan. When the discussions became vehement, the monks came to Suruga - the Tōshō Daigongen was staying there in his castle in Sunpu -with the Provisional High Priest (*gon-sōjō*) Gōsei at the head of one of the two factions, and appealed to him. The Divine Lord (*shinkun*) heard their case, distinguished right from wrong, and expelled the wrongdoers from the Mountain. Then he said to Zeyakuin-nyūdō Sōhaku, that in their stead a monk who had gained fame should be selected from the Kantō and sent [to the Enryakuji]. When he was selecting a man of great virtue from among the major Tendai temples of the Kantō, people told him that the Provisional High Priest Tenkai of the Sōkōji in Naganuma truly was a man [perfect in] wisdom and demeanour. Thereupon [Ieyasu] decided to place him in the Nankōbō in the Southern Valley (Nangoku) of the Main Compound (*hon'in*) of the Enryakuji, and Sōhaku brought Tenkai to Sunpu [in order to introduce him to Ieyasu]. When the Divine Lord met

him, he said: "Although this is the first time we meet, it
would not be right to let you live only on the Mountain.
I have heard that the Kitain in Senba, somewhere in the
neighbourhood of Kawagoe in Musashi, is an unrivalled
temple of the Tendai sect in the East. If you were abbot
there, I would extend my patronage to that temple. Since,
however, I cannot go back on my given word, you will
first have to climb the Mountain and encourage the
practising monks of the chief temple [of the Tendai sect].
However, be sure to come down again in about a year."
What bond from a former incarnation [was this]? People
remarked among themselves, how strange it was that at
this first meeting [Ieyasu] spoke like this.
Well then, when he was living on the Mountain, the
monks of the Enryakuji said, that a High Priest from the
country was only a quasi-official and according to the old
statutes equivalent to a Seal of the Law (*hōin*) or an
Assistant High Priest (*sōzu*) of the chief temple, and he
received the house appellation (*kamon no shōgō*) of
Chirakuin and was for the second time appointed Provisional High Priest. If you think of the logical rule (*dōri*)
that the minister of a small country loses his ranking
when he visits the court of a large state, you will see it
is the same.
While he was living there, he was very poor. Were it not
for a solitary firefly he would hardly have had the means
wherewith to illuminate his solitude, and only thin wisps
of smoke trailed [from his dwelling] at daybreak and
nightfall. When he was living there so wretchedly, Sōhaku
sewed the rents in his robes and whenever his bowl was
empty, he did something about it and thus provided for
everything.[37]

A beautiful story, well told, as is often the case in the *Engi*,
but hardly a truthful account of the facts. Not only the internal
inconsistency - Ieyasu's handpicked emissary living in abject
poverty in the Nankōbō - indicates this, but also the differences
with the older *Jigen-daishi denki* and the *Jigen-daishi den*.[38] In
their broad outlines the three biographies agree: all report the
dispute that arose in Keichō 12 amongst the monks of the
Enryakuji, leading to Ieyasu's arbitration, and all say that it was
Ieyasu who sent Tenkai to live on Hieizan. That, however, is as

far as the agreement goes. The older biographies do not mention the names of Gōsei or Sōhaku, they claim that Tenkai's name was brought forward unanimously by the monks of both warring factions, and they specify that Ieyasu ordered Tenkai to be appointed *tandai shugyō*.[39] The *Engi*, here, is satisfied with the more general phrase "to encourage the practising monks" (*gaku-ryo o susumetamau*). Finally, neither text reports that Tenkai met Ieyasu before he left for the Enryakuji, nor do they mention the extremes of poverty the *Engi* says Tenkai was living in.

In order to understand the background of these entries, it is important to remember that on Keichō 13/7/17 the *bakufu* confirmed the landholdings of the Enryakuji and promulgated its regulations for this temple. A letter, signed by Hidetada and addressed to the *shugyōdai* of the Shōkakuin, Shōkan'in and Eshin'in of the Enryakuji, gives the Enryakuji *in perpetuum* landholdings to the amount of 5000 *koku*. This was again confirmed in a letter from Ieyasu dated on the eighth of the eighth month, specifying the gift of these same holdings. The regulations are dated on the same date (Keichō 13/8/8), and contain the following provisions:

(1) Who does not practise Buddhism will have to leave the Mountain;
(2) who practises Buddhism but does not behave, will be expelled;
(3) only practitioners will succeed each other as heads of the "residences" (*bō*) that are famous for their teaching of the esoteric and exoteric doctrines (*kenmitsu no meishitsu*);
(4) no one will "have" more than one residence; empty residences will not be allowed;
(5) the head (*jūji*) disposes over the holdings of the residence;
(6) the holdings of the residence may not be sold or put up as a collateral;
(7) those monks who sign petitions and form factions will be banished.[40]

Tsuji Zennosuke has remarked that "many of these regulations were enacted as a result of judgements rendered in cases brought before [the *bakufu*]. The reasons were that [with a case pending before the *bakufu*] many opportunities were available to get to know the precedents within the sect and that it was the most opportune moment to enact legislation. Even when no lawsuit had been brought in order to decide a dispute, the usual procedure seems to have been to invite all eminent monks from within the sect, have them prepare a draft, and revise that."[41] The *Enryakuji hatto* was only the second set of such regulations promulgated by the *bakufu*, the first one being the regulations for the Kōyasan of 1601.[42] The supposition that, after the pattern obtaining on the Kōyasan[43], on Hieizan, too, disputes between the monks had been brought before Ieyasu and had provided the *bakufu* with an opportunity to impose its regulations is not, as such, unlikely. It is, however, unattested. At least, no disputes within the Enryakuji or expeditions of its monks to Sunpu are mentioned in the sources consulted by this writer for the year Keichō 12.

If the story of the "dispute of the monks" is false, the implication would seem to be that Tenkai was not sent by Ieyasu, but went to the Enryakuji on his own initiative, in order further to improve his own fortunes. In that case, the abject poverty he lived in may have been more than a literary *cliché*.

A second problem concerns the dating. "Keichō 12 or 13", say the biographies, but that does not tally with the definite dates that are provided by a *kuzen'an*, dated Keichō 14/12/9, in which "Seal of the Law Tenkai" is appointed Provisional High Priest (*gon-sōjō*)[44], and a letter, also dated on the ninth of the twelfth month and addressed to the "High Priest (*sōjō*) Sōkōji Tenkai", that was written by the *monzeki* of the Myōhōin, Prince Jōin:

> I take the trouble to write you. Since the matter at hand, [your promotion to] the supreme office (*kyokkan*), is a matter of grave concern, both according to the ancient precedents and according to the present customs, I petitioned [the emperor], and immediately an imperial appointment was given. This, however, is [due to] the extreme grace [of the Buddha], about which we cannot do a thing (i.e. for which we can only be grateful - W.J.B.). You would do well to excel yourself more and more in prayers for the long life of our emperor and in a single-

minded sincere [devotion] to the prosperity of Buddhism: these are the most important things.[45]

The *kuzen'an* and Jōin's letter are generally, if rather tenuously, constructed as the answer to the following letter by Tenkai:

> This time I have come to the capital on the command of the *shōgun* (?) (*jōi ni yori*), with orders to climb the Mountain in order to encourage [the monks to improve] their practice of Buddhism. Therefore, as regards the matter of my supreme office (*kyokkan*), I would appreciate it very much if you would petition the emperor, that according to the precedents I may receive an imperial appointment. Since the purport of the above has also, from my patrons (*danna-shū*) in the Kantō, been communicated to Itakura Iga[-no-kami Katsushige (1542-1624)], he will have told Lord Kajūji [Mitsutoyo (1575-1612)]. He will announce that these things will indeed come to pass. Respectfully.
> Signed: Sōkōji Tenkai
> Dated: nineteenth day, twelfth month (no year specified)
> Addressed to: Toriikōji-dono.[46]

The object of Tenkai's letter clearly was to ask the *monzeki* of the Shōren'in to intercede with the emperor on his behalf and to get Tenkai what Tenkai and his patrons wanted, i.e. a "supreme office" (*kyokkan*). In view of the *kuzen'an* of Keichō 14/12/9 and the letter I assume to be Jōin's, the supreme office he solicited must have been that of Provisional High Priest (*gon-sōjō*). Unless, however, as Tsuji suggests, both the *kuzen'an* and Jōin's letter were antedated,[47] this means that it took almost a whole year (from Keichō 13/12/19 till Keichō 14/12/9) for Tenkai's initial letter to Toriikōji to have the desired effect. If the backing he claimed he had in his letter existed at all, it had singularly failed to impress the courtiers, and his patrons had been singularly uninterested in supporting Tenkai, leaving him to cool his heels in Kyōto for nearly a year. Moreover, the appointment brought him not much nearer to his (and Ieyasu's) alleged goal, for the title of Provisional High Priest (*gon-sōjō*) carried no special authority on Hieizan. Since it does not seem likely that Tenkai was bragging, and I see no reason to arrange the letters in a different sequence, the likeliest remaining supposition is that, indeed, Tenkai's backers let him down.

Following on the documents we have discussed above, a second series of letters and diary entries exists all of which concern Tenkai's appointment to the office of *tandai*. This series starts with a formal request that Tenkai wrote on the sixth of the ninth month of Keichō 15, asking to be appointed. Together with the letters of three other candidates his letter was forwarded to the court on the fourteenth through Imakōji, the *bōkan* of the Myōhōin. Imperial approval was given on Keichō 15/9/18, the decrees were drafted on the thirtieth, and on the first of the tenth month the four monks came to court and received their appointments.[48]

Tandai ("they who select the themes") were appointed in connection with the celebration of the "Great Seminar", the *Tendai Hokke-e* or *Shimotsuki-e*, which in Keichō 15 was celebrated from the eleventh till the seventeenth of the tenth month.[49] Even though it was an *ad hoc* office, Tenkai's appointment must be regarded as a distinction and an acknowledgement of his scholarly qualities.

The reconstruction of this sequence of events is threatened somewhat by one last document, that nobody knows what to do with. It is the undated draft of a letter (*bun'an*) that was preserved amongst the papers of Kajūji Mitsutoyo and must be assigned to the beginning of the eighth month of Keichō 15:

> In connection with the coming Great Seminar there are some problems regarding Sōkōji's fulfilling this duty. Anyhow, a temple-name of a temple that is equal [to the Enryakuji] will not do. Therefore, you must ask and see whether the emperor is of the opinion that [Tenkai] will be able to fulfill his duties without [the name of] one of the monk's residences (*bō*) of Hieizan or having received a new *in*-name. If [the emperor] agrees, I will instruct [Tenkai] to return the oral decree (*kuzen*) ... [50]

The rest of the letter is too garbled to make sense, though it is interesting to note that the name Nankōbō, that in future will be Tenkai's sobriquet, here makes its first appearance. The problem seems to have been that Tenkai up till then had used the title "of the Sōkōji", and that the Sōkōji was a temple in its own right, on par with the Enryakuji. In other words, Tenkai did not belong to the Enryakuji, and as an outsider he could not fulfill any of its offices. Apparently this irregularity was noticed only after a first imperial decree, appointing Tenkai (to the office of *tandai* ?), had been given out, so protocol demanded that this first decree be rescinded, that a new, correct title be given to Tenkai, and that a second decree be handed down. Logic seems to demand that this new title was the one used on the second occasion, at the end of the ninth month, when Tenkai and his three fellow *tandai* were appointed. In that case the title newly given to Tenkai must have been "Chirakuin", as is used by Mibu Takasuke in his diary, and not yet "Nankōbō".[51]

In the extant sources, Sōkōji appears for the last time at the end of Keichō 14[52], while Nankōbō is used currently in reference to Tenkai from the third month of Keichō 18 on- ward.[53] The earliest passages, however, in which Nankōbō is used in reference to Tenkai seem to be an entry in Sūden's diary for Keichō 16/9/29, and an entry in the *Sunpu-ki* for Keichō 16/11/1.[54]

It seems to me that two key figures in these events must have been Zeyakuin Sōhaku and Ex-Emperor Go-Yōzei. Sōhaku was a physician, highly regarded by Ieyasu and with connections at the imperial court; he was the adopted son of Zensō, who had studied under Manase Shōkei and had become Hideyoshi's attending physician. Zensō had been one of the people who persuaded Hideyoshi to allow the Enryakuji to be restored, and his son apparently continued this family tradition of Tendai patronage.[55] Someone with his connections might have given Tenkai a wrong impression of the extent to which Ieyasu was interested in sending him to Hieizan, but might, on the other hand, have finally managed to gather sufficient support in the capital to carry the project through to a satisfactory conclusion. If the report that in the course of Keichō 14 Tenkai was summoned several times by Go-Yōzei to come to court were otherwise attested, this would form an important link in the chain of events. It is just the kind of meeting Sōhaku could have engineered, and the *Denki* and the *Den*, though their account is marred by factual mistakes and is not supported by the *Engi*, contain a vague suggestion of a causal relation between Tenkai's attendance on Go-Yōzei and his appointment to *gon-sōjō*.[56]

Sōhaku's continuing interest and his air of authority, also in his dealings with *monzeki*, are apparent in the following letter (from Sōhaku to Imakōji, dated sixteenth day of the sixth month, no year specified):

Since last year I have had no contact with you. Though I should have waited upon the *monzeki* (of the Myōhōin-W.J.B.) quickly in order to thank him, this has been delayed, contrary to my intentions. I want you to intercede for me. I would especially like to ask you to mediate, in order that [the *monzeki*] instructs lord Kajūji that also in the case of the supreme office (*kyokkan*) of Kitain he gets imperial consent and finishes the business. I am very grateful that in regard to Nankōbō you were willing to mediate. I look forward to meeting you. Respectfully.
(signed) Yakuin Sōhaku
P.S. As you have obtained in regard to Nankōbō an imperial decree, I would like to ask you to obtain at the same time [the emperor's] consent in regard to Kitain.[57]

First meetings with Ieyasu

The main paradox in Tenkai's biography is that, while his meeting with Ieyasu was of crucial importance to his career, it occurred so late in his life. Tenkai's biographers apparently regarded this situation as less than satisfactory, and as a result all biographies have a tendency to place the first meeting as early as they dare; in fact, one could say that the less reliable the biography, the earlier it places such a meeting.

The palm must go to the *Asakusa-dera shi* that claims Ieyasu summoned Tenkai as early as the fourth month of Tenshō 18 (1590), when the siege of Odawara had barely begun.[58] The *Tenshō nikki*, a spurious source if there ever was one, comes in a good second. It describes a meeting in Tenshō 18/10/1, a mere two months after Ieyasu had moved into his new residence Edo. The idea is that Tenkai, the abbot of one of the major temples in the Kantō, came to pay his respects to his new overlord. Tenkai appears as Senba no Kitain and Shinoda no Fudōin. "'Call him in,' spoke Ieyasu."[59] Another source claims that in the seventh month of Keichō 5 two months before the battle of

Sekigahara, Tenkai "prayed for the protection of country" in the Yakushidō in Kanda. When he presented the tallies (indicating the number of prayers and of *sutra* recitations) to Ieyasu, he received an undergarment.[60]

The *Engi*, as we have seen, settles for Keichō 12, and claims that Ieyasu and Tenkai met before the latter left for the Enryakuji. The *Denki*, finally, places it in Keichō 13 (1608), and tells a most moving story:

> He received Ieyasu's command and went to Sunpu for the first time. The monks of the Mountain gave a farewell party in the Wood of the Seven Shrines (i.e. the shrine complex where the Sannō, the tutelary deity of Hieizan, was worshipped - W.J.B.), in order to enliven his departure. At that time a monkey suddenly appeared. Its appearance was very extraordinary. It was not afraid of the men and remained at Tenkai's side. Tenkai was glad and thought that it must be an incarnation of the god (i.e. Sannō - W.J.B.). Thereupon he spoke to the multitude, saying: "Today for the first time I have gone down the Mountain. On this day this spiritual animal has mingled with our farewell party. This is an auspicious omen. *Sannō ichijitsu shintō* and the deep meaning of the Three Kinds of Truth of Tendai certainly are something to be held up for this frivolous and decadent world [as an ideal] worth striving for."[61]

The *Denki* then proceeds to relate how Tenkai made his first impression on Ieyasu one evening when Ieyasu, having given a rough rendering of the fundamentals of the Pure Land teachings, asked whether "this was not a very secret and deep doctrine?"[62]
Tenkai had to disappoint him: "In Tendai circles ideas of this level are considered to have a very inferior and shallow meaning. [They are the same ideas] young novices, too, are always spouting." Ieyasu, rather taken aback, commanded him to organize on a short term a disputation in order to prove his assertion. Tendai monks were gathered, and a disputation was duly held. This, the *Denki* concludes, was the first of such religious debates held in the castle at Sunpu, and to drive home this point it follows with a lyrical description of such gatherings:

At the opinions expressed by those who asked the questions and those who responded, lions frowned and roared
and the elephant kings turned round to watch. Tenkai, as
the arbiter (*shōgi*), was even like a gold-winged bird up in
the air. Now they hold forth on the secret meaning of the
senju nenbutsu teachings, and gradually they reach the
point at which the young monks of one summer sitting in
the back rows admit defeat. But what is discussed and
concluded by the monks of two summers and more on the
front rows is [of a level] quite unreachable for anybody
of inferior intelligence. Ieyasu, however, is endowed with
a fine natural understanding, and thus he is at least able
to tell shallow from deep opinions.[63]

Still according to the *Denki*, Tenkai left Sunpu in Keichō 14
(1609), to return there only in Keichō 16. On his return, Ieyasu,
glad to see him back, told him that he was now ready to change
his religious conviction and would take Tenkai as his teacher
(*shihan*). This request was introduced with quite a speech:

It has been some years now that I have ruled the empire
with military virtue. Looking back maturely over the past,
I wanted to destroy my unjust enemies and I have lost
quite a lot of my own soldiers. [However, as the saying
goes,] "When all is in a state of order, he does not forget
that disorder may come."[64] Nowadays I have to enforce
punishments, but I imagine that this cannot but have some
unforeseen, detrimental influence on my chances of
rebirth. If I am not succoured by the force of the [Bud-
dhist] Law, how can I throw off this body of accumulated
worldly defilement?[65]

Tenkai, however, asked Ieyasu "first to invite famous monks of
the various sects and to study in depth the tenets of their
sects." It was his intention, so the writer of the *Denki* explains,
first to extirpate the one-sided opinions of the various schools
by confronting representatives of exoteric, esoteric, and Zen
sects with each other and then to come out with his *Sannō
ichijitsu shintō*, thus letting Ieyasu know "the perfection of both
worlds".[66] Eventually Ieyasu, "delighting in the subtle [teachings
of the three] wondrous aspects sat in forgetfulness in his room
and discovered the abstruse [truth that] 'the essential nature as

such is bright'."[67] Thereupon, Tenkai transmitted to him the "blood-veins" of Tendai.[68]

It becomes monotonous but, again, nothing of this can be proven. We have seen how the biographies contradict each other: while the *Denki* and the *Den* place Tenkai's first return to Sunpu in Keichō 13 and 14 respectively, the *Engi* places it *after* his appointment to *gon-sōjō* and yet has him come back from Sunpu to Kyōto in Keichō 14. The *Tokugawa jikki* mentions Keichō 13 in one account and Keichō 15 in the other. Sudō, who has made an honest effort to rework the various sources into one coherent story, has to put off the first meeting to the beginning of Keichō 15, situating it between Tenkai's appointment to *gon-sōjō* and his appointment to *tandai*.[69] Tenkai, of course, had every opportunity to return to the Kantō, but proof that he did so at any given time before the ninth month of Keichō 16 is lacking.[70]

Neither is there any proof that at that time he already knew Ieyasu. There are, to the contrary, some indications that he did not: in connection with the succession of Emperor Go-Yōzei by Emperor Go-Minoo in Keichō 16, Ieyasu stayed in Kyōto from the seventeenth of the third till the eighteenth of the fourth month; he even found the time to organize a religious disputation by a number of Shingon monks.[71] Yet we are asked to believe that during this whole month Tenkai did not once try to meet him[72], though we possess a letter in the hand of Go-Yōzei himself, dated the twentieth of the same third month, in which Go-Yōzei personally ordered that "the Provisional High Priest (*gon-sōjō*) Tenkai of the Bishamondō was to be promoted to High Priest (*shō-sōjō*)."[73] Tenkai must have visited the capital on that occasion. Apparently he had not yet been properly introduced to Ieyasu; he could hardly have regarded him as a patron not important enough to wait upon, if he had known him.

Sometime between the fourth and the seventh month, however, relations between the *bakufu* and Tenkai must have become closer. The *terminus ante quem* is provided by a letter by Tenkai, dated on Keichō 16/7/20 and addressed to Honda Masanobu (1538-1616). It is contained in the *Nenpu* and runs as follows:

Senba has been founded by the three patriarchs[74], it is the original lineage of the Eshin School.[75] Amongst the Buddhist temples it is a spiritual place, unrivalled in the empire. Yet in recent years the place has gone to waste- a thing our whole sect lamented. But though we grieved, we were powerless. Now, however, the *bakufu* ("*ryūei*") has directed that it should be restored. An excellent opportunity! The time has come! I would like you to report [to the *shōgun*] that we intend to remain in this place for ever, to preach with all our might and to exert ourselves in spreading the Law of the Buddha. Respectfully.[76]

The letter reads not as a solicitation for funds, but rather as the confirmation ("lest you forget") of promises made by the *bakufu*. Masanobu was the obvious person to whom to send this reminder, for he was one of the most important officials of the *bakufu*, in good standing with both Ieyasu and Hidetada, and one of the three intendants (*sōbugyō*) of the Kantō. By whom these promises had been made, and to whom, is unclear. The use of the word "*ryūei*", however, suggests Hidetada, rather than Ieyasu, who would be referred to as *ōgosho-sama*.

The first recorded meeting between Tenkai and Ieyasu did finally take place on the first of the eleventh month of the same year, when Ieyasu visited Kawagoe in the course of a hawking trip. After dark, so the *Sunpu-ki* informs us, he received in audience "Sanmon Nankōbō, Senba Kitain and others"[77] and directed that, as "fields of charity" (*kanninryō*) for its monks, land should be given to the temple in Senba.[78] The following year (Keichō 17/4/19) "Sanmon Nankōbō *sōjō* Tenkai" visited Ieyasu in Sunpu and told him of his intention to go to Senba. The implication was that he would remain there as abbot, for Ieyasu made him a present of thirty pieces of silver and gave the temple landholdings to the amount of 300 *koku*, while he remarked that "he considered this High Priest a teacher (*gakushō*) of the Tendai sect whom all the monks of the Tendai sect in the Kantō should follow."[79]

These are the only entries the *Sunpu-ki* contains for the years Keichō 16 and 17, in which Tenkai is mentioned, and neither of them is confirmed in Sūden's diary, the *Honkō-kokushi nikki*. This changes drastically in the following year. Beginning with the eighteenth day, second month of Keichō 18, the *Sunpu-ki* mentions him during that year in ten different entries, and Sūden, too, refers to him often. Tenkai's movements during this year can be reconstructed as follows: he arrived in Sunpu on the twenty-eighth of the first month and stayed on till at least the twenty-second of the third[80]. Most of his time was taken up with religious disputations. In a letter to Itakura Katsushige, dated Keichō 18/3/12, Sūden writes that four disputations by Tendai monks had already been held that year, to the great delight of Ieyasu[81], and from a letter to the same addressee we learn that on the twenty-second of the third month Ieyasu ordered yet another disputation to be held by monks of the Shingon Shingi sect.[82]

One of the things to notice is the change of address: in its entry for Keichō 18/2/18 the *Sunpu-ki* carefully mentions Tenkai not, as it used to, as "Sanmon Nankōbō", but as "Bu-shū Kawagoe Senba Nankōbō *sōjō*", and on the twenty-eighth of the same month it is "Senba Nankōbō *sōjō*" who is invited by Ieyasu for a meal.[83] Sūden, too, stresses that Tenkai "arrived from Senba" and once distinguishes "Shōkakuin of Hieizan and Nankōbō of Senba."[84]

In Senba in the meantime a small revolution must have taken place, but the sources are very uninformative about what actually happened there. The ordinary reference works tell us that the Seiyasan Muryōjuji originally, i.e. after its restoration by Sonkai, consisted of three *tatchū*, the Nakain, Kitain, and Minamiin. The temple was burnt down by Hōjō Ujitsuna (1486-1541) in 1537, but it must have been restored after a fashion, for we read that in the course of the Tenshō period (1573-1591) the Kitain became more important than the other two *in*, finally excluding the Nakain from the temple[85] and usurping the other. As a result the temple as a whole came to be called Kitain, now written with two *ateji* instead of the character for "north", and its original name Muryōjuji disappeared. Moreover, in Keichō 17 the temple received the new appellation (*sangō*) Tōeizan, and a board inscribed with this name by Ex-Emperor Go-Yōzei was presented to it. After the Kan'eiji in Edo was founded, however, the name Tōeizan was ceded to this temple and the Kitain returned to its former appellation Seiyasan.[86]

Hardly any of these things is mentioned in the biographies. It is understandable that they passed over the matter of the appellation Tōeizan in silence, as it could only create complications vis-à-vis the Kan'eiji. Apart from that, the biographies take the line that the Kitain had been Tenkai's ever since Keichō 4 at the latest, and that all its monks were glad to see him back and in charge again. Who these monks were, however, is not mentioned in the biographies, but we find references in other sources.

A revealing document in this connection is a letter from Sūden to Honda Sado-no-kami Masazumi, dated Keichō 18/3/9:

> Senba Nakain recently took part in a disputation, and the *ō-gosho-sama* (= Ieyasu) was very much taken in with his performance. In secret he even told Kakusan (a monk from the Zōjōji in Edo - W.J.B.) that, when the temple is built, he will extend his help. Overjoyed he has returned to his temple, saying that he wanted to have an audience with the *shōgun*. I send him on, [that] he may avail himself of your mediation to this effect. Details will have to wait for a later communication. ... [P.S.] Minamiin is also saying that he wants to thank the *shōgun*. Him, too, I send on, [that] you may arrange this for him. Nakain will tell you about it.[87]

The disputation where Nakain made such a good impression will have been the one that took place on the eighteenth of the second month; Senba Nakain is listed as one of the participants.[88]

At the end of Keichō 18 Nakain is mentioned again, together with Tenkai, as having had a meeting with Ieyasu. They "talked about Buddhism for more than two hours, and Ieyasu was very cheerful. Thereupon he gave the High Priest a temple fief of five hundred *koku* near Senba, and Senba Nakain he gave ten pieces of gold. Both priests then took their leave."[89] This Nakain will have been Jisson, who was appointed *gon-sōjō* in Keichō 12.[90]

Because of the way in which the sources have been complied and edited, it is very difficult to find out anything about these other monks, who were in the Muryōjuji before Tenkai came to live there and who were his closest colleagues during these years. Illustrative is the way in which even the *Senba konryū ki* is silent about the fate of the Nakain or the Minamiin. Though its account for the years from Keichō 17 till 19 seems exhaustive, in fact it only tells of the buildings that were put up for Tenkai, i.e. for the Kitain.

According to the *Konryū-ki* building activities began in Keichō 17, eighth month, with the "Great Sleeping Hall" (*daishinjo*) of the Kitain. The building was commissioned by Hidetada, who acted on the instructions of Ieyasu.[91] Apparently it was ready by the eleventh month, when Ieyasu visited the temple. In Keichō 18, again in the eighth month, the Jiedō, the storehouse and Tenkai's living quarters (*ima*) were built, also by Hidetada. The total cost of these buildings was 8.000 *ryō*.

In the eleventh month of Keichō 18 Ieyasu visited the temple again, and gave orders for the Great Hall to be built. Ieyasu also personally measured out the plots for the three *in*.[92] The next year, again in the eighth month, but this time on the orders and at the expense of Ieyasu himself, a Great Hall (*daidō*) was built. The expenses were considerable: not counting the 16.000 *ryō* for the foundation stones, which were supplied by a number of *daimyō*, Ieyasu had to lay out 8.000 *ryō* for the buildings themselves. Enshrined were Amitabha Buddha (Amida), Shakyamuni Buddha (Shakuson) and Bhaisajya-guru (Yakushi), and the Twelve Gods. Sakai Bingo-no-kami Tadatoshi was the responsible intendant in Keichō 17 and 19, and probably also, though his name is not mentioned, in Keichō 18.[93]

In the meantime Tenkai's position as - Ieyasu's words - "the *gakushō* of the Tendai School" had been confirmed in the eighth month of Keichō 18, when the *Kantō Tendai hatto* were enacted. They conferred great powers and prestige on the Kitain and on Tenkai personally. According to these regulations the Kitain held full authority over all the temples of the Tendai sect in the Kantō: no abbots could be appointed or monks admitted without the consent of the Kitain, and orders of the Kitain overrode even those of the Enryakuji itself.[94]

In a letter dated Keichō 18/3/12 that he wrote to Itakura Katsushige, Sūden confirms that he has handed these *hatto* and several other documents with vermillion seals to Tenkai.[95]

Compare this to the account that is given in the *Denki* and the *Den*! Sometime in Keicho 16, they say, Ieyasu ordered Tenkai back to Sunpu.[96] In the following year (Keichō 17, = 1612) Ieyasu asked Tenkai in which temple in the Kantō he would want to live. Tenkai answered that the Seiyasan Muryōjuji in Senba, founded by Sonkai and the wellspring of the Eshin School, was the most revered Tendai temple in the Kantō. He himself had been there, and he had had a miraculous experience during his stay. Ieyasu looked the place over, but found it rather small. Had it always been this way, he asked. No, Tenkai replied, formerly is was much larger. So Ieyasu summoned Sakai Bingo-no-kami Tadatoshi (1559-1627), the *daimyō* of Kawagoe, in whose fief the temple was located, and ordered him to rebuild and extend the temple.

In Keichō 18 (1613) Tenkai invented the so-called *ikku mondō* in answer to Ieyasu's complaint that the long sessions were too tiring for him. In the same year - "in the tenth month," says Sudō, as usual without identifying his source - Ieyasu gave the Nikkōsan to Tenkai, with the intent, apparently, that it should be his last resting place.[97] "For this reason," the *Denki* adds, "he gave the adjacent villages to the Nikkōsan."[98]   T h e biographers knew where they were going: to Nikkō. For in Nikkō Ieyasu was buried, and Nikkō therefore had become the cornerstone of Tenkai's empire and of their own. Nikkō, however, is a name that does not surface in any of the independent sources. The weight of Ieyasu's appointment or donation, whichever form it took, was only appreciated with hindsight.

Conclusions

During the researches, not yet finished by far, that have led to the writing of the present article, two things especially attracted my attention. One has to do with the nature of the sources, the other with the status of religion in Edo Japan. In my conclusions, therefore, I shall restrict myself to these two aspects.

The sources, though they call themselves *Denki*, *Den* or *Engi* are biased, selective and unreliable. Of the three, the *Denki* was not only the earliest, but also the most influential. The *Den* merely excerpts it, and hardly adds any information of its own. The *Engi*, written nearly three decades later, seems to be an attempt to set up a different tradition. It offers many details and stories that do not overlap with the *Denki*. I think that the explanation is that its writer, Inkai, had a father, Zeyakuin Sōhaku, whose important role had to be rescued from obscurity. Nearly all other biographies, including those of the various temples Tenkai led, as the *Nikkōsan resso den*, *Kitain setai fu* or *Sōkōji rekidai shi*, are posterior the the major biographies and base themselves in the main on the *Denki*. The *Nenpu*, finally, is an impressive collection of materials, but its backbone is formed by the *Denki* and its author, in his occasional editorial comments, is more interested in merging the various sources into one coherent story than in finding out which of them would be closer to the truth. This approach and this attitude are shared by Tenkai's only modern biographer, Sudō Kōki. For all practical purposes Tenkai's image has been designed by the compiler of the *Denki*, Tōgen, who has fashioned Tenkai's early life into a fitting preparation for his meeting with Ieyasu and his resulting career.

In this article I have tried to show that Tenkai's career was not as simple and straightforward as it seems when one takes into account only its major stages: Keichō 14 - *gon-sōjō*, Keichō 15 - *tandai*, Keichō 16 - *(shō-)sōjō*. When one takes a closer look the evidence of Ieyasu's backing, which the pattern suggests, evaporates and other possible patrons (Go-Yōzei, Sōhaku) obtrude themselves.

As I reconstruct it, Tenkai's career started in the (late) 1590's, when we find him, as abbot of the Fudōin, intriguing in Kyōto. His position in the Fudōin he owed to the local *daimyō*, Ashina Morishige, to whom he was distantly related. Then the battle of Sekigahara struck; his patrons were re-enfeoffed in Akita and Tenkai was on his own. He found a new temple, the Sōkōji, with new patrons, the Mizunoya, and managed to rid himself of the original abbot, Ryōben. After a few years, however, he decided that he could do better for himself if he went to Kyōto; perhaps this move was suggested to him by Sōhaku, who also may have helped him in various ways and introduced him to the imperial court. Between the winter of Keichō 13 and the early summer of Keichō 16 he rose from being a provincial nobody to *sōjō* and *tandai*. Perhaps his newly won status within the Tendai sect made the monks of the Muryōjuji, to which he may have had older links, approach him and ask him to support the request for subsidies that they had submitted to the *bakufu*. When this request met with success it gave him a hold on the Muryōjuji that he exploited. In the course of the events that followed he then met Ieyasu, whom he impressed.

Sōhaku's letter to Imakōji and the entry in the *Sunpu-ki* for Keichō 16/11/1 show that there was a "Kitain" who was Tenkai's equal. This "Kitain" was ousted sometime in the first few months of Keichō 17 when Tenkai decided to "enter" the Kitain. The

Nakain, originally the most important of the three *in*, whose principal also enjoyed Ieyasu's favour, was excluded from the temple and assigned subaltern status. The Seiyasan Muryōjuji became the Tōeizan Kitain, and Tenkai proceeded to turn it into the Eastern counterpart of the Enryakuji, with the full support of Ieyasu and of the *bakufu*.

It is a career that indicates a strong ambition, an alertness and agility of mind, a willingness to take chances, and a strong, if not charismatic personality. It also offers exiting glimpses of motives for and patterns of religious patronage that need further investigation.

The other conclusion regards what I called "the status of religion". The *Denki* unabashedly gives Tenkai credit for Ieyasu's sudden addiction to religious disputations. Tōgen has a *prima facie* case, for between Keichō 16 (1611) and Genna 1 (1615) Ieyasu attended 108 of such disputations: one in Keichō 16, three in Keichō 17, the remaining 104 during the following three years.[99] Chronologically this coincides with Tenkai's appearance in Sunpu. The question is of course, whether this *post hoc* is also a *propter hoc*.

Ieyasu's sudden liking for Buddhist disputations cannot very well be ignored. Yet Tsuji shirks the issue, when he calls it "a hero's policy to capture the minds of men."[100] A more acceptable theory, that Sasaki Kunimaro formulated in line with Tsuji's argument, is that it was not an idiosyncracy of Ieyasu, but must be interpreted as part of the efforts of the *bakufu* at organizing the Buddhist church. Attending these disputations gave Ieyasu the firsthand knowledge of precedents, beliefs and personalities that he needed for his regulations and appointments.[101] Yet it seems to me that this theory, too, seriously hampers our understanding of the relation between Ieyasu and Tenkai.

We can, with Tsuji, think of Ieyasu as a very rational and therefore tolerant leader of men who "was exceedingly fair towards all Buddhist sects" and "did not discriminate against either Shinto, Confucianism or Buddhism."[102] If we do this, however, we run into the kind of problems that plague Tsuji when he cannot accept that the "transmission of the Tendai blood-veins", mentioned several times in the *Sunpu-ki*, really took place. Such a "transmission", in fact the presentation of the teacher's (initiator's) religious pedigree to his disciple at the time that this disciple takes the vows, would effectively have made Ieyasu Tenkai's disciple and an adherent of the Tendai sect. Since this does not at all agree with the idea Tsuji has formed of Ieyasu and his religious policy, he uses four pages to prove that this "transmission" did not occur and that the interviews which the *Sunpu-ki* mentions in reality were dedicated to the formulation of the policy to be followed vis-à-vis ōsaka.[103] Why a contemporary chronicler in the employ of Ieyasu should have felt compelled to disguise a policy deliberation as a religious rite is not explained.

It seems to me that Tsuji's reading of Ieyasu's actions is wrong. Religious tolerance as an ideal has no place in seventeenth century Japan. It is quite true that the *bakufu* was, as such, pursuing a policy of religious *Gleichschaltung*[104], but why should Ieyasu have had to occupy himself with this personally, in this very time consuming and tiring way of listening to endless theological disputations? Unless Ieyasu had a genuine predilection for this kind of pastime, he could have left it all to Sūden and other members of his or Hidetada's staff. This predilection, moreover, had arisen very sudden, in the last years of his life, with his final battle against the Toyotomi looming ahead. The karmic considerations Tōgen mentions may very well have been a major motive.[105] In other words, why not acknowledge the personal religious convictions of Ieyasu as a possibly relevant explanatory factor?

Another aspect Tsuji's and Sasaki's explanations fail to account for is the sheer cost of this "tolerant and evenhanded" approach to religious unification. In the three years between Keichō 17 and 19, not counting occasional gifts, Tenkai netted 32.000 thousand *ryō* in gold and 800 *koku* in land[106] for his Kitain, and this is only a small part of the total outlay of the *bakufu*, of Ieyasu, of the *daimyō*, for the upkeep and renovation of religious establishments and the patronage of eminent Buddhists.

Various rationales might be imagined that explain this largesse: the new warrior lords wanted to underscore their legitimacy by conspicuous spending within the established tradition of the imperial court and the Muromachi *bakufu*; the *bakufu* was set on upgrading the Kantō as against the Kansai by the embellishment of its religious centres and it was trying to gain control of the Buddhist church through smothering it with subsidies.

These rationales, however, are all predicated on a generally shared belief in Buddhism, which made Buddhism into a worthy object of subsidies and into a potential force that had to be allayed. This belief could, in itself, without the mediation of these "rational" considerations, have constituted a sufficient ground for Ieyasu to occupy himself with Buddhism intellectually and to give it his patronage.

NOTES

1. Tsuji Zennosuke, *Nihon Bukkyō Shi* VIII, Tōkyō: Iwanami Shoten, 1970, pp. 148-161.
2. *Dai-sōjō Tenkai*, Tōkyō: Fusanbō, 1916.
3. Tsuji, *Nihon Bukkyō shi* VIII, pp. 88-172.
4. Besides Sudō's book, the *Nihon jinbutsu bunken mokuroku* (Tōkyō: Heibonsha, 1974) lists only sixteen articles for the years from 1898 to 1958. To these can be added Sasaki Kunimaro, "Tenkai to Kantō Tendai-shū", *Kushida-hakase shōju kinen Kōsō-den no kenkyū*, Tōkyō: Sankibō Busshorin, 1973, pp. 491-506; Sasaki Kunimaro, "Tenkai no zainin seisha", *Tendai Gakuhō* XVI (1974), pp. 107-110; Okami Kanchū, "Ei-zan Tenkai-zō Gikashōrui no kōsei", *Ei-zan Bukkyō Kenkyū*, 1974, pp. 40-71; Tamamuro Fumio, "Sūden to Tenkai", Wakamori Tarō (ed.), *Nihon shūkyōshi no nazo* II, Tōkyō: Kōsei Shuppansha, 1976, pp. 53-63.
5. Kan'eiji (comp.), 2 vols., Tōkyō, 1916; rpt, 2 vols., Tōkyō: Kokusho Kankōkai, 1976 (hereafter referred to as *JDZ*).
6. *JDZ* I, pp. 279-345 (hereafter referred to as *Denki*).
7. *JDZ* I, pp. 346-369; appendix *ibid.*, pp. 369-372 (hereafter referred to as *Den*).
8. *JDZ* I, pp. 373-394 (hereafter referred to as *Engi*). Inkai was a Fujiwara by birth, a son of Zeyakuin Sōhaku and the adoptive son of Kazan'in Sadayoshi. He was ordained in 1624 by Saiin, the *monzeki* of the Sanzen'in, and became Tenkai's disciple in 1626 (*JDZ* II, p. 20, *Tōeizan nikki*). Cf. also *Dai-Nihon shiryō* XII.10, p. 410, *Kitain monjo*, where he is referred to as Inkai-*sōjō*, "a disciple of Tenkai, Tōei *gakutō* and Hagurosan *bettō*."
9. Work in 6 + 2 *kan*; *JDZ* I, pp. 417-708, appendices *ibid.*, pp. 709-859 (hereafter referred to as *Nenpu*).

10. *JDZ* I, pp. 404-409 (hereafter referred to as *Ryakki*); no year of completion is given, but the work must date from the seventeenth century.

11. This is at least suggested by a remark, purportedly made by Tenkai in response to such questions, that is reported in the *Engi*: "When Tenkai was [still among us] people asked him about his family, but he said that he had forgotten both his family and his clan names and also his age, and did not know them. 'Once one has entered the gate of emptiness,' [he said,] 'whatever they may have been, it is useless to know them.' Since he did not tell, it is difficult to know anything for sure." (*JDZ* I, p. 373)

12. *Tokugawa jikki* III (*Kokushi taikei*, Tōkyō: Yoshikawa Kōbunkan, 1981), p. 333.

13. The Bishamondō is an old Tendai temple. It was founded in Nara in 703, and moved to Kyōto in 794. It was known as the Izumo-ji, until Saichō placed there a statue of Bishamon-ten which he had sculptured himself. In the beginning of the Edo period it was moved to the place where formerly the Ankōji had been. From the Kanbun era onwards it was an imperial temple (*monzeki*).

14. The *Furoku* of the *Tōshōgū go-jikki* contains another biographical entry concerning Tenkai: *TJ* I, pp. 377-378. The only factual difference with the other entry is that here it says that Tenkai was summoned by Ieyasu only in Keichō 15 (1610).

15. Cf. Tsuji, *Nihon Bukkyō shi* VIII, pp. 97-98. Cf. also Sudō, *Dai-sōjō Tenkai*, p. 96. As regards his biographies, cf. *JDZ* I, p. 286 (*Denki*); p. 349 (*Den*); p. 375 (*Engi*); p. 401 (*Kitain sedai fu*); p. 405 (*Ryakki*).

16. *JDZ* I, p. 286. The ritual Tenkai performed will have been the *Hsü-k'ung-ts'ang ch'iu wen-ch'ih fa* (J. *Kokūzō kumonji hō*). The object of this ritual is the Bodhisattva Ākāśagarbha; it is performed in order to perfect one's power of memory. The ball of light falls within the framework of traditional associations: between the sun, the moon, and the stars, the "bright stars" are usually paired off with Ākāśagarbha. For further details see Oda, *Bukkyō daijiten*, pp. 458-459, p. 313.

17. *JDZ* I, pp. 286-287.

18. Cf. *JDZ* I, p. 291.

19. *JDZ* I, p. 349 (*Den*); p. 405 (*Ryakki*); pp. 375, 377, 379 (*Engi*).
20. *JDZ* I, pp. 132-136. Cf. also Sudō, *Dai-sōjō Tenkai*, p. 110, where a copy Tenkai made of the *Nakatomi harai* for his patron Ashina Morishige is mentioned, signed "Fudōin Zuifū"; where this copy is kept Sudō does not indicate. The *kaidai* (*JDZ* I, *furoku*, p. 4) notwithstanding, the *Edosaki Fudōin kakochō* (*JDZ* I, pp. 400-401) does not qualify as an independent source.
21. Cf. *Dokushi biyō*, p. 929.
22. Jōin received the title of imperial prince (*hōshinnō*) in 1575, he became *monzeki* of the Myōhōin in 1581, and he was Tendai *zasu* (the 168th) from 1597 till 1612.
23. *JDZ* I, pp. 132, 135.
24. *JDZ* I, p. 135.
25. Cf. *JDZ* I, p. 117. He was, however, eventually initiated into the Sanmai-ryū by the *monzeki* of the Sanzen'in, Saiin (1563-1639; *monzeki* since 1598 and the 169th Tendai *zasu* from 1612 till 1639): *JDZ* I, pp. 103-106. The *Denki* (*JDZ* I, p. 287) and the *Den* (*JDZ* I, p. 350), without giving the name of an initiator, report that Tenkai was initiated into the Sanmai-ryū in 1603 (Keichō 8/12/14), after he had settled in the Shin-Sōkōji. Cf. also Sudō, *Dai-sōjō Tenkai*, p. 120.
26. Cf. *JDZ* I, pp. 287-288 (*Denki*); pp. 349-350 (*Den*); p. 375 (*Engi*); p. 402 (*Sōkōji rekidai shi*); *Naganuma Sōkōji engi*, quoted in Yoshida Tōgo (comp.), *Dai-Nihon chimei jisho: Bandō*), 2nd edn, Tōkyō: Fusanbō, 1937, p. 3524.
27. The *Denki* (*JDZ* I, p. 287) and the *Den* (*ibid.*, p. 350) give Tenshō 19 as the year in which Ryōben moved to Kugeta, and place the destruction of the original Sōkōji by Shigetsune in Bunroku 1 (1592), *after* Ryōben had left. A *Tagaya gunki*, quoted in Yoshida, *Dai-Nihon chimei jisho: Bandō*, p. 3524, says that the temple buildings were impounded by Shigetsune and turned over to a Kannonji newly built in his residence Shimotsuma (Yui-gōri, Shimotsuke). Other sources, however, say that Shigetsune used the materials of the Sōkōji to repair his castle in Shimotsuma (cf. Yoshida, *op. cit.*, p. 3446). Cf. also *Dai-sōjō Tenkai*, p. 117.
28. Biography in *Kan'ei chōshū shokafu* XIV, pp. 119-120.
29. Biography in *Kan'ei chōshū shokafu* XIV, pp. 120-121. Cf. *JDZ* I, p. 287 (*Denki*); p. 350 (*Den*).

30. Sudō, *Dai-sōjō Tenkai*, p. 123. Cf. *JDZ* I, p. 402 (*Sōkōji rekidai shi*). Cf. Yoshida, *Nihon chimei jisho: Bandō*, p. 3524.

31. *JDZ* I, p. 402.

32. *JDZ* I, p. 287. Cf. *JDZ* I, p. 350 (*Den*); p. 375 (*Engi*).

33. Enton Shikan'in was an *in-gō*, given to the temple by Emperor Fushimi on the occasion of its restoration in Shōō 5 (1292). Cf. Sudō, *Dai-sōjō Tenkai*, p. 117.

34. Letters in *JDZ* II, pp. 721-722.

35. *JDZ* I, pp. 519-529 (*Nenpu*).

36. *JDZ* I, pp. 136-137. Both the letter and the poem are signed "Mushin" ("Without Intentions"); as "Zuifū" ("Following the Wind"), it contains a reference to clouds. For the *gō* Mushin, cf. also the *JDZ* I, p. 66 (*Han'on-shō*), where the signatures Shaku Mushin and Senba Kitain Tenkai appear together. For Benkai, cf. *JDZ* II, p. 23 (*Tōeizan nikki*): he was born in Naganuma, a disciple of Jōkai, Nōkai's teacher, and tonsured by Ryōben.

37. *JDZ* I, pp. 375-376.

38. Cf. *JDZ* I, p. 288 (*Denki*); p. 350 (*Den*).

39. *JDZ* I, p. 288. Both *tandai* and *shugyō* were functions connected with the organization of the Great Seminars (*hōe*) of the Enryakuji.

40. *DNS* XII.5, pp. 653-655. Cf. *JDZ* II, *Tōeizan nikki*, pp. 4-5.

41. *Nihon Bukkyō shi* VIII, p. 177.

42. Cf. the chronological list of *hatto* in Tsuji, *Nihon Bukkyō shi* VIII, pp. 173-176.

43. For the disputes on the Kōyasan, cf. Tsuji, *Nihon Bukkyō shi* VIII, pp. 11-13, 178-185.

44. *JDZ* II, p. 738; *DNS* XII.6, pp. 796-797. A *kuzen'an* is a written memo in which the emperor's intentions are transmitted through the Kurōdo-dokoro (Sovereign's Private Office) to the *shōkei*, the "duty official" or "presiding *kugyō*".

45. *DNS* XII.6, p. 797; *JDZ* II, p. 313. The editors of the *JDZ* attribute the letter to Prince Sonjun (1591-1653), the *monzeki* of the Shōren'in. Tsuji, *Nihon Bukkyō shi* VIII, p. 99, however, supposes that this letter was sent by Jōin. In view of Sonjun's age and Jōin's position as Tendai *zasu*, this seems to be the more probable supposition.

46. Letter kept in the Gansenji in Izumi. Text in *JDZ* I, p. 138; Tsuji, *Nihon Bukkyō shi* VIII, pp. 98-99; *DNS* XII.6, pp.

797-798; Sudō, *Dai-sōjō Tenkai*, p. 132. N.B. From Keichō 8 till his death in Keichō 17 Kajūji Mitsutoyo was one of the two *buke densō*, and as such in charge of the relations between the court and the *bakufu*. Toriikōji was a *bōkan* of the Shōren'in.

47. Tsuji suggests this in *Nihon Bukkyo shi* VIII, p. 99, but refers only to the *kuzen'an*, not to the letter. Sasaki, "Tenkai to Kantō Tendai-shū", p. 492, follows Tsuji in both respects. The editors of the *JDZ* assign Tenkai's letter to Keichō 13, those of the *DNS* to Keichō 14.

48. Letters (*kanjō*) and decrees (*senji*) in *DNS* XII.7, pp. 652-657, and *JDZ* II, pp. 439-441; diary entries by Mibu Takasuke, *ibid.*, resp. pp. 657-658 and 430-431. Cf. also Sudō, *Dai-sōjō Tenkai*, pp. 137-138, 141-143.

49. See the letters etc. in *DNS* XII.7, pp. 660-662. About the "seminars", cf. also Sudō, *Dai-sōjō Tenkai*, pp. 138-140. According to precedent, the *Shimotsuki-e* should be held from the fourteenth till the twenty-fourth of the eleventh month, in commemoration of the founder of the Tendai sect, Chih-i (538-597), who died on the twenty-fourth of the eleventh month. Why these dates were not adhered to in Keichō 15 is not explained.

50. *DNS* XII.7, p. 659; *JDZ* II, p. 427. Cf. Tsuji, *Nihon Bukkyō shi* VIII, pp. 99-100; Sudō, *Dai-sōjō Tenkai*, pp. 144-145.

51. Entry for Keichō 15/10/1, *DNS* XII.7, p. 658; *JDZ* II, p. 431. According to Sudō, *Dai-sōjō Tenkai*, p. 145, "Chiraku-in" was not the name of a residence of the Enryakuji, but an *ingō* in the gift of the Shōren'in. Cf. *JDZ* II, p. 546 (*Kachō yōryaku* 14; entry for Kan'ei 3), where the name Chirakuin is given to Chūson of the Asakusa Kannon'in.

52. I.e. in Jōin's letter of Keichō 14/12/9 (*JDZ* II, p. 313).

53. Diary of Nishi no Tōin Tokiyoshi, entry for Keichō 18/3/23 (*JDZ* II, pp. 403-404); *Honkō-kokushi nikki*, entry for Keichō 18/4/19, 5/8, 6/2 (*JDZ* II, pp. 479-480); *Gien jūgō nikki*, entry for Keichō 19/4/3 (*JDZ* II, p. 401); letter by Tenkai, dated Keichō 19/9/12 (*JDZ* I, p. 139).

54. *Honkō-kokushi nikki* I, Tōkyō: Gunshoruijū Kanseikai, 1966, pp. 107-108; quoted in *JDZ* I, p. 535 (*Nenpu*). *Sunpu-ki*, edn in Hayakawa Junzaburō (ed.), *Shiseki zassan* II, Tōkyō: Kokusho Kankōkai, 1911, p. 221.

55. Cf. the few remarks in Sudō, *Dai-sōjō Tenkai*, pp. 128-129; cf. also *JDZ* I, pp. 414-415 (*Honchō kōzō den*).

56. See *JDZ* I, p. 289 (*Denki*); p. 351 (*Den*); p. 378 (*Engi*). The factual mistakes are, that the *Denki* and the *Den* describe Go-Yōzei as the retired emperor, while he stepped down only in Keichō 16 (1611), and that the *Denki* mentions Madenokōji Takafusa (1592-1617) as the *sachūben* involved in Tenkai's appointment to *gon-sōjō*, instead of Seikanji Tomofusa.
57. *JDZ* II, p. 314.
58. Quoted *JDZ* II, p. 3.
59. *JDZ* II, p. 454. Cf. Sudō, *Dai-sōjō Tenkai*, pp. 104-105.
60. *JDZ* I, pp. 512-514 (*Nenpu*, quoting "old records of the Tōfukuji in Azabu, Edo"). Cf. Sudō, *Dai-sōjō Tenkai*, p. 112.
61. *JDZ* I, p. 288 (*Denki*); pp. 350-351 (*Den*).
62. *JDZ* I, pp. 288-289 (*Denki*); p. 351 (*Den*).
63. *JDZ* I, p. 289 (*Denki*); p. 351 (*Den*). Cf. Sudō, *Dai-sōjō Tenkai*, p. 172, where the seating arrangement of such a discussion is drawn after the *Sunpu-ki*. For these disputations in general, see Sasaki Kunimaro, "Ieyasu no Sunpu-jidai ni okeru gozen rongi", *Bukkyōshi kenkyū* V (1971), pp. 103-106.
64. *I-ching*, "Hsi-tz'u (hsia)", 4. Cf. Legge, *The I-ching*, New York: Dover Publications, 1963, pp. 391-392.
65. *JDZ* I, p. 290 (*Denki*); p. 351 (*Den*).
66. *JDZ* I, p. 290. "Both worlds" (*nise*; Ch. *erh shih*) in this context probably refers to the world of man and the world of the gods; "perfection" (*shitchi*; Ch. *hsi-ti*) is a term of esoteric Buddhism and refers to the final state of perfection to be reached through ascetic practices.
67. *Tenshin doku rō* (Ch. *t'ien-chen tu lang*; "the essential nature as such is bright") is said to be an oral teaching, imparted to Saichō by his Chinese master Tao-sui as the summation of the ideas related to the concept of *i-hsin san-kuan* (J. *isshin sankan*; "one heart, three views"). Cf. Oda, *Bukkyōgo daijiten*, p. 1250. Cf. also Sudō, *Dai-sōjō Tenkai*, pp. 196-197.
68. *JDZ* I, pp. 290-291 (*Denki*). Sudō, *Dai-sōjō Tenkai*, pp. 196-197, maintains the same story (with many more details), but adapts the chronology to the *Sunpu-ki*, where a "transmission of the blood-veins" is mentioned for the first time under Keichō 19/5/21 (*Shiseki zassan* II, p. 258). Cf. Sudō, *Dai-sōjō Tenkai*, p. 199, where also the six other occasions are listed.

69. Sudō, *Dai-sōjō Tenkai*, pp. 133-136.
70. *JDZ* I, p. 535; *Honkō-kokushi nikki* I, pp. 107-108: "A letter, dated in the tenth of the ninth month, arrived from the Zenjōin in Yokawa on Hieizan; on the twenty-ninth [of the ninth month of Keichō 16] it was brought by Nankōbō. I sent a reply."
71. *Shiryō sōran* XIV, p. 222, entry for Keichō 16/4/8. Sasaki Kunimaro, "Ieyasu no Sunpu-jidai ni okeru gozen rongi", pp. 103-104.
72. Sudō, *Dai-sōjō Tenkai*, p. 149.
73. Letter in *JDZ* II, p. 313. Cf. *JDZ* I, p. 290 (*Denki*); *JDZ* I, p. 351 (*Den*).
74. These patriarchs are Senpō-sennin, who according to the legend first reclaimed this place and built a temple, Ennin, who founded the temple in Tenchō 7 (830), and Sonkai, who restored the temple in Einin 4 (1296). Cf. *JDZ* II, pp. 528-529 (*Kitain engi*).
75. Cf. *JDZ* I, pp. 137-138, where we find this same phrase in a letter dated in Keichō 13. It is not clear to whom this letter is addressed or to which temple Tenkai is referring.
76. *JDZ* I, p. 534; cf. Sudō, *Dai-sōjō Tenkai*, p. 152, and *DNS* XII.10, p. 410 (*Kitain monjo*).
77. Sudō, *Dai-sōjō Tenkai*, p. 152, says "Tenkai together with Jisson-sōzu of the Nakain", without any corroboration. Sasaki, however, identifies Kitain as Songei (cf. Sasaki Kunimaro, "Ieyasu no Sunpu-jidai ni okeru gozen rongi", p. 105).
78. *Sunpu-ki*, entry for Keichō 16/11/1 (*Shiseki zassan* II, p. 221); not mentioned in *Shiryō sōran*.
79. *Sunpu-ki*, entry for Keichō 17/4/19 (*Shiseki zassan* II, p. 232). Cf. *DNS* XII.9, pp. 680-682, esp. the quotation *ibid.* from the *Kachō yōryaku*: *Daimei ni yori Bu-shū Senba Kitain o jūshoku-su.*
80. Cf. *Honkō-kokushi nikki*, quoted *JDZ* I, p. 537 (*Nenpu*), for the first, and *ibid.*, p. 544, for the second date.
81. *Honkō-kokushi nikki*, quoted *JDZ* I, pp. 542-543 (*Nenpu*).
82. *Honkō-kokushi nikki*, quoted *JDZ* I, p. 544 (*Nenpu*); cf. *Sunpu-ki*, entry for Keichō 18/4/8 (*Shiseki zassan* II, p. 241).
83. *Sunpu-ki*, entries for Keichō 18/2/18 and 28 (*Shiseki zassan* II, p. 240). Cf. *JDZ* I, pp. 537-539 (*Nenpu*).

84. *Honkō-kokushi nikki*, quoted resp. in *JDZ* I, p. 537 and p. 538 (*Nenpu*).
85. Thus Sudō, *Dai-sōjō Tenkai*, pp. 169-170. In the *Kitain monjo* (quoted *Koji ruien: Shūkyō-bu* 4, p. 476), however, in a set of regulations dated Kan'ei 19, Tenkai himself speaks of *Nakain hajime jike-shū shoke-shū* ..., as if the Nakain still were part of the temple.
86. Cf. Yoshida, *Dai-Nihon chimei jisho: Bandō*, p. 3013; Mochizuki, *Bukkyō daijiten* I, p. 524. Cf. the accounts given in *JDZ* II, pp. 528-530 (*Kitain engi*), and *JDZ* II, pp. 531-532 (*Senba Kawagoe yūrai kenmon ki*; this source esp. mentions the matter of the *sangō*). Tenkai himself, in Genna 1, uses the address "Senba *Tōeizan* Muryōjuji Kitain" (*Kitain monjo*, quoted in *Koji ruien: Shūkyō-bu* 4, p. 476).
87. *Honkō-kokushi nikki* II, p. 2.
88. *Sunpu-ki*, entry for Keichō 18/2/18 (*Shiseki zassan* II, p. 240). Cf. *JDZ* I, p. 538 (*Nenpu*).
89. *Sunpu-ki*, entry for Keichō 18/12/1 (*Shiseki zassan* II, p. 249). Cf. *JDZ* I, p. 556 (*Nenpu*).
90. Cf. *DNS* XII.4, pp. 743-744.
91. I read "*Ieyasu shōgun, seiishōgun Hidetada-kō* ni *go-konryū* o *ōseraru*". Otherwise the building would have been commissioned by both together.
92. *DNS* XII.10, p. 408; cf. Sudō, *Dai-sōjō Tenkai*, p. 172. What is meant with the "three *in*", if not the Nakain, Kitain and Minamiin, is not clear to me. Sudō makes a similar supposition (*op. cit.*, p. 172).
93. *DNS* XII.10, pp. 407-408.
94. Cf. Tsuji, *Nihon Bukkyō shi* VIII, pp. 135-137, 231-232. For no apparent reason the *Kantō Tendai hatto* were promulgated two times. The first time was in Keichō 18/2/28 (cf. *DNS* XII.10, pp. 795-799; *Honkō-kokushi nikki* II, pp. 2-4, quoted *JDZ* I, pp. 539-542, *Nenpu*), the second time in Keichō 18/8/26 (cf. *DNS* XII.11, pp. 452-453; *JDZ* I, pp. 548-549, *Nenpu*). The purport is the same, but the wording of the two versions differs considerably. The *Tokugawa kinrei kō* (Ishii Ryōsuke (ed.), 3d impr., Tōkyō: Sōbunsha, 1978; *zenshū* V, pp. 42-43) contains both versions (nos. 2613 and 2614), as does the *Tokugawa jikki* (I, pp. 613-614, 630-631). Both Sūden, *op. cit.*, p. 4, and the *Tokugawa kinrei kō* add, that these *hatto* were to be handed to

Nankōbō Tenkai. Cf. also Sudō, *Dai-sōjō Tenkai*, pp. 168-169, where the *hatto* of 18/8/26 are quoted in full.

95. *Honkō-kokushi nikki* II, p. 5 (quoted in *JDZ* I, pp. 542-543, *Nenpu*): "[Monks of] the Tendai sect had come down to Sunpu, and disputations haven been held four times in the castle. Ieyasu was delighted and gave silver and clothing to everyone, according to his station. Shōkakuin will return presently to Kyōto, and it seems that Nankōbō, too, will from here go to the capital. *I have given him the Regulations for the Tendai sect in the Kantō and other documents with vermillion seal, five or six in all.*"

96. *JDZ* I, p. 290 (*Denki*); *JDZ* I, p. 351 (*Den*). The *Engi*, following a chronology of its own, has no entries for the year Keichō 16 (cf. *JDZ* I, p. 387). Sudō, *Dai-sōjō Tenkai*, p. 149, says that Tenkai left for Sunpu in the beginning of the sixth month, i.e. the middle of July, after the rainy period is over, but this seems to be no more than an educated guess.

97. Sudō, *Dai-sōjō Tenkai*, p. 173. Sudō's source may have been the *Nikkōsan honbō narabi ni sōto kyūseki ki* (*JDZ* II, pp. 533-536), where the date (Keichō 18, tenth month) is given and the donation by the *bakufu* of the villages of Imaichi, Hisaga and Kusaku is mentioned. Cf. *DNS* XII.13, pp. 234-236, where the same two sources are quoted.

98. *JDZ* I, pp. 291-292.

99. Figures in Sasaki Kunimaro, "Ieyasu no Sunpu-jidai ni okeru gozen rongi", p. 103.

100. Tsuji, *Nihon Bukkyō shi* VIII, p. 127: *eiyū ga jinshin shūran no saku ni hoka naranu*.

101. Sasaki Kunimaro, "Ieyasu no Sunpu-jidai ni okeru gozen rongi", pp. 105, 106.

102. Tsuji Zennosuke, *Nihon Bukkyo shi* VIII, p. 126. He quotes several instances to prove this: Gen'yo, the abbot and founder of the Zōjōji, got into his bad books because he presumed too much and tried to persuade him to "destroy the four temples of the Tendai sect", and at the last minute he cancelled an appointment with Bonshun, who would impart to him "the secrets of the Shinto tradition". He cancelled it - so Tsuji supposes - in order not to lose his impartiality towards the various Ways.

103. Tsuji, *Nihon Bukkyō shi* VIII, pp. 129-133; his conclusions, *ibid.*, p. 133

104. Interesting parallels exist with similar policies pursued in the beginning of the Ming dynasty. Cf. Ter Haar, B.J., *The White Lotus Society and the White Lotus Teachings. Reality and Label*, dissertation, Leiden, 1990, pp. 134-135.

105. Sasaki, "Gozen rongi", p. 106, says that "in his private religious life Ieyasu was sincerely devoted to the beliefs of the Pure Land sect, as we know from his daily *nenbutsu* recitations (*nikka nenbutsu*), but from his political standpoint he was fair to all sects." For these *nikka nenbutsu*, cf. *DNS* XII.24, pp. 400-405. All sheets date from Keichō 17.

106. 300 *koku* in Keichō 17/4/19 (cf. *DNS* XII.9, p. 681, quotation from *Sunpu-ki*, entry for Keichō 17/4/19) and another 500 *koku* in Keichō 18/12/1 (cf. *DNS* XII.13, p. 149, and *Sunpu-ki*, entry for this date). The *Senba Kawagoe yūrai sono ta kenmon ki*, quoted in *Koji ruien: Shūkyō-bu* 4, pp. 475-476, specifies 750 *koku* as landholdings of the Kitain: fifty *koku* as the original holdings, 500 *koku* given in Keichō 17, and 200 *koku* given in Kanbun 1.

IN THE HOUR OF THE OX:
A STRUCTURAL ANALYSIS OF A CASE OF "ENVOUTEMENT" IN JAPAN

W.R. van Gulik

In a curious publication issued in 1924 under the intriguing title *Hentai chiseki*, dealing with "unusual information", reference is made to a remarkable ritual which may be described as an act of sorcery directed at a victim who would eventually meet with a certain death.[1]

The ritual in question takes place in the Hour of the Ox, between one and three o'clock at night, usually in the quiet precincts of a temple, and is invariably performed by a woman full of vengeance upon her unfaithful lover or her rival. The woman carries with her a small effigy made of straw which is supposed to represent her victim and is furthermore equipped with a mallet and a few nails. Her dress is white and her hair is hanging loose. On her head she wears a metal crown with three spikes upon each of which a burning candle is stuck. A large round mirror hanging from the neck is carried upon the breast and on her feet she wears wooden clogs with only a single high support instead of the usual two. On one of the trees in the temple compound she fastens the straw image with the hammer and nails making sure that one of the nails pierces the heart of the effigy. The performance needs to be accompanied by reciting certain magical formula's and would have to be repeated in a sequence of three times in seven days ultimately leading to the conviction that the victim would have been tortured to death.

In the example as described above, the practitioner is consciously and directly involved in a ritual which is performed to attain a specific objective of a malevolent nature, usually conducted in solitude and in secrecy. Ritually injuring or destroying an enemy symbolically represented by an effigy, image or object is a familiar practice in witchcraft, sorcery and comparable magico-religious rites. By burning or burying the object associated with the victim, or otherwise by manipulating and working it over with needles, nails and other sharp instruments, it is believed that the one affected endures pain and ultimately suffers death in like manner. The ritual performance of a certain activity is hoped and thought to be reproduced in similar fashion and under the same circumstances as in reality.

This principle of similarity is perhaps more commonly known as an act of "envoûtement" as described by Mauss[2] based on the idea that certain actions are "wished for" to be reproduced in analogy of the desired objective or that the effect of a certain action is evoked and initiated as if under real circumstances. This concept of "same-influencing" has first been labeled by Frazer[3] as a type of imitative or homoeopathic magic.

The occult ritual of visiting the temple grounds at the midnightly hour of the ox and known as *Ushi (no) toki mairi*, may well be designated as one of the most distinctive examples of imitative magic in Japan.

It is naturally understood that the ritual in question, here described as a magical practice of the imitative type, does not stand alone as a singular pattern of action related to occultism or the supernatural. It would seem more appropriate to consider the rite as part and parcel of a body of beliefs connected to folk religion (*minkan shinkō*) and popular lore which combines many elements of the more organized religious systems such as Buddhism, Confucianism, Taoism and Shintō including also *yin-yang* thought and shamanistic elements. It comprised a system of traditional folk beliefs, customs and festivals still alive in present-day Japan which are observed and shared by the members of society bound together in family and communal ties. By means of spells, omen lore, talismans and charms, directional taboos, calendrical divination and excorcism, rites of passage, annual observances and ritual practices, people sought to influence the course and circumstances of daily life. Particularly relevant in the ushi toki mairi ritual would seem to be the mystic aspects connected with the esoteric Shingon sect of Buddhism.

In the following, an attempt will be made at the analysis of the structural elements comprising the enactment of the ushi toki mairi ritual with an interpretation of the functional relation between these various constituent elements in order to elucidate the significance of the performance.

Colourprint by Kuniyoshi (1798-1861). From the series *Mitate jūnishi no uchi*, "Comparisons with the twelve zodiac signs", here compared with the ox. The actor Kume no Heinaizaemon in the role of *Ushi toki mairi* practitioner. Coll: Rijksmuseum voor Volkenkunde (National Museum of Ethnology), Leiden. No. 1353-940.

It will not seem surprising that the hour in which the ritual is performed, the hour of the ox, may be associated with the general notion of the midnight hour when ghosts, goblins and witches become active and occult rites are put into practice.

According to the traditional system, the hours of the day were divided into twelve equal intervals (*toki*), each called after the twelve signs of the zodiacal cycle (*jūnishi*). The day of twenty-four hours was divided into four phases (morning, day, evening and night) each of which consisted of three *toki* or "double-hours". Thus, the nighttime phase included respectively the *ne no toki* (hour of the rat) from 23.00 to 01.00 hours; the *ushi no toki* (hour of the ox) from 01.00 to 03.00 hours and the *tora no toki* (hour of the tiger) from 03.00 to 05.00 hours. The hour of the ox therefore represents exactly the middle part of the night-phase, the midnight hour corresponding with 02.00 a.m. The association of the midnight hour of the ox with malevolent spirits and unfavourable influences is equally relevant within the system of directional rules (*hōgaku*) that determine the arrangement of space in the compound and the precincts of residences. If the zodiacal wheel is projected on a houseyard with the main dwelling in its centre, the hour of the ox corresponds exactly with the northeast, the direction from which bad fortune is regarded to flow on the axis towards the southwest. The inauspicious zodiacal zone of the ox, located in the northeast of the houseyard is called the *kimon*, the devil's gate, considered as a permanent directional taboo (*kata-imi*).[4] The correlation between the inauspicious hour of the ox and its corresponding zodiacal zone of the ox located in the northeastern section of a houseyard from which bad fortune is believed to flow inwards, all the more corroborates the occult significance of the ushi toki mairi performance, adding to the mystic and essentially maleficent quality of the ritual.

Of importance in the relational order between the central dwelling and its confines as well as its orientation in regard to the various directional zones of the zodiacal wheel, is the position of the symbolic central pillar (*daikoku-bashira*) of the house from which point the zodiacal zones determining the fortunate and unfavourable directions around the house are plotted.[5] The emphasis on the main supporting pillar of the house as the symbolic centre of the dwelling itself and as the central pivot of the zodiacal wheel with its directional zones, calls to mind the comparison of the central pillar support as symbolic for the cosmic tree that stands in the centre of the world, while the roof of the house or tent is thought of as the firmament of the sky supported by the pillar. As such, the sacred pillar associated with the cosmic tree, serves as the point of support upon which heaven rests on earth. Consequently, this support is regarded as a living force, the creator of the world, holding everything together and keeping everything in existence.[6]

The function of the supportive pillar as the "axis mundi", the cosmic tree as a creative force representing divine power, naturally exemplifies the notion that trees in one way or the other are sacred or imbued with the power of spirits and gods. It is to such trees, that the attention will now be directed.

According to popular lore, several trees in Japan appear to serve as the haunt of ghosts and spirits. Examples of such "ghost trees" (*bakemono-ki*) are the *enoki* (Celtis Sinensis), the *yanagi* (willow) and the *tsubaki* (Camellia Japonica).[7] Cryptomerias, especially the tall ones, are the preferred abode of a demon-like creature called the *tengu*, described as "one of the most interesting figures in Japanese demonology",[8] who, as will be made clear, plays an important part in the ushi toki mairi ritual.

The *tengu*, closely associated with trees and birds, are alternately distinguished as red-faced humans with extraordinary long noses, sharp teeth, wings instead of arms and claws on their feet. Otherwise, they appear as bird-like creatures with a beak instead of nose and mouth, usually clad in leaf-skirts.[9]

It is said that the tengu live in communities under the leadership of a chief, the *dai-tengu*, together forming a wild bunch with a particular interest in persecuting priests on their wanderings in lonely places. Because of their misdeeds, they were condemned to live between heaven and earth thus thought of as the creators of heavy mists (*kasumi*), so often formed in mountain forests and confusing the solitary traveller.[10]

Hovering mid-way between heaven and earth as clearly expressed by the association with heavy fog-banks, not only signifies the intermediary position of the tengu between two opposing elements but is equally indicative of their dual role as culture hero (benefactor) and as deceiver (trickster). This ambivalent nature of the tengu incorporates the oppositional qualities of both good and evil. While they are likely to deceive the people with playful pranks and occasionally also threatening them with violent outbursts, they are not altogether malevolent. Particularly so in their virtuous role as protector of the oppressed, punishing those disliked in society. In their benevolent aspect, tengu are considered as very wise, good-humoured and often willing to give sound advice to the people, even providing those who deserve it with riches and prosperity.

In sharp contrast to their various good qualities, the tengu are capable of venting their anger full force on any individual considered to have offended them in any way. Particularly unfortunate would be the victim who had ventured to damage the trees in the mountain-forest abodes of the tengu. Such persons would not be likely to escape certain death after finding themselves suddenly enclosed by dark clouds, followed by thunder and lightning. "Even if somebody would dare to take only a single leaf from a tree", so it is recorded in a tengu legend, "certainly calamity will come upon him. Neither gods nor Buddhas can save such a man's life."[11]

Aside from the destructive features of the tengu there are also definite procreative characteristics, already evidenced by the phallic symbolization as commonly represented by the long-nosed tengu masks. In this connection, the tengu are closely related to the fertility of the paddy-fields and commonly identified with the Shintō deity Saruta hiko no mikoto, the *kami* of the crossroads (*chimata no kami*), with a vermilion face and a huge protruding nose.[12] The identification of the tengu with a kami deity is interesting in that we are once more faced with its ambiguous functions, partly as a deity of the forests, trees and mountains (*yama no kami*) and partly as the protective spirit safeguarding the crops and the process of rice cultivation as a field god (*ta no kami*). Thus, the tengu would seem to play a part in the traditional rites and annual observances related to agricultural festivals, specifically in view of the phenomenon known in Japanese folk religion as *kisetsu kōtai*, involving the seasonal alternation of the mountain gods descending to the rice-fields in spring in order to be worshipped as field gods, followed by the return to their mountain abodes in autumn when they again assume their mountain-god identity.[13]

The tengu, then, may naturally be identified with the tree itself in which his spirit (*tama*) is believed to reside. Tree and tree spirit are identical and defined as a "sacred entity", both with equal functions, namely as mediator between heaven and earth. Together they constitute an entity of oppositional terms or, in other words, the opposition of extreme qualities at the same time implies a correlation. This ambivalence in a deity or sacred entity is defined as *ryōmensei* or *nigensei*, affirming that the whole spirit of the gods (*zentai no mitama*) is actually divided into two parts, namely the *nigimitama* (gentle spirit) and the *aramitama* (rough spirit).[14] In the same way, as we have noted earlier, the tengu combines the oppositional qualities of a virtuous god (*zenshin*) and evil god (*akujin*), making it clear that the good and evil aspects of one and the same spirit, although seemingly inclined to develop into disparate entities, are in fact embodied in a single manifestation of the spirit or god who is by nature of a neutral disposition, being benevolent when appeased or satisfied and malevolent when arroused to anger.

Thus we have observed that the tengu, like certain other deities involved in folk rituals, could be made to alternate from one aspect to another, at the same time bringing about a shift from one particular quality to a completely opposite quality. The process of the transition in qualities or values is characterized by a strongly defined opposition of polar terms which are progressively weakened and inverted according as the neutral point has been reached where all values are ultimately assimilated and a situation of complete balance has been attained. The process is identical to the one demonstrated by Lévi Strauss[15] in his structural analysis of myths and mythological transformations in a given set of "extreme" variant terms arranged in a permutation group where these terms compare with each other in a symmetrical but inverted structural relationship. This relationship can be made clear in the following diagram.

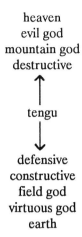

heaven
evil god
mountain god
destructive

tengu

defensive
constructive
field god
virtuous god
earth

Here we may observe that the tengu occupies the position halfway between the two polar terms of heaven and earth and equally identified as a tree spirit, fulfills the typical function of the trickster figure retaining the dualism as expressed by his ambiguous nature. The tengu acts as the mediator in a balanced, neutral position where his negative aspects (but not wholly negative) belong to the upper sphere (heaven) and his positive aspects (but not wholly positive) belong to the lower (earth) sphere.

Leaving aside the discussion for the moment concerning the phenomenon of oppositional relationships represented by the dual aspects incorporated in the tengu entity, the attention will now briefly be reverted to the protagonist of the ushi toki mairi ritual. As may be recalled, the female practitioner has a metal three-pronged crown on the head with burning candles. The combination of flames with the metal "trident" reminds us of the *trisūla* (S.), the three-forked flame represented as a Buddhist emblem in the shape of a trident. This usually serves as the crown of a round object, symbol of the sun-disc.[16] On the basis of the association between the sun and the the mirror (cf. Amaterasu), we may notice the similarity between the attributes worn by our protagonist and the trisūla. In this combination, the sun-disc which is surmounted by a trident is commonly called the *sūrya-mani* (S.) or the "sun-jewel".[17] In the Mantrayāna context, this symbol corresponds with the *vajra* (S.) or *kongō* (J.), which in its literal sense stands for "diamond" or "indestructible" and is generally translated as the "indestructible thunderbolt", that which destroys but is itself indestructible. The "diamond sceptre", symbol of creation through destruction and the prime symbol of Buddhist Tantrism, commonly reveals itself in Japan as a bronze-metal sceptre with three prongs (*sankō*) mainly put to use for spells and excorcising rituals.[18]

The relation of the above-mentioned attributes with the Mantrayāna aspects as revealed in the esoteric rituals of Shingon Buddhism with the emphasis on magical formulas, spells and invocations, becomes even more evident when we consider the attire of the ushi toki mairi practitioner, which is quite similar to the appearance of the *yamabushi* (literally "mountain sleepers"), the Buddhist priests who wander around in the mountains. In the *Kokonchomonshū*[19] for example, we are told how priests are constantly being plagued by tengu in the guise of yamabushi. These yamabushi were invariably dressed in white, often decorated with metal discs, the hair kept long and untidy and on their feet wearing unusually high geta's sometimes made of iron with a single cross-support. Specialized in magico-religious practices, very much like the esoteric Shingon-dō rituals, the yamabushi were the followers of the seventh century historical En-no Shōkaku, supposed to be the great lord of the tengu.[20] Thus, the correlation between the tengu and the yamabushi seems to be apparent, even to the extent of a certain identification between practitioner and tengu.

Returning to the association of practitioner, tengu and tree, we have seen that they correspond with each other in a dualistic relation of mutually opposing values which are arranged in a diametric dualism with an implicit mediator that keeps both spheres in a harmonious state of balance. It is in this position of equal balance that the two oppositional, yet complementary and interrelated attributes of one and the same force are reconciled as it were, in that the force in question is actually confronted with itself and where the gap between the good and evil sides of one force, deity or spirit is bridged over.[21] It is in this structure that the function of the ritual may be determined. In its elementary form, the structure can graphically be represented in the following figure.

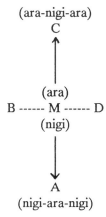

(ara-nigi-ara)
C

(ara)
B ------ M ------ D
(nigi)

A
(nigi-ara-nigi)

The dual spheres in the figure are represented by joining the points ABD, thus marking off the lower segment, while the upper segment is formed by the points CBD. Both segments or dyads are divided by the horizontal axis BMD. The upper dyad CBD represents the sacred sphere (heaven), whereas the lower dyad ABD represents the profane sphere (earth). The mediator on the axis BD is M, which is identical with the tree. A is the practitioner, designated as ego, while the counterpart C represents the alter-ego.

The various elements in the structure are related to each other in such a way that A and C stand to M in an inversely proportioned equation, expressed in the following formula.[22]

$$A : M \asymp C : M$$

In the confrontation of A and C with M, A is equally gentle as C is rough, which leads to the formula

$$A(AC) / B(M)D \asymp C(CA) / B(M)D$$

By analogy and in other words, we may assume that any action in any function or quality of ego (A) performed in the profane sphere evokes precisely the inverted opposite results of the action in the form of a logical reaction which takes place in the sacred sphere. To induce such a reaction, naturally some sort of specific action would have to be performed to influence and alter the balanced marginal situation in the dual structure of oppositional relationships. The crucial moment that the shift

Colourprint by Hiroshige (1797-1858). Numazu, from the series *Tōkaidō gojūsan tsugi no uchi*, the "Fifty-three stations of the Tōkaidō". Three pilgrims on their way to Konpira shrine at dusk. The last pilgrim carrying a large mask of the *tengu* on his back.

Coll: Rijksmuseum voor Volkenkunde (National Museum of Ethnology), Leiden. No. 1353-25.

from one sphere to the other (profane to sacred) or from one quality to the other (gentle spirit to rough spirit) takes place, is forcefully induced at the moment when the nail transfixes the straw effigy to the tree. By this act, the balance is clearly disturbed, evoking a fierce reaction in the sacred sphere discharging all evil and destructive qualities incorporated in the predominantly rough aspects of the tree spirit. Thus, the effigy representing the victim will be struck with all the released malevolent forces as a typical scapegoat and all the more so since the effigy is actually firmly attached to the tree from which the negative influences flow directly in the effigy through the principle of contact magic.[23]

From the foregoing we may conclude that the common model of imitative magic as revealed in the ushi toki mairi ritual, involves a secondary, additional dimension. As we have noted, the transfixing of the effigy with needles is not the only objective to be imitated in reality, but the performance of the ritual in its totality is equally a "wished for" situation to be imitated on a different level, namely in the sacred sphere. The effects of the ritual also involve more than one dimension. The direct effect of the envoûtement performed in the ritual is of course wishing the victim's death by piercing its symbol with nails. The secondary, but no less effective result is evoked by wounding the tree with the same nails that pierce the effigy, thus affecting the balanced state of the tree as mediator. The transition is made to the tree as a rough spirit with a surplus of evil qualities which are provoked by the deed and directly released on the ill-fated victim.

As we have observed, the correlation between tree-spirit, tengu and practitioner in fact implies that they are identical to each other. Consequently, the ritual killing of a symbolic victim at the same time entails the inflictment of the tree (spirit) and in similar fashion therefore also the self-sacrifice of the practitioner. In this stiuation, ego is confronted with itself, implying that the dual aspects of its ambivalent nature, the peaceful spirit as opposed to the rough spirit are reconciled to such an extent that only the inherent benignant forces remain predominant. Thus, positively fierce deities may turn into tutelary gods. An appropriate example would be the for Shingon important deity of fierce countenance, Fudō Myō-ō (Acala Vidyārāja), the

"Immovable". He is surrounded by a large halo of flames, in one hand holding the sword and in the other a rope with which he subdues and controls all evil. These potentially destructive attributes, particularly expressed by his sword as thunder emblem and his association with fire, acquire an inversed function and subsequently turn into purifying attributes. The rough and terrifying deity turns into a guardian spirit. While the release of rough qualities in a spirit is usually put to use in folk rituals and rites for beneficial purposes, namely to ward off or to destroy evil influence[24] these qualities are however emphatically employed for malevolent purposes in the ushi toki mairi ritual. The anger of the spirits is provoked and strengthened and their destructive qualities are released at the victim. In this situation of reconciliation and self-confrontation, oppositional forces are confronted with part of themselves, potentially destroying themselves in order to protect themselves. In the rite in question, the ritual self-destruction of the practitioner is employed to protect herself from falling victim to the calamities released by the enactment of the ritual.

The reconciliation which in fact means a self-confrontation, subsequently leads to a process of transition where the tree spirit embodied by the tengu shifts from a terrestrial, basically beneficent power to a celestial, basically maleficent power. The shift from one sphere to the other is induced as it were and set in motion by striking the nails into the tree.

In conclusion, the imitative aspect of the ushi toki mairi rite is further enhanced by a process of induction and reaction in an interrelated cycle in which the "wished for" results are supported and expressed in a ritual of dramatized performance.

NOTES

1. Haisei (Miyatake) Gaikotsu, *Hentai chishiki*, Tōkyō: Hankyō-dō, vol. 2 (8), 1924, p. 9.
2. Mauss, Marcel, "Esquisse d'une Théorie Générale de la Magie", *Sociologie et Anthropologie*, Paris, 1980, pp. 60-65.
3. Frazer, J.G., *The Golden Bough*, London, (repr.) 1970, p. 16.
4. Beardsley, K., J.W. Hall and R.E. Ward, *Village Japan*, Chicago, 1965, p. 79.
5. Beardsley, *Village Japan*, p. 462.

6. Cf. Aston, W.G., *Nihongi*, London, 1965, p. 12; Hermanns, M., *Mythen und Mysterien, Magie und Religion der Tibeter*, Köln, 1956, pp. 24-25; Batchelor, J., *The Ainu and their Folk-lore*, London, 1901, pp. 582-583.

7. Hearn, L., *Glimpses of Unfamiliar Japan*, London, 1905, vol. 1, p. 303, vol. 2, pp. 359, 427.

8. Visser, M.W. de, "The Tengu", *Transactions of the Asiatic Society of Japan* (Tōkyō, 1909), p. 25.

9. The former are designated as *karasu-tengu*, ("crow" tengu) and the latter as *konoha-tengu* ("small-leaf" tengu). The tengu corresponds with the *t'ien-kou*, the "celestial dog" known in China from ancient times as associated with the god of storms, thunder and lightning. Cf. Casal, U.A., "The Tengu", *Occasional Papers, Kansai Asiatic Society* V (December 1957), pp. 3-4.
    See also Van Gulik, W.R., "De Tengu, een merkwaardig langneus-demon in Japan", *Verre Naasten Naderbij* V, 3 (December 1971), p. 85.

10. Casal, "The Tengu", pp. 7, 19.

11. Recorded in the *Sanshū kidan* written by Hotta Bakusui in 1764. Cf. De Visser, "The Tengu", p. 77.

12. Herbert, Jean, *Shintō, at the Fountainhead of Japan*, London, 1967, pp. 167, 359.

13. Van Gulik, W.R., *Irezumi, the Pattern of Dermatography in Japan*, Leiden, 1982, p. 119.

14. Ouwehand, C., "Some Notes on the God Susa-no-o," *Monumenta Nipponica* XVI, 3-4 (1958-1959), pp. 401-402. See also Herbert, *Shintō*, p. 61 ff.; Van Gulik, *Irezumi*, p. 126.

15. Cf. Lévi-Strauss, Claude, "The structural Study of Myth", *Structural Anthropology*, New York, 1967, pp. 202-228.

16. Getty, A., *The Gods of Northern Buddhism*, Oxford, 1928, p. 197.

17. *Ibidem*, p. 195.

18. Van Gulik, *Irezumi*, p. 156. See also Zimmer, H., *Myths and Symbols in Indian Art and Civilization*, New York, 1947, p. 124.

19. *Kokushi taikei* XV, ch. 17, p. 545. Cf. De Visser, " The Tengu", p. 55.

20. Casal, "The Tengu", pp. 16-17.

21. The position of equal balance is designated by Lévi-Strauss as the "borderline state" (*état limite*), the gap which is bridged over. Cf. Lévi-Strauss, *Anthropologie Structurale*

Deux, Paris, 1973, p. 216.

22. Based on the formulas applied by Lévi-Strauss, especially within the framework of his structural analysis of myths. Cf. Lévi-Strauss, *Anthropologie Structurale*, Paris, 1974, p. 252. See also Van Gulik, *Irezumi*, pp. 131, 171.

23. As an example of similar contact-magic, reference can be made to the *hitogata*, human figures cut out of paper used in Shintō and folk-religious ceremonies to transfer evil influences from the body to the paper figurine, by rubbing it against the body. Afterwards, the figures are thrown in the river. Cf. Herbert, *Shintō*, p. 190.

24. Van Gulik, *Irezumi*, p. 131 ff.

THE REMAKING OF AN UNFILIAL HERO: SOME NOTES ON THE EARLIEST DRAMATIC ADAPTATIONS OF "THE STORY OF HSŪEH JEN-KUEI"

W.L. Idema

I

One day in the eighteenth year of the Chen-kuan reign-period (647), when the whole world is at peace and all countries pay tribute to China, Emperor T'ai-tsung, the second emperor of the T'ang and the *de facto* founder of that dynasty, holds court. The arrival of an envoy from the king of Paekche is announced but when this man is ushered in, the assembled officials cannot but notice that he has covered his face with a black hood. He refuses to remove it and informs them that passing through Koguryŏ he has been robbed of his tribute gifts by the fierce general Kai (or Ko) Su-wen, who carries the title of Mo-li-chih and has usurped the power in that country. The reason that he does not want to uncover his face, he continues, is that Kai Su-wen has had some lines tattooed on his face. These lines are highly insulting to the Emperor. When the envoy from Paekche eventually is persuaded to reveal his face, Li Shih-min reads a defiant challenge to war, which spells out the horrid details of his own accession to the throne:

> You killed your brothers in the outer court,
> You kept your father prisoner inside the palace:
> Your generals are old, your troops overbearing,
> Utterly incapable of accomplishing anything.[1]

Despite the protests of his courtiers, who refer to the dismal failure of Sui Yang-ti's Korean campaigns, T'ai-tsung decides to go to war against Koguryŏ and to lead the campaign in person.

That night T'ai-tsung has a dream about his impending Korean campaign: when all alone he is trapped in a marsh and about to be killed by Kai Su-wen, he is saved by the sudden appearance of a young soldier clad in white and riding a red horse, who counters Kai Su-wen's throwing knives by his well-aimed arrows, but disappears before he can tell the Emperor his name. The next morning, the Emperor's counselors explain the dream to him and conclude that this young hero will be found in Chiang-chou. Accordingly, the general Chang Shih-kuei is ordered to recruit troops there. Among those who enlist is a certain Hsüeh Jen-kuei, who does so at the urging of his wife. Despite his obvious excellence, Chang Shih-kuei loathes him right from the start. Throughout the long and arduous campaign, he will systematically claim Hsüeh Jen-kuei's many merits in the eventual subjugation of Koguryŏ for himself, until, of course, in the end, when Hsüeh Jen-kuei has saved the Emperor's life, the true state of affairs is brought to light: Chang Shih-kuei is punished, while Hsüeh Jen-kuei is duly honoured for his numerous and astounding feats of arms.

Such is the outline of the story of Hsüeh Jen-kuei as it enjoyed a great and lasting popularity ever since the Yüan dynasty. As in other stories of this kind, fact and fancy have been freely mixed. The historical Hsüeh Jen-kuei did distinguish himself during the campaign against Koguryŏ of 645 which was personally led by T'ai-tsung, but the campaign itself was not very successful, to say the least.[2] Actually, the long and expensive involvement of the T'ang dynasty in the Korean imbroglio of the seventh century barely achieved any lasting gains. Hsüeh Jen-kuei's many feats of arms in Korea and Central Asia were all projected into a single campaign by the popular imagination and it is unclear why Chang Shih-kuei, a deserving general in his own right, had to become the villain of the piece. However, the basic outline of the story of Hsüeh Jen-kuei would appear to have been well established by the middle of the thirteenth century.

The earliest dramatic adaptation of these materials is a *tsa-chü* entitled *Hsüeh Jen-kuei i-chin huan-hsiang* ("Hsüeh Jen-kuei, Clad in Brocade, Returns to his Home-Village") by the actor-playwright Chang Kuo-pin, who was active in the second half of the thirteenth century and held a leading function in the Court Entertainment Bureau.[3] This play is not only preserved in an edition in the early seventeenth century *Yüan-ch'ü hsüan* under the slightly different title of *Hsüeh Jen-kuei jung-kuei ku-li* ("Hsüeh Jen-kuei Returns in Glory to his Native Village"), but also in a Yüan printing which establishes its Yüan provenance beyond doubt. Because the two versions of Chang's play show major differences, they will be treated as two separate works in this study. The earliest narrative versions may also very well date from the Yüan dynasty, but they are only known through fifteenth century editions. These early narrative versions are the *Hsüeh Jen-kuei cheng Liao shih-lüeh* ("A Brief Account of Hsüeh Jen-kuei's Subjugation of Korea"), a *p'ing-hua* text which was found in one of the remaining volumes of the *Yung-lo ta-tien* (1407), and the *T'ang Hsüeh Jen-kuei k'ua-hai cheng Liao ku-shih* ("The Story of how Hsüeh Jen-kuei of the T'ang Dynasty Crossed the Sea and Subjugated Korea"), one of the recently discovered *tz'u-hua* texts, that were originally printed during the Ch'eng-hua period (1465-1487). While these two texts show some striking textual parallels, which may argue for a common source, they are wide apart in style and purpose. Whereas the *p'ing-hua* presents a bleak picture of the horrors of war, the *tz'u-hua* celebrates the exploits of a supernatural hero. The *p'ing-hua* provides a circumstantial narrative of an extremely complex action, whereas the *tz'u-hua* only focuses on some major episodes.[4] From the first century of the Ming dynasty, we also have two further *tsa-chü*, viz. *Mo-li-chih fei-tao tui-chien* ("The Mo-li-chih's Throwing Knives against Arrows"), and *Hsien-ta-fu Lung-men yin-hsiu* ("A Wise Wife Hides her Excellence in Lung-men"). Both these plays are anonymous and have been preserved as manuscript copies from the Wan-li era.

Also from the Wan-li period we have printed editions of *ch'uan-ch'i* dramatizations of the story of Hsüeh Jen-kuei. The first of these, *Pai-pao-chi* ("The Tale of the White Gown") is yet another dramatization of the story of Hsüeh Jen-kuei's rise from obscurity to glory. The second of these, *Chin-tiao chi* ("The Tale of the Golden Sable"), provides our hero with a son, Hsüeh Ting-shan: Hsüeh Jen-kuei once again journeys east to subdue the Koreans but finds himself besieged and has to be rescued by his son. The campaign ends of course in a Chinese victory.[5] In the Ming novels on the founding of the T'ang, Hsüeh Jen-kuei only plays a minor part, but in Ch'ing times the story of his exploits developed into a novel, which is best known as *Hsüeh Jen-kuei cheng tung* ("Hsüeh Jen-kuei Subdues the East"). In the genre of the military romance, a heroic father is bound to have an equally heroic son, and the *Cheng tung* had a sequel in the *Hsüeh Ting-shan cheng hsi* ("Hsüeh Ting-shan Subdues the West"), which greatly develops the story of *Chin-tiao chi* and marries Hsüeh Ting-shan to the barbarian princess Fan Li-hua. Their children, Hsüeh Kang and Hsüeh Chiang, became the protagonists in yet another sequel to the saga, viz. *Hsüeh Kang fan T'ang* ("Hsüeh Kang Revolts against the T'ang").[6] The adaptations of scenes from these novels in Peking opera and the other forms of regional drama are far too numerous to be listed here. This also applies to the adaptations in the various forms of prosimetric literature and narrative song.[7] The popularity of the story of Hsüeh Jen-kuei even spread to Korea and resulted in Korean adaptations.[8]

In recent years a growing number of studies on the Hsüeh Jen-kuei saga in its various stages of development have been published. In this article, I intend to limit my discussion to the thematic aspect of the earliest dramatic adaptations of the story. These *tsa-chü* constitute a closely interrelated group of texts, which may have had relatively little influence on the further growth of the saga in *ch'uan-ch'i* and novel but nevertheless are interesting in their own right for what they tell us about the fate of *tsa-chü* during the transition from Yüan to Ming.

II

While the earliest narrative and dramatic adaptations of the Hsüeh Jen-kuei saga date from the Yüan and early Ming dynasties, it would appear that the saga had established itself in the popular mind at a much earlier date. Our earliest play, viz. Chang Kuo-pin's *Hsüeh Jen-kuei*, focuses on the detail of our hero's homecoming but does not have to provide an extensive account of Hsüeh Jen-kuei's military career. The author limited himself to a few hints, because, one assumes, the story was too well known to need elaboration.

Apparently, the seventh century campaigns on the Korean peninsula left an ineradicable impression on the Chinese imagination. Perhaps the earliest evidence of this in popular literature is found in the *Yen-tzu fu* ("Prose-poem on the Swallow"), a witty composition discovered at Tun-huang, concerning a court-case of the swallow and the sparrow, which is usually dated to the first half of the eighth century.[9] When eventually the sparrow is found guilty by the phenix of illegally occupying the swallow's nest, he asks for mercy on account of his meritorious service during T'ai-tsung's Korean campaign:

> ""In the nineteenth year of Chen-kuan
> During the great attack on Liao-tung
> I, sparrow, was called up
> And took part in the campaign,
> Being allotted a place in the vanguard.
> I did not ride on horseback, I had no bow in my hand,
> But in my mouth held lighted tinder
> Which I launched down the wind,
> And the Koreans were destroyed.""[10]

One is even led to wonder whether these lines could contain an oblique reference to the Hsüeh Jen-kuei saga when the sparrow claims to have been a member of the vanguard like our hero, but not a horseman or a bowman. If this supposition is not too far-fetched, one might even guess a connection between the last three lines quoted and the attempt by Chang Shih-kuei on the life of our hero by luring him into a closed-off canyon and setting fire to it (in the *p'ing-hua* version Hsüeh Jen-kuei is saved by timely rains, in the *tz'u-hua* version by divine intervention).

Another reflection of the growing popularity of our saga may perhaps be detected in a discrepancy between Hsüeh Jen-kuei's biographies in the tenth-century *Chiu T'ang shu* and the eleventh-century *Hsin T'ang shu*. The latter work introduces his wife, *née* Liu. When troops are recruited for the Korean campaign, Hsüeh Jen-kuei at first hesitates to enlist as he has not yet reburied his (apparently recently deceased) parents, but *née* Liu urges him to grasp the opportunity.

> "Hsüeh Jen-kuei hailed from the village of Lung-men in Chiang-chou. In his youth he was poor and lowly and lived by tilling the fields. He was about to rebury his ancestors, but his wife *née* Liu said to him: 'When a man has the talents to rise above his generation, he has to meet with the right situation in order to advance. Right now the Son of Heaven will personally lead a campaign against Korea and recruits fierce generals: this is a rare opportunity. So why don't you scheme for merit and fame in order to distinguish yourself. It will be early enough to give them a burial when you return to the village as a rich and noble man.' Thereupon Hsüeh Jen-kuei went to see general Chang Shih-kuei and enlisted."[11]

It is not just her family name (which *née* Liu shares with many
heroines from popular fiction) that suggests that the historical
foundation for her existence may be slight.[12] Her impassioned
plea to her husband to forget about his parents and pursue his
own career is a distinctive stock scene in all later narrative
versions of the saga. That it became such a distinctive element
doubtlessly was due to the fact that it efficiently encapsulated
the main theme of the Hsüeh Jen-kuei saga: the conflict between filial piety and self-interest, the conflict between the
selfless devotion to the patrilineal family and the individual
pursuit of one's own fancy. Throughout the development of the
Hsüeh Jen-kuei saga this conflict is played out again and again.
Hsüeh Jen-kuei, in pursuing his own career, will not only
neglect his parents but also kill his own son (lack of posterity
is one of the gravest forms of lack of filial piety); his (resurrected) son Hsüeh Ting-shan will not only marry a barbarian
wife against his parents' express wishes but even kill his father
(stressing the link between unfilial behaviour and the introduction of a new wife as a foreign element into the patrilineal
family); Hsüeh Kang will cause the extirpation of the whole
Hsüeh family because of his uncontrolled behaviour.[13]

Once we realize the centrality of the conflict between filial
piety and self-interest to the Hsüeh Jen-kuei saga, the ap-
propriateness of the opening of the early narrative versions
becomes clear: the case of our hero is not different from the
one of Li Sih-min who had to kill his brothers and dethrone his
father in order to achieve his manifest destiny and fully realize
his personal virtue. The barbarian challenge discloses the ugly
truth of filiality: a son can only continue the family line if he
supplants the father. And if the integrity of the Chinese empire
can only be maintained by the subjugation of all barbarians, the
continuity of the patrilineal family can only be guaranteed if
the son's wife selflessly submits herself to her husband's
relatives. However, by reestablishing the macrocosmic social
order of the body politic, Hsüeh Jen-kuei successfully upsets the
microcosmic social order of the family: Chang Shih-kuei in his
ineffective attempts to stop the career of our upstart hero,
repeats the failure of supplanted parental authority.

Our discussion of the early dramatic adaptations will show
that, whereas Chang Kuo-pin chose to stress Hsüeh Jen-kuei's
unfiliality by resurrecting his parents from their grave, the
other *tsa-chü* authors did their best to defuse this potent

conflict, first by reformulating it as a conflict between two positive values (filial piety towards one's parents vs. loyalty to one's prince) and next by arguing that there need not be a conflict at all between these terms.

III

Whereas the two early narrative versions of the saga end with the public recognition of Hsüeh Jen-kuei's military merits by the Emperor, Chang Kuo-pin chose to focus on our hero's return to his native village, a subject which is not even touched upon in these early narrative versions. According to the Yüan printing, the action of *Hsüeh Jen-kuei* may be summarized as follows:[14]

Wedge. After the Emperor (*chia*), Chang Shih-kuei (*ching*), and Hsüeh Jen-kuei (*wai-mo*) have consecutively appeared on stage, the latter's father Hsüeh Ta-po (*cheng-mo*) appears with his wife. He complains about their only son, who doesn't want to till the fields but "only likes to twirl a spear and handle a stave" and intends to enlist with the army. When Hsüeh Jen-kuei enters, his father urges him to return as soon as possible.

Act I opens with the consecutive appearances of the Emperor, of Hsüeh Jen-kuei, of Chang Shih-kuei, and of a conflict between Hsüeh and Chang concerning their relative merits. The Emperor reenters and summons Tu Ju-hui (*cheng-mo*), who is ordered to decide between Hsüeh and Chang. Tu Ju-hui listens to their claims, knowing full well that Hsüeh is a hero and Chang an impostor. Eventually he arranges an archery contest to decide their claims. When Hsüeh hits the target and Chang fails to do so repeatedly, Chang is degraded to the status of commoner, while Hsüeh is appointed to high rank.

Act II. Hsüeh Jen-kuei has fallen asleep and dreams that he returns to his native village [as a common soldier]. When he knocks at the door of his parents' house, Hsüeh Ta-po (*cheng-mo*) is just telling his wife how he has been humiliated at a wedding because he has no son. When he has recognized his son, he tells his wife to spend their last

money in order to prepare their son a festive welcome meal.
But then Chang Shih-kuei suddenly appears to arrest our
hero and take him away.
When Hsüeh Jen-kuei wakes up from his dream, the Emperor
orders him to return to his native village [together with his
wife, the Emperor's daughter].

Act III is set in the countryside outside Hsüeh Jen-kuei's
home village on the day of Clear and Bright (*Ch'ing-ming*).
Hsüeh Jen-kuei's boyhood friend, the peasant Pan-ko is on
his way to the family graves, together with his thoroughly
soused wife. Questioned by a high official about Hsüeh Jen-
kuei, Pan-ko narrates their common youth, and adds that
Hsüeh should be struck down by lightning for leaving his
parents without any support. When the high official reveals
himself to be none other than Hsüeh Jen-kuei, Pan-ko
implores his mercy and describes at length the misery of
Hsüeh Jen-kuei's parents.

Act IV. While Hsüeh Ta-po (*cheng-mo*) complains about the
heartlessness of his only son, who has left him and his wife
without any support, a high official enters who asks whether
this is the house of the father of Prince-Consort Hsüeh.
Hsüeh Ta-po provides a detailed account of his poverty, he
cannot believe that his son has risen to such a rank and
fears the ridicule of his fellow-villagers. When he discovers
that the high official *is* his own son, he panics: how could
he and his wife be the in-laws of the Emperor? When the
princess pays her respects to him, he collapses. Eventually
the princess, in her sedan-chair, is taken into the house.

As the Yüan printing only provides the stage directions and the
words for the leading role (the *cheng-mo*), it is not always
possible to reconstruct the action with full certainty. Usually
the *Yüan-ch'ü-hsüan* version is helpful in this respect, but it
fails us in the fourth act, which is completely different in these
two editions.[15]
  If Chang Kuo-pin resurrected Hsüeh Jen-kuei's parents in
order to stress the conflict between his filial duties and his
desire to pursue his own career, he probably suppressed the
existence of *née* Liu out of the same motive. In many plays-
one only has to think of Kao Ming's *P'i-p'a-chi* ("The Lute")-

the conflict between filial piety and the pursuit of fame and riches is blunted because the protagonist, when departing from home, leaves his aged parents in the care of his devoted and capable wife.[16] Chang Kuo-pin does not permit our hero such an excuse: Hsüeh Jen-kuei is from the outset portrayed as a single son, who never has been willing to earn a decent living by working the fields and who joins the army despite his father's protests. Hsüeh Jen-kuei not just fails to give his parents a proper burial after their death, he wilfully neglects to take care of them during their life. The further development of the play is based both on Hsüeh Jen-kuei's conspicuous lack of filial piety and his feelings of guilt on this account. As soon as Hsüeh Jen-kuei, after eleven years of service in the army, has indeed achieved his ambition, he is overcome with anxiety about the fate of his parents, as is shown in the extensive dream scene of the second act. In his dream, our hero imagines how his parents blame him for their unavoidable poverty and how his father is humiliated at a wedding because he has no son - while he hopes for his parents' forgiveness (the simple meal paid for by his parents' last money), he also fears that he may not be able to see them again (the sudden appearance of Chang Shih-kuei who drags him away).

The imagined return as a common soldier is followed by the actual return as a high official, but the eventual reunion of Hsüeh Jen-kuei with his parents is postponed by his meeting with Pan-ko, who, unaware of his identity, curses him to his face for his unfilial behaviour. Despite the background of his type in farce, which is fully exploited in the opening songs of this act, Pan-ko becomes the spokesman for the basic notions of good and evil of the honest and simple country folk.[17] Hsüeh Jen-kuei might now expect a stern lecture and hope for forgiveness upon his arrival at home but the outcome is opposite. While his parents are on the verge of despair because of their approaching death and his continued absence ("When death has arrived, / Who will wear mourning, / Bring sacrifice?"),[18] the eventual reunion turns into farce because of misunderstandings and because Hsüeh Po-ta physically falls down when his daughter-in-law kowtows for him. Hsüeh Jen-kuei may have wished to return as a filial son (cf. his dream in Act II), but the extent of his success makes this impossible. The very success of his career (represented in the flesh by the imperial princess) overpowers the father, who warns his wife not to anger her daughter-in-law:

> How could I dare to be the equal
> > of the Emperor of Great T'ang?
> As soon as my son
> And daughter-in-law
> Have a misunderstanding,
> There's a gold and purple mace, as thick as a cudgel,
> That has me scared stiff!
> My wife, don't upset that sweet little thing![19]

Although Hsüeh Jen-kuei is the central character of the play, his role is not assigned to the *cheng-mo*. This authorial decision may at first sight seem puzzling. However, it would appear to be in line with the main theme of the play. If the author had decided to have Hsüeh Jen-kuei played by the *cheng-mo*, he would have found it difficult to avoid to assign our hero some songs about his concern for his parents, lessening the impact of Hsüeh Jen-kuei as the personification of unfiliality. Now other characters can expound at length on Hsüeh Jen-kuei's perverse neglect of duty.[20]

So far, critical discussion of *Hsüeh Jen-kuei* has focused on its satire. *Hsüeh Jen-kuei* is not unique in having a country setting, but it is remarkable for the extent to which it is indebted to the tradition of skits on country yokels. But, as has been pointed out before, the country yokel on stage in his simplicity is both an object of ridicule and a source of wisdom.[21] This dual nature of the country yokel is fully exemplified by Pan-ko in Act III. This act has often been compared to Chü Ching-ch'eng's *san-ch'ü* suite *Kao-tsu huan-hsiang*, which describes the triumphal return to his native village by the founding Emperor of the Han dynasty, as seen through the eyes of an old peasant, who suddenly realizes that this special visitor is no one else but good-for-nothing Liu Bang, who still owes him some money.[22] While both works poke fun at the "glorious return" and exploit to the full the social distance between a simple villager and a former friend who has achieved fame and glory, the situation is quite different. Liu Bang and his former friend never come face to face, whereas Pan-ko roundly curses Hsüeh Jen-kuei to his face but only because he does not recognize his true identity.[23] Both Hsüeh Jen-kuei's (dreamed) return as a common soldier and his being scolded by Pan-ko rather find their parallels in the "all-keys-and-modes" on Liu Chih-yüan.[24] The broad similarity of the careers of Hsüeh Jen-kuei and Liu Chih-yüan have been pointed out before.[25] However, in many episodes these two sagas rather are each other's mirror image. Liu Chih-yüan, who almost immediately after leaving his pregnant wife has betrayed her by remarrying, returns, upon achieving high rank, in the disguise of a common soldier to the village in order to test his wife's chastity, whereas Hsüeh Jen-kuei in his dreamed return wants to be reassured of the continued love of the parents he left without any support. Pan-ko's scolding of Hsüeh Jen-kuei may be compared to the complaint against Liu Chih-yüan laid before the governor by Liu Chih-yüan's brothers-in-law, who do not realize the governor *is* Liu Chih-yüan! But whereas the complaint by Liu Chih-yüan's brothers-in-law is unjustified, Pan-ko's scolding is not, and he can continue at length even after Hsüeh Jen-kuei has revealed his identity. The "all-keys-and-modes" concludes with the reconciliation of Liu Chih-yüan's two wives, whereas the finale of our play is devoted to the confrontation of Hsüeh Ta-po and his daughter-in-law, but her attempt at a smooth integration into her husband's family would appear to fail dismally. Hsüeh Jen-kuei's unfiliality culminates when the wife he has won through his own efforts is forcefully carried into his parental home.[26]

IV

Hsüeh Jen-kuei could not be performed anymore in the stifling intellectual atmosphere of the first century of the Ming dynasty, to begin with because it was strictly forbidden to impersonate Emperors and other members of the imperial family on stage. The anonymous *Fei-tao tui-chien*, which was in existence by the early fifteenth century (the title is listed in the *T'ai-he cheng-yin p'u* and in the *Lu-kuei-pu hsü-pien*),[27] probably was written to fill this gap by a more acceptable dramatization of the forever popular Hsüeh Jen-kuei saga. The contents of *Fei-tao tui-chien* may be summarized as follows.[28]

> *Act I, Scene 1.* Hsü Shih-chi (*ch'ung-mo*) informs the public that Koguryŏ has appointed Kai Su-wen as its Mo-li-chih and that Kai Su-wen now obstructs the tribute missions from the

eastern states and even has challenged the T'ang to war! As T'ai-tsung in his dream has seen a general clad in white, Hsü Shih-chi has sent Chang Shih-kuei to Chiang-chou to recruit troops, he will now follow Chang to Chiang-chou.

Scene 2. In Chiang-chou, Hsüeh Ta-po (*po-lao-erh*), who enters with his wife and daughter-in-law Liu Ying-ch'un (*tan*), complains about his son Hsüeh Jen-kuei, who does not want to become a farmer. When Hsüeh Jen-kuei (*cheng-mo*) enters, he voices his dislike of a farmer's life and his desire to make a career in the army. When his father hears how little he has plowed that day, he wants to give him a beating and even threatens to accuse him before the magistrate of unfiliality. At his parents' request, Hsüeh Jen-kuei gives a demonstration of his military prowess. To their dismay he announces his intention to enlist in the army. Even his wife cannot change his mind.

Act II. At the district capital Hsüeh Jen-kuei presents himself to Chang Shih-kuei (*ching*), who is quickly annoyed by the arrogance of this recruit. When Chang hears his name, he is angered because their personal names share a character. When Chang thereupon tests our hero's bowmanship, Hsüeh Jen-kuei rejects all common bows as too soft for his strength. When eventually he snaps a precious stiff bow, Chang Shih-kuei orders him beheaded. At this moment Hsü Shih-chi arrives. Hsüeh Jen-kuei implores his help and Hsü intercedes on his behalf with Chang. As the Chinese troops are challenged to battle by the Mo-li-chih, Hsüeh Jen-kuei is set free in order to fight the barbarian.

Wedge, Scene 1. Kai Su-wen deploys his troops near the Yalu river, waiting for the arrival of Chang Shih-kuei and his men.

Scene 2. Chang Shih-kuei enters, is defeated by Kai Su-wen, and flees. Next Hsüeh Jen-kuei enters, thrice he counters Kai Su-wen's throwing knife by an arrow from his bow. Kai Su-wen flees, with our hero in pursuit.

Act III. The Commander-in-chief of Koguryŏ is expecting a report on the battle. A messenger (*cheng-mo*) arrives and describes, in reply to questions, the victory of Kai Su-wen over Chang Shih-kuei, the appearance of Hsüeh Jen-kuei, the battle between him and the Mo-li-chih, and the latter's defeat. The messenger concludes his report with a eulogy on the Emperor's omnipotence and the Commander-in-chief decides to quickly prepare a tribute mission to China.

Act IV. At the Capital, Hsü Shih-chi informs the public that he has sent for Hsüeh Jen-kuei's parents.
Chang Shih-kuei reports back to Hsü and claims the credit for the victory. He is degraded to the status of commoner and chased away.
Hsüeh Ta-po, his wife and his daughter-in-law arrive at Hsü Shih-chi's place. Hsü asks them to wait at the side.
Now Hsüeh Jen-kuei (*cheng-mo*) arrives, overjoyed at the high flight of his career. But when Hsü Shih-chi transmits an imperial appointment to him, our hero refuses to accept it because he wants to take care of his parents. Thereupon Hsü Shih-chi calls out the parents, who at first do not recognize their son. To his great satisfaction, Hsüeh Ta-po also receives an official appointment. Hsüeh Jen-kuei jokingly reminds his father of his former opposition to his son's ambition. Hsü Shih-chi summarizes all the appointments in his closing lines.

Pei-tao tui-chien shows many of the typical features of the early Ming *chiao-fang-chü* (plays commissioned by the Court Entertainment Bureau): the plot is simple, even hackneyed; the song-suites are relatively short, while the language of the arias is rather undistinguished; and the dialogues are fully scripted, including the comic routines of the *ching*. Yet the play is not without some merit. Wang Chi-lieh overstated his case when he called this play a "masterwork",[29] but certainly the first two acts present lively comedy in the confrontations of Hsüeh Jen-kuei with his father, an honest peasant exasperated by his son's laziness, and of Hsüeh Jen-kuei with Chang Shih-kuei, an archetypical *miles gloriosus*, whose farcical self-introductions and exit-speeches are remarkable for their comic invention.[30] The third act is, as a messenger's act, a conventional set-piece,[31] but the expressed eagerness of the Koreans to establish tribute relations with China must have made *Fei-tao tui-chien* in

Chinese eyes a very suitable play for performance on the occasion of the reception of envoys from the Yi dynasty.

The many correspondences in points of detail[32] strengthen the hypothesis that *Fei-tao tui-chien* was written to replace Chang Kuo-pin's *Hsüeh Jen-kuei*. The Wedge of the latter play has now been developed into a full-length act. The Emperor and his daughter had to disappear from the play and his role is taken over, as in other *chiao-fang-chü* on the founding of the T'ang dynasty, by his minister Hsü Shih-chi. At the same time the dispute between Chang Shih-kuei and our hero at the conclusion of the campaign has been transformed into a confrontation at its outset, when there is no need for the Emperor's presence. Again, Hsüeh Jen-kuei's bowmanship is tested, but it is now rather his strength than his marksmanship which is at issue. The "omission" of any scene of actual warfare is now remedied by the inclusion of Hsüeh Jen-kuei's victory over Kai Su-wen (in the Wedge) and the verbal amplification of the preceding action in the messenger's report (of Act III). Hsüeh Jen-kuei's appointment to high office and his reunion with his parents have been fused together in the final act; by having the parents come to the Capital, our anonymous author precluded the possibility of Hsüeh Jen-kuei meeting with any unpleasant surprises on his way home - quite possibly the early Ming court was over-sensitive to scenes in which persons in authority were chided for their moral failings.

Still, the issue of Hsüeh Jen-kuei's lack of filial piety in leaving his parents and pursuing his own career, which we identified as the central theme of Chang Kuo-pin's play, is explicitly addressed in *Fei-tao tui-chien*. Hsüeh Ta-po, exasperated by his son's neglect of the family farm, threatens to accuse his son before the magistrate of unfilial behaviour. Hsüeh Jen-kuei, who is now played by the *cheng-mo*, gladly accepts the charge but he now defines his desire to join the army as *chung* (loyalty), and simply states that the dictates of these two values cannot be met at the same time: "Father, if your son shall be completely loyal, he cannot be completely filial."[33] However, this blunt denial of the primacy of filial piety is mitigated by the presence of a capable and filial daughter-in-law, and Hsüeh Jen-kuei instructs his wife to look after his relatives during his absence; "My wife, you stay at home and take good care of my parents!"[34] Liu Ying-ch'un now does not urge her husband to pursue his own career, on the contrary, she urges him to stay home as a filial son, but all to no avail as Hsüeh Jen-kuei's mind is made up "to shed his blood for the T'ang dynasty!"[35]

If Act I of *Fei-tao tui-chien* posits the irreconcilable incompatibility of filial piety and loyalty towards one's prince, Act IV attempts to show that, although the dictates of these two values cannot be met at the same time, they can be met by the same person. By refusing appointment to a high office in order to take care of his parents, Hsüeh Jen-kuei conspicuously reasserts his filial piety, and an admiring Hsü Shih-chi concludes: "This man is both completely loyal and completely filial!"[36] And while in *Hsüeh Jen-kuei* our hero's rise in status upset the traditional hierarchical relations of father and son, now Hsüeh Ta-po is also given official rank and so shares in his son's glory. As the emphasis is on the reestablishment of correct hierarchical relations within the family, there is no need for any high-born bride to scare the old peasant out of his wits.

V

Fei-tao tui-chien has its counterpart in *Lung-men yin-hsiu* in which Liu Ying-ch'un has become the central character. *Lung-men yin-hsiu* is not listed in any of the early catalogues,[37] but in view of its stylistic characteristics it probably may be dated to the first century and a half of the Ming dynasty. The action of the play may be briefly summarized as follows.[38]

Wedge, Scene 1. Kai Su-wen has confiscated the tribute gifts of all the fifteen eastern statelets and now expects a Chinese attack.

Scene 2. In Chiang-chou, during a cold winter night, the poor farmhand Hsüeh Jen-kuei lies down to sleep in the hay. When, later that night, Liu Ying-ch'un (*cheng-tan*), the daughter of his employer squire Liu, comes out to burn midnight incense, she sees a white tiger: Hsüeh Jen-kuei. She covers, despite the protests of her servant girl, the farmhand with her red-lined jacket to protect him from the cold.

Act I, Scene 1. Liu Ying-ch'un's servant decides to inform on her mistress.

Scene 2. Liu Ying-ch'un's servant informs squire Liu, who has entered with his wife, son, and daughter-in-law, that his daughter has given her jacket to the family's farmhand. Squire Liu sends for Liu Ying-ch'un. When she has confessed, he sends for Hsüeh Jen-kuei, gives him his daughter in marriage and orders the couple to leave his house on that same day. Liu Ying-ch'un expresses her willingness to share her husband's poverty as she is convinced of his future greatness.
Following the departure of the couple, squire Liu feels remorse.

Act II, Scene 1. Fang Hsüan-ling and Hsü Shih-chi order Chang Shih-kuei to proceed to Chiang-chou and recruit troops there, as the Emperor has seen in his dream a young hero clad in white.

Scene 2. Liu Ying-ch'un assures her parents-in-law that she gladly shares their poverty. Hsüeh Jen-kuei returns from the district capital, where he has seen the announcement of recruitment. He wants to enlist but has not yet made up his mind as he is concerned about his parents. When he asks his father's permission, he is told to ask his mother and she tells him to ask his wife. Liu Ying-ch'un strongly urges her husband to enlist - she will take care of his parents during his absence. Following Hsüeh Jen-kuei's departure, she once again assures her parents-in-law of her willingness to take care of them.

Act III, Scene 1. Fang Hsüan-ling orders Chang Shih-kuei to march forth with his newly recruited troops. Chang, who loathes Hsüeh Jen-kuei, appoints him commander of the vanguard and departs.

Scene 2. Hsüeh Jen-kuei's father has asked Liu Ying-ch'un to borrow a sack of rice from her parents.

Scene 3. Squire Liu and his wife heave heard that Hsüeh Jen-kuei has left for the army. Liu Ying-ch'un, who feels greatly ashamed at having to beg food from her parents, nevertheless enters and asks to borrow some rice. Her father gives her a sack of grain and tells her to return when she needs more, but instructs her to leave by a back door to avoid her brother.

When Liu Ying-ch'un does so, she is surprised by her brother and his wife, who hold and search her. Her sister-in-law steals her rice and chases her away. Liu Ying-ch'un bemoans her fate and hopes for Hsüeh Jen-kuei's speedy return.

Squire Liu berates his son for his coldheartedness.

Act IV, Scene 1. Chang Shih-kuei is on his way to attack Kai Su-wen.

Scene 2. Kai Su-wen defeats Chang Shih-kuei, to be defeated himself by Hsüeh Jen-kuei, who counters his throwing knives with well-aimed arrows.

Scene 3. Following the subjugation of Koguryŏ and the degradation of Chang Shih-kuei, Fang Hsüan-ling proceeds to Chiang-chou for the ennoblement of Hsüeh Jen-kuei.

Scene 4. Hsüeh Jen-kuei sets out for Chiang-chou together with a daughter of a commander Li, who has been bestowed on him as a bride. He instructs her to honour his wife Liu Ying-ch'un.

Scene 5. Hsüeh Jen-kuei and *née* Li arrive in Lung-men village. *Née* Li greets his parents and Liu Ying-ch'un, who accepts her as a younger sister.

Squire Liu and his wife arrive to welcome their son-in-law. They are followed by their son and his wife. Liu Ying-ch'un chides them for their former callous cruelty towards her.

A villager enters to offer a cup of wine.

Fang Hsüan-ling arrives on horseback and reads out an imperial edict.

As *Fei-tao tui-chien, Lung-men yin-hsiu* most likely belongs to the *chiao-fang-chü*.[39] However, the plot is more complex than usual as our anonymous author not only wanted to display Liu Ying-ch'un's exemplary filial piety, but also wanted to include the outline of Hsüeh Jen-kuei's career. In his development of the story of Liu Ying-ch'un, the playwright heavily relied on popular tradition, especially the parallels to the "all-keys-and-modes" on Liu Chih-yüan are very striking.

In *Lung-men yin-hsiu* Liu Ying-ch'un is portrayed as the ideal filial daughter-in-law. She immediately recognizes the signs of future greatness in her husband, she is willing to share his poverty, she takes care of his parents during his absence and accepts their most humiliating demand (to beg for food from the father who had thrown her out of the house), and she gracefully accepts a second wife into her marriage when her husband has achieved high status. (This "daughter of commander Li" probably is a pale reflection of Li Shih-min's daughter in *Hsüeh Jen-kuei*). But Liu Ying-ch'un's husband also has been transformed into a model of filial piety right from the start. Out of concern for his parents, he is willing to miss his opportunity for greatness. Liu Ying-ch'un again plays her traditional role in urging Hsüeh Jen-kuei to enlist, but now she does not persuade him to forget about his filial obligations and pursue his own career, rather she assures him that she will substitute for him in fulfilling the demands of filial piety. Once Hsüeh Jen-kuei has become a filial son, the memory of Pan-ko's lecture is suppressed by the introduction of an episode in which the fellow-villagers congratulate Hsüeh Jen-kuei on his newly acquired honours by offering a toast.

If *Fei-tao tui-chien* at least admitted the possibility of a clash of values, *Lung-men yin-hsiu* even denies this possibility. The rebels against traditional norms have finally been reduced to perfect paragons of virtue, and whereas *Hsüeh Jen-kuei* was an iconoclastic comedy, *Fei-tao tui-chien* and *Lung-men yin-hsiu* are melodramas, which increasingly need a villain for dramatic interest.

VI

The version of *Hsüeh Jen-kuei* that was included by Tsang Mou-hsün (1550-1620) in his *Yüan-ch'ü hsüan* of 1615/1616, shows such extensive deviations from the Yüan printing of Chang Kuo-pin's play, that it is difficult to believe that all these changes should solely be credited to Tsang Mou-hsün's heavy-handed editing of his texts.[40] A more likely assumption would be that, despite the existence of *Fei-tao tui-chien* and *Lung-men yin-*

hsiu, Hsüeh Jen-kuei was readmitted into the Court repertoire of the Ming dynasty at some later date and was heavily revised for that occasion.[41] The *Yüan-ch'ü-hsüan* version of *Hsüeh Jen-kuei* therefore would incorporate three types of revisions: ideologically motivated adaptations by Court censors, theatrically motivated changes by generations of actors, and textually motivated emendations by a literary editor. At this remove in time, however, it will be impossible to differentiate clearly between these three types of revision in the presently available text in the *Yüan-ch'ü-hsüan*.[42]

In this edition of *Hsüeh Jen-kuei*, the wedge has been reduced to the single scene of Hsüeh Jen-kuei taking leave of his parents. However, his parents are now accompanied by his wife. The character of Liu Ying-ch'un probably has been added under the influence of the narrative tradition and of *Fei-tao tui-chien* and *Lung-men yin-hsiu*; her appearance here is closely connected to the drastic rewriting of the final act and closely tied to the retouching of the characterization of Hsüeh Jen-kuei. Our hero now defends his decision to enlist in the army by an appeal to *ta-hsiao* (greater filial piety), the duty to bring glory to one's family by making a public career, and before he leaves he enjoins his wife to take good care of his parents.

The opening of the wedge by the appearance on stage of the Emperor has disappeared without a trace, while the opening scene by the Emperor in Act I of the Yüan printing of *Hsüeh Jen-kuei* is now replaced by a scene in which the king of Koguryŏ sends Ko Su-wen to the Yalu with orders to challenge the T'ang to war. The basic conception of the original first act has been maintained in the *Yüan-ch'ü-hsüan* edition but the Emperor has been replaced by Hsü Shih-chi, a number of arias have been dropped, and the wording of the remaining songs have been extensively revised. Chang Shih-kuei now argues against rewarding Hsüeh Jen-kuei for his meritorious service because of his lowly background. This increased stress on status-consciousness may perhaps be interpreted as a reflection of the rigidified social structure of the first half of the Ming. The second act in the *Yüan ch'ü-hsüan* edition shows the smallest number of changes. As the act now starts with words of praise by Hsüeh Jen-kuei's mother for the efforts of her daughter-in-law in taking care of her and her husband, one of the arias by Hsüeh Ta-po on his physical toil has been dropped. Hsüeh Jen-kuei is allowed to defend his long absence by a reference to the proverbial incompatibility of loyalty and filial piety. He is now given Hsü Shih-chi's daughter as a bride. The changes are also very limited in act III. Near the beginning of the song-suite, two arias by Pan-ko on the drunken behaviour of his wife are turned into a peasant's awed description of a high official. Pan-ko still has no words of praise for the filial daughter-in-law, but at the end of his suite three areas on the deprivations of Hsüeh Jen-kuei's parents have been dropped, no doubt because they had become inappropriate in view of the efforts of Liu Ying-ch'un.

As Hsüeh Jen-kuei has not become a Prince-Consort and his filial wife has taken care of his parents during his absence, a completely new ending is called for. Act IV of the *Yüan-ch'ü-hsüan* edition of *Hsüeh Jen-kuei* only shares one song with Chang Kuo-pin's original work. It clearly shows the influence of the final acts of both *Fei-tao tui-chien* and *Lung-men yin-hsiu*. In a short introductory scene Tu Ju-hui now orders Hsü Shih-chi to proceed to Chiang-chou. In Chiang-chou, in the second and major scene, Hsüeh Ta-po, his wife and their daughter-in-law are eagerly expecting the return of Hsüeh Jen-kuei who, accompanied by his new bride, arrives home and introduces her to his parents. Liu Ying-ch'un also greets Hsü Shih-chi's daughter. Hsüeh Ta-po praises Liu Ying-ch'un highly for her efforts during her husband's absence. Hsüeh Jen-kuei orders the new bride to greet his wife, and his father orders his two daughters-in-law to treat each other as elder sister and younger sister. Now Hsü Shih-chi arrives, bringing imperial gifts and titles, also ordering Hsüeh Jen-kuei to return to the Capital in three months' time. The play concludes on a note of general rejoicing.

As should be obvious from the above summary, nothing remains of the farcical and iconoclastic atmosphere of the original play in this act. Hsüeh Jen-kuei pays his respects to his parents as a dutiful filial son and his father correctly exercises his authority as head of the family by settling the relative statuses of his son's wives. The unruly son at last has been fully domesticated. If Chang Kuo-pin's original play dramatized the successful rebellion against the fetters of filial piety by the pursuit of an individual career, the rewritten version never endangers the integrity of the patrilineal family, and the emphasis has shifted to the spectacular change in social status, from lowly peasant to high official. In the *Yüan-ch'ü-hsüan* version, *Hsüeh Jen-kuei* is still an enjoyable comedy, but

together with the original theme much of the originality has
been written out of the play. If the *Yüan-ch'ü-hsüan* version
maintains the original third act of *Hsüeh Jen-kuei*, although only
in a mitigated form, it could find no place for the hilarious
final act in the original version, but replaced it by a most
conventional grand reunion scene. Both the weight of popular
tradition and of upper class feelings of decorum and decency,
conspired against the intellectual audacity and theatrical invention of a Chang Kuo-pin, and the *Yüan-ch'ü-hsüan* version of
his *Hsüeh Jen-kuei* is yet another example of the extent to
which the daring originality of Yüan playwrights may have
become muted in the late Ming editions of their works.

NOTES

1. *Hsüeh Jen-kuei cheng Liao shih-lüeh*, ed. by Chao Wan-li,
    Shanghai: Ku-tien wen-hsüeh ch'u-pan-she, 1957, p. 1. In
    the *Hsin-k'an ch'üan-hsiang T'ang Hsüeh Jen-kuei k'ua-hai
    cheng Liao ku-shih*, reprinted in *Ming Ch'eng-hua shuo-
    ch'ang tz'u-hua ts'ung-k'an*, Shanghai: Shang-hai po-wu-
    kuan, 1973, p. 2a, these four lines have been developed
    into the following eight-line poem:
    > Alas, the T'ang Son of Heaven
    > Knows no limit in his greed:
    > He has killed his elder brothers in the outer court,
    > His imprisoned father sorrows inside the palace.
    > However large your empire may be,
    > Still you don't have fourhundred prefectures:
    > In just a single battle I will have
    > Your blood flow all over the ground!

2. Hsüeh Jen-kuei has biographies both in the *Chiu T'ang-shu*
    ch. 82 (*Lieh-chuan* ch. 33) and the *Hsin T'ang-shu* ch. 111
    (*Lieh-chuan* ch. 36). For a brief summary of the career of
    the historical Hsüeh Jen-kuei, see Li Wen-pin, "The
    Changing Image of a Popular Hero: Hsüeh Jen-kuei in
    History and Literature", *Tamkang Review* XI (1980), pp.
    190-195. Also see Lo Chin-t'ang, *Hsien-ts'un Yüan-jen tsa-
    chü pen-shih k'ao*, Taipei: Chung-kuo wen-hua shih-yeh,
    1960, pp. 231-232 and pp. 387-388, and Chang Chung-liang,
    "Hsüeh Jen-kuei ku-shih yen-chiu", in *Shih-ta Kuo-wen
    yen-chiu-so chi-k'an* XXVII (1983), pp. 941-944. I have not

seen Wei Chü-hsien, *Hsüeh Jen-kuei cheng-tung k'ao*, Shanghai, 1939 and Li Wen-pin, *The Evolution of the Hsüeh Jen-Kuei Story in Chinese Popular Literature*, Taipei, 1986.

3. Chung Ssu-ch'eng in his *Lu-kuei-pu*, in *Chung-kuo ku-tien hsi-ch'ü lun-chu chi-ch'eng* II, p. 489 credits him with three titles. His *Han Kao-tsu i-chin huan-hsiang* has not been preserved, but his *Hsiang-kuo-ssu Kung-sun han-shan-chi* has been preserved in a Yüan printing, a late Ming manuscript, and a *Yüan-ch'ü-hsüan* edition. The latter version was translated into French by M. Bazin, as "Ho-han-chan ou La tunique confrontée, drame en quatre actes", in his *Théâtre chinois, ou Choix de pièces de théâtre composées sous les empereurs Mongols*, Paris: Imprimerie royale, 1838, pp. 135-256. The *Yüan-ch'ü hsüan* also credits Chang Kuo-pin with the authorship of *Lo-Li-lang ta-nao Hsiang-kuo-ssu*. Cf. Fu Hsi-hua, *Yüan-tai tsa-chü ch'üan-mu*, Peking: Tso-chia ch'u-pan-she, 1957, pp. 83-86.
    The exact nature of Chang Kuo-pin's function within the Court Entertainment Bureau is not clear. The *Lu-kuei-pu* calls him *chiao-fang kou-kuan*. Charles O. Hucker, in his *A Dictionary of Official Titles in Imperial China*, Stanford: Stanford University Press, 1983, p. 281, explains "*kou-kuan*" as a "common title for relatively low ranking officials who were normally in charge of minor government agencies such as storehouses". Bazin mistakenly assumed that Chang Kuo-pin was a woman but his biographical notice on her in his *Le siècle des Youên...*, Paris: Imprimerie nationale, 1850, pp. 296-297, is too curious not to quote: "Tchang-koue-pin, courtisane, actrice, poête dramatique ... Il est à présumer qu'elle avait des relations avec Kouan-han-king [Kuan Han-ch'ing] et que ce fut cet académicien qui lui apprit à composer des vers ... On a de Tchang-koue-pin trois drames ... J'en ai déjà fait la remarque, il y a moins de sensibilité, moins de naturel et moins de grâce dans la composition de cette femme que dans les drames de Ma-tchi-yuên [Ma Chih-yüan], de Pe-jîn-fou [Pai P'u] ... On s'aperçoit trop facilement qu'elle s'était adonnée, comme les courtisanes de son temps, à l'étude de la philosophie."

4. Both texts have been reprinted together in *Ming Ch'eng-hua shuo-ch'ang tz'u-hua ts'ung-k'an*, Taipei: Ting-wen shu-chü, 1979, pp. 177-288. For a statement on the textual correspondences, see e.g. David T. Roy, "The Fifteenth

Century *Shuo-ch'ang Tz'u-hua* as Examples of Written Formulaic Composition", *Chinoperl Papers* X (1981), p. 18. The huge intellectual gap between these two texts has been stressed by Hashimoto Yō, "Setsu Jinki - atarashii mono-gatari taipu no tanjō", *Wakō daigaku jinbun kagakubu kiyō* XXI (1986), pp. 19-29.

5. For a detailed discussion of these two plays, and related fragments, see Li Wen-pin, "Ming-tai ch'uan-ch'i chung ti Hsüeh Jen-kuei ku-shih", *Han-hsüeh yen-chiu* VI (1988), pp. 581-594.

6. For a first discussion of some themes in these novels, see C.T. Hsia, "The Military Romance", in Cyril Birch (ed.), *Studies in Chinese Literary Genres*, Berkeley: University of California Press, 1974, pp. 339-390. More detailed discussions are provided by Li Wen-pin, "The Changing Image of a Popular Hero ...", *Tamkang Review* XI (1980), pp. 211-217, and Chang Chung-liang, "Hsüeh Jen-kuei ku-shih yen-chiu", *Shih-ta Kuo-wen yen-chiu-so chi-k'an* XXVII (1983), *passim*.

7. See Chang Chung-liang, *op. cit.*, pp. 985-996, pp. 1013-1026, pp. 1032-1036.

8. W.E. Skillend, *Kodae Sosol: A Survey of Korean Traditional Style Fiction*, London: School of Oriental and African Studies, 1968, p. 111; A.F. Trotcevich, "The Influence of the Plots of Chinese Fiction on Korean Vernacular Novels", in Claudine Salmon (ed.), *Literary Migrations, Traditional Chinese Fiction in Asia (17-20th centuries)*, Peking: International Culture Publishing Corporation, 1987, pp. 88-93.

9. Wang Chong-min et al. (eds.), *Tun-huang pien-wen chi*, Peking: Jen-min wen-hsüeh ch'u-pan-she, 1957, pp. 249-261; Chang Hung-hsün (ann.), *Tun-huang chiang-ch'ang wen-hsüeh tso-p'in hsüan-chu*, Lan-chou: Kan-su Jen-min ch'u-pan-she, pp. 44-62; Chou Shao-liang (ed.), *Tun-huang wen-hsüeh tso-p'in hsüan*, Peking: Chung-hua shu-chü, 1987, pp. 294-313.

10. Arthur Waley, *Ballads and Stories from Tun-huang*, London: George Allen and Unwin, 1960, p. 22.

11. *Hsin T'ang-shu*, Peking: Chung-hua shu-chü, 1975, p. 4139.

12. The propensity of the editors of the *Hsin T'ang-shu* for *hsiao-shuo* was already pointed out during the Sung dynasty. See Chang Chung-liang, *op. cit.*, p. 942.

13. Yen Yüan-shu, in his "Hsüeh Jen-kuei and Hsüeh Ting-shan: A Chinese Oedipal Conflict", *Tamkang Review* I (1970), pp.

223-232, has shown that in the Peking opera version of Hsüeh Jen-kuei's homecoming as *Fen ho wan* the theme of the father-son conflict is combined with the theme of sexual jealousy (Hsüeh Jen-kuei, who has returned in the disguise of a common soldier, suspects his wife of having a young lover, but this young man turns out to be their son who had been born following his departure for the army). In *Hsüeh Kang fan T'ang*, Hsüeh Kang causes the extirpation of the Hsüeh clan but his mother Fan Li-hua escapes.

14. The following summary of *Hsüeh Jen-kuei* is based on the critical editions of the Yüan edition in Cheng Ch'ien (ed.), *Chiao-ting Yüan-k'an tsa-chü san-shih-chung*, Taipei: Shih-chieh shu-chü, 1962, pp. 211-225; and in Hsü Ch'in-chün (ed.), *Hsin-chiao Yüan-k'an tsa-chü san-shih-chung*, Peking: Chung-hua shu-chü, 1980, pp. 383-410.

15. My reconstruction of the action accompanying the final arias of Act IV differs considerably from the one proposed by Takahashi Bunji in his "Gen kanbon Setsu Jinki ikin kankyō geki wo megutte", *Tōhōgaku* LXXVI (1988), pp. 63-68, but would seem to be supported by Yen Ch'ang-k'o's understanding of the text in "I-chin huan-hsiang ti pien-tsou: t'an Chang Kuo-pin Hsüeh Jen-kuei tsa-chü", *Hsi-ch'ü yen-chiu* XXII (1987), pp. 87-88.

16. Cf. Jean Mulligan (transl.), *The Lute, Kao Ming's P'i-p'a chi*, New York: Columbia University Press, 1980, pp. 18-23.

17. For the links between the skits on country yokels (*tsa-pan*) and *Hsüeh Jen-kuei*, see Hu Chi, *Sung Chin tsa-chü k'ao*, Shanghai: Chung-hua shu-chü, 1959, p. 43; and Takahashi Bunji, *op. cit.*, pp. 68-69.

18. Cheng Ch'ien, *op. cit.*, p. 219; Hsü Ch'in-chün, *op. cit.*, p. 405.

19. Cheng Ch'ien, *op. cit.*, p. 221, and Hsü Ch'in-ch'un, *op. cit.*, p. 406.

20. Also cf. Chang Chung-liang, *op. cit.*, p. 1001.

21. Tanaka Kenji, "Inbon kō", *Nihon Chūgokugakkai hō* XX (1968), pp. 175-178.

22. For a critical edition of "Kao-tsu huan-xiang", see Sui Shu-sen (ed.), *Ch'üan Yüan san-ch'ü*, Peking: Chung-hua shu-chü, 1964, pp. 543-545. For an English translation, see e.g. J.I. Crump, "The Ch'ü and its Critics", *Literature East and West* XVI (1972), pp. 961-979.

23. Cf. Yen Ch'ang-k'o, *op. cit.*, pp. 81-84; Takahashi Bunji, *op. cit.*, pp. 69-71.

24. For critical, annotated editions of the preserved fragments of the *Liu Chih-yüan chu-kung-tiao*, see Uchida Michio et al. (ann.), "Kōchū Ryu Chi'en shokyūchō", *Tōhoku daigaku bungakubu kenkyū nenpō* XIV (1974), pp. 240-319; and Ling Ching-yen and Hsieh Po-yang (ann.), "Liu Chih-yüan chu-kung-tiao", in their *Chu-kung-tiao liang-chung*, Chinan: Ch'i Lu shu-she, 1988, pp. 4-87. The text has been translated into English by M. Dolezelová-Velingerová and J.I. Crump as *Ballad of the Hidden Dragon, Liu Chih-yüan chu-kung-tiao*, Oxford: Oxford University Press, 1971.

25. Hashimoto Yō, *op. cit.*, pp. 23-25. For a more detailed discussion of the structural affinity between the Liu Chih-yüan saga and the Hsüeh Jen-kuei saga, see Kim Moon-kyung, "Ryu Chi'en no monogatari", *Tōhōgaku* LXII (1981), pp. 66-82, Section III (pp. 71-75).

26. In the view of Yen Ch'ang-k'o the satirical thrust of this play is primarily directed against the many social upstarts of the early Yüan, who during the unsettled times of the mid-thirteenth century made a spectacular career in the military; accordingly the author rather stressed the misery for others resulting from Hsüeh Jen-kuei's career than its benefits to himself. Yen Ch'ang-k'o, *op. cit.*, pp. 82-88.

27. Fu Hsi-hua, *op. cit.*, pp. 293-294.

28. Typeset editions may be found in Wang Chi-lieh (ed.), *Ku-pen Yüan Ming tsa-chü*, Peking: Chung-kuo hsi-chü ch'u-pan-she, 1958, and in Sui Shu-sen (comp.), *Yüan-ch'ü hsüan wai-pien*, Peking: Chung-hua shu-chü, 1959, pp. 876-882. The manuscript has been reproduced as part of the *Mai-wang-kuan ch'ao-chiao-pen ku-chin tsa-chü* in *Ku-pen hsi-ch'ü ts'ung-k'an ssu-chi*.

29. Wang Chi-lieh, "T'i-yao", p. 14b, in Wang Chi-lieh, *op. cit.*.

30. Hu Chi, *op. cit.*, p. 250, has identified Chang Shih-kuei's self-introduction as an adaptation of the Chin dynasty farce *Chen-erh hsien* ("Needle and Thread"). For a translation of this passage, see J.I. Crump, *Chinese Theater in the Days of Kublai Khan*, Tucson: University of Arizona Press, 1980, pp. 130-131.

31. Chang Chung-liang, *op. cit.*, p. 998, approvingly quotes extensively from this song-suite.

32. Shang Tao, *Lun Yüan-tai tsa-chü*, Chinan: Ch'i Lu shu-she, 1986, p. 61: "The action of *Fei-tao tui-chien* is basically identical to that of *Hsüeh Jen-kuei*."

33. *Fei-tao tui-chien*, in Wang Chi-lieh, *op. cit.*, p. 3a; Sui Shu-sen, *Yüan-ch'ü-hsüan wai-pien*, p. 870.

34. *Fei-tao tui-chien*, in Wang Chi-lieh, *op. cit.*, p. 3b; Sui Shu-sen, *Yüan-ch'ü-hsüan wai-pien*, p. 870.

35. *Ibidem*.

36. *Fei-tao tui-chien*, in Wang Chi-lieh, *op. cit.*, p. 11b; Sui Shu-sen, *Yüan-ch'ü-hsüan wai-pien*, p. 881.

37. Fu Hsi-hua, *op. cit.*, p. 324.

38. A typeset edition has been provided by Wang Chi-lieh, in *Ku-pen Yüan Ming tsa-chü*. The manuscript has been reproduced as part of the *Mai-wang-kuan ch'ao-chiao-pen ku-chin tsa-chü* in *Ku-pen hsi-ch'ü ts'ung-k'an ssu-chi*.

39. Wang Chi-lieh, "T'i-yao", pp. 37b-38a (in Wang Chi-lieh, *op. cit.*), praises the arias for their simplicity. Chang Chung-liang, *op. cit.*, pp. 998-999, approvingly quotes the arias of the third act.

40. Tsang Chin-shu (ed.), *Yüan-ch'ü-hsüan*, Peking: Chung-hua shu-chü, 1958, pp. 315-331. M. Bazin provided an extensive French summary in *Le siècle des Youên...*, pp. 261-268.

41. A comparable triad is provided by the Yüan printing of Shang Chung-hsien's *Ch'i Ying Pu*, the anonymous early Ming play *Pien Ying Pu*, and the *Yüan-ch'ü-hsüan* edition of *Ch'i Ying Pu*.

42. Also see Yen Ch'ang-k'o, *op. cit.*, pp. 88-90 for a discussion and evaluation of the differences between the two versions of *Hsüeh Jen-kuei*. For a critical appreciation of the *Yüan-ch'ü-hsüan* version, see Chao Ching-yü, "Hsüeh Jen-kuei tsa-chü ti i-shu t'e-se", in *Yüan tsa-chü chien-shang chi*, Peking: Jen-min wen-hsüeh ch'u-pan-she, 1983, pp. 89-98.

CHARACTER LIST

Chang Kuo-pin	張國賓
Chang Shih-kuei	張士貴
Chen-erh hsien	針兒綫
cheng-mo	正末
Ch'i Ying Pu	氣英布
chia	駕
Chiang-chou	絳州
chiao-fang-chü	教坊劇
chiao-fang kou-kuan	教坊勾管
Chin-tiao chi	金貂記
ching	淨
Chü Ching-ch'eng	睢景臣
chung	忠
Chung Ssu-ch'eng	鍾嗣成
Fan Li-hua	樊梨花
Fang Hsüan-ling	房玄齡
Fen ho wan	汾河灣
Han Kao-tsu i-chin huan-hsiang	漢高祖衣錦還鄉
Hsiang-kuo-ssu Kung-sun han-shan-chi	相國寺公孫汗衫記
Hsien-ta-fu Lung-men yin-hsiu	賢達婦龍門隱秀
Hsü Shih-chi	徐世勣
Hsüeh Chiang	薛強
Hsüeh Kang	薛剛
Hsüeh Kang fan T'ang	薛剛反唐
Hsüeh Jen-kuei	薛仁貴
Hsüeh Jen-kuei cheng Liao shih-lüeh	薛仁貴征遼事略
Hsüeh Jen-kuei cheng tung	薛仁貴征東

Hsüeh Jen-kuei i-chin huan-hsiang	薛仁貴衣錦還鄉
Hsüeh Jen-kuei jung-kuei ku-li	薛仁貴榮歸故里
Hsüeh Ta-po	薛大伯
Hsüeh Ting-shan	薛丁山
Hsüeh Ting-shan cheng hsi	薛丁山征西
Kai (or Ko) Su-wen	蓋（葛）蘇文
Kao Ming	高明
Kao-tsu huan-hsiang	高祖還鄉
Liu	柳
Liu Ying-ch'un	柳應春
Lo-Li-lang ta-nao Hsiang-kuo-ssu	羅李郎大鬧相國寺
Lu-kuei-pu	錄鬼簿
Lu-kuei-pu hsü-pien	錄鬼簿續編
Mai-wang-kuan ch'ao-chiao-pen	
ku-chin tsa-chü	脈望館鈔校本古今雜劇
Mo-li-chih	摩利支
Mo-li-chih fei-tao tui-chien	摩利支飛刀對箭
Pai-pao-chi	白袍記
Pan-ko	伴哥
P'i-p'a-chi	琵琶記
Pien Ying Pu	騙英布
po-lao-erh	孛老兒
Shang Chung-hsien	尚仲賢
ta-hsiao	大孝
T'ai-he cheng-yin p'u	太和正音譜
T'ang Hsüeh Jen-kuei k'ua-hai	
cheng Liao ku-shih	唐薛仁貴跨海征遼故事
tsa-pan	雜扮

Tsang Mou-hsün	藏懋循
Tu Ju-hui	杜如晦
wai-mo	外末
Yen-tzu fu	燕子賦
Yüan-ch'ü hsüan	元曲選
Yung-lo ta-tien	永樂大典

CH'IU CHIN AND THE CHINESE WOMEN'S EMANCIPATION: A BEGINNING IN JAPAN

Liu Mei Ching

Ch'iu Chin (1877-1907) is the first woman martyr of the 1911 Revolution and is known as a heroine of the modern history of China.[1] Her public execution at Shaoshing, Chekiang, by the Manchu provincial authorities on July 15, 1907, made her a lasting model of a revolutionary.

In the ensuing period, as a result of the public outburst of protests aroused by the demonstration of cruelty, news in the press regarding Ch'iu Chin tended only to promote the cause of the Revolution. Moreover, the single verse she had written in prison: "Amidst autumn storm and rains, the grief for killing"[2] had become a handy slogan and password for the Revolution, referred to time and again in the press.

Ch'iu Chin's life as a revolutionary was but a brief one, lasting from 1904 to the time she was beheaded in 1907: three short years. But the history of the last three years of her life is very much the story of her endless efforts for the benefit of the emancipation of Chinese women, which in fact began with her own struggle for independence. The hardships she had encountered during her own development had given her the strength with which she undertook to accomplish her dedication, i.e., for the Revolution and for the emancipation of the Chinese women.

That the years in Japan had helped to accelerate the process of her own development into an emancipated woman and a full-fledged revolutionary is without doubt. For her as well as for many other, mainly male, students from China, Japan was just the right nurturing ground they needed, a country that had known some thirty years of development into a modern nation could well point out to them the way to achieve nationhood; the cultural similarity and the geographic proximity were also advantageous. Perhaps of greater significance still was the fact that their sojourn in Japan was free of the ethical norms and duties of their home society which would otherwise have withheld them from certain actions and whipped them into line as social requirements demanded, especially so where women were concerned.

This was obvious from an address made by a woman student, Wang Lien, who came to Japan around the beginning of 1902. She addressed a gathering of the Hupei fellow-students during which a farewell party was given in honour of the first batch of students from Hupei to return to China at the beginning of 1903. The speech was published in the second issue of the journal *Hu-pei hsüeh-sheng chieh* (*Hupei Students' Circle*), which had appeared for the first time in February 1903.[3] Wang Lien recounted her first moments of embarrassment when travelling together with unacquainted male passengers on board of a ship to Japan; the experience of freely associating with male friends who often visited her in Japan was entirely new to her. How surprised she was to note that all girls in Japan received education and hence were able to read newspapers and write as well, how different it was from women in China, most of whom were illiterate.

She told of the care given her by the school authorities and the doctor when she first got rid of the painful bandages binding her feet into the required form of what were called the "golden water-lilies". How happy she felt now that she could walk back and forth from the boarding house to the school, a thing she had been unable to do before. The practice of foot-binding was officially prohibited in the summer of 1902. Undoubtedly Wang Lien must have decided to discard the inhuman custom as soon as the ban had been announced. Had she been at home in China instead of being at school in Japan, it would presumably have taken her much longer to take the step.

Favourable climate and aspects

By the close of the 19th century and in the beginning years of this century the climate in Japan was, of course, conducive to the development of the Chinese students. International rivalry in China reaching the stage of "the mad scramble for concessions" at the end of the 1890's had not only stirred up the concern of many in China with the imminent threat of territorial partition-ment (hence stimulating reform attempts), in Japan it had activated initiatives too, as those expounded, among others, by the *Tōa Dōbunkai*, working for the preservation of China through efforts supporting the development of education and the press in China, in accordance with Japan's policy of Asianism.[4]

Consequently, guided by this motive, the schools set up for the purpose provided the Chinese students with a fitting milieu that ensured their quick development. Main emphasis of the curricula was on subjects needed for the building of a modern nation, and lectures were given on the political writings of Western philosophers, including Rousseau's *Contrat social*, Montesquieu's *Esprit des lois*, Mill's *On liberty* and *Representative Government*, etc., while health education and physical training were not neglected.[5] Obviously in line with the school practice in Japan at the time, public speaking and discussions were also encouraged.

The example of Japanese students' actions

At the end of the 19th century, two remarkable aspects of the Japanese students' activism, especially of the middle and high schools were: *jichi* (self-government) and *gakkō sōdō* (school disturbances) which could entail a *dōmei kyūkō* (student strike) in protest of certain actions effected by the school authorities.[6] For the Chinese students these examples served their purposes as evidenced from their own administration of the Chinese Students' Clubhouse which opened in 1902. The Clubhouse became a center of extracurricular activities and an information center for the students, offering possibilities for student gatherings, Japanese language lessons for newcomers, lectures, speech and debating sessions on Sundays, sports activities, etc. Publication activities also became a notable aspect of the students at the Clubhouse.

Significance of news on Russian moves

Inasmuch as the news concerning Russian occupation of Port Arthur and Dairen, two ports on the Liaotung Peninsula, in December 1897 were disconcerting, further Russian manoeuvres in Manchuria were equally distressing to the Chinese students, who in fact were alerted on every single new move of Russia by the press in Japan. Although the Boxer uprising had brought forth a joint action of the foreign powers in China, international rivalry did not abate; instead a tendency towards aggravation persisted while relations between Japan and Russia deteriorated.

At the end of April 1903, the Japanese press published the news concerning Russia's demand on China pertaining to the Three Eastern Provinces (Manchuria), accompanied by the threat not to withdraw her forces from that territory despite the earlier agreement reached. This had an agitating effect on the Chinese students, who held meetings to discuss possible counter-measures. Finally at a gathering convened by the radical Tokyo Youth Club which was formed in the winter of 1902, a voluntary corps to resist Russia was organized with the main objective of "facing the enemy at the front". More than 130 students regis-tered for the corps, while more than 50 signed up to man the headquarters, and it was decided to send telegrams to important government authorities and to other groups in Shanghai as well as other places in the interior, etc., notifying them of the intention of the corps. Soon the Japanese police intervened and the student corps dissolved itself, but only in name: another body was set up called the National Military Education Society (*Chün kuo-min chiao-yü hui*) with outward emphasis in physical drill and sports.[7]

In line with the actions of their male counterparts, the woman students also held a meeting of their own and set up a nursing corps to second those fighting at the frontline; many of the participants in fact belonged to the Mutual Love Society (*Kung-ai hui*) which was founded in April 1903 with the aim of "saving the two hundred million Chinese women by restoring their rights, so that they would have some understanding of the nation and would be able to contribute their share as citizens".[8] One of those to sign up for the nursing corps was Wang Lien, whose speech and poems were published by the monthly journal *Hupei Students' Circle* in early 1903, hence marking the begin-ning of participation by female students in the media world of the Chinese students in Japan.

In fact many of the attending girl-students studied at the Jissen Girls School of Shimoda Utako, a pioneer in education for women in Japan and chairwoman of the Imperial Society for Women (*Teikoku fujin kyōkai*). Her school was one of the first to open a section for the education of Chinese women. Although dedicated to the training of her students, Shimoda nevertheless deplored their public commitment, and hence pleaded with them for non-involvement in the burning issue, but her efforts were in vain and to no avail.[9]

The political implication of this step taken by the woman students was that by transforming their fervent patriotism into a public action, they had succeeded in making themselves equal partners with the male students in the venture, and thus had achieved an own platform for their struggle, although, admittedly, in their reasoning, the struggle for emancipation was subordinated to the dire need for patriotism, the call for which was nation-wide. But the basic understanding of the duties and obligations of the people towards the nation lay with education and development of the public in general and in particular of the women, who lagged far behind because of the traditional norms embedded in the Confucian ethical order requirements of the three dependencies (*san-ch'ung*) and the four virtues (*szu-te*) for women.[10] Fundamental in the issue was therefore the right to receive education, and since the social ethics had robbed the women of this right, the Mutual Love Society made it a first objective to restore it.

Ch'iu Chin's arrival in Japan in 1904

Inasmuch as events in 1902 in the Chinese students' world in Japan had brought forth the publication of various journals in 1903 by the respective societies of fellow-provincials such as: the *Hupei Students' Circle* (*Hu-pei hsüeh-sheng chieh*), *Chekiang Tide* (*Che-chiang ch'ao*), *Kiangsu Journal* (*Chiang-su*), *Straight Talk* (*Chih-shuo*), *Journal of Politics and Law* (*Cheng-fa hsüeh-pao*), etc., the salient anti-Russian action of 1903 meanwhile had consolidated the patriotic fervor of the students, while subsequent circumstances further caused it to disperse into underground revolutionary activities. It was against this background of students' activism that Ch'iu Chin arrived in Japan in the spring of 1904.

Born out of well-off civil servant parentage originating from Chekiang Province, Ch'iu Chin had received considerable education in her youth, during which she had been able to practise such sports as horse riding and fencing with her male kinsmen. When her father assumed an appointment in Hunan as chief executive at the Likin Administration Bureau in 1890, the family

went with him. At the age of 19, in 1896, Ch'iu Chin was
wedded to Wang T'ing-chün, a distant relative of the famous
statesman, general and scholar from Hunan, Tseng Kuo-fan
(1811-1872). Two children were born out of this wedlock, a son
in 1897, and a daughter in 1901. The family moved in 1902 to
Peking where her husband acquired a civil servant post. It was
here that Ch'iu Chin first came under the direct influence of
reform ideas through her friend and neighbour, the well-known
woman calligrapher Wu Chih-ying, whose husband was a colleague of Wang and originated as well from Hunan.

Since her marriage did not work out well, a separation
settlement was agreed upon and Ch'iu Chin decided to study in
Japan. Arriving at Tokyo in 1904, she registered at the language
class organized for newcomers at the Students' Clubhouse, which
was efficiently run by the students themselves, and by then had
become a headquarter for the students. A Chekiangese by birth
and a Hunanese by marriage, she attended the meetings of
fellow- students from both Chekiang and Hunan, and participated
in the speech and debating sessions as well as sports activities.
Her personal acquaintanceship with some soon brought her into
contact with T'ao Ch'eng-chang from Chekiang who had secret
society relationships and who had also formed together with
others from Chekiang, including Ts'ai Yüan-pei from Shanghai,
the Restoration Society (*Kuang-fu hui*); her relations with the
Canton group from Yokohama associated her with the Three
Points Society (*San-tien hui*), a secret society having strong ties
with the revolutionary group around Sun Yat-sen.[11]

Conscious of the significance of the media, the Chinese
students in Japan had by 1904 succeeded in publishing many
journals to help disseminate to their fellow-students and countrymen the necessary knowledge for nation-building, keeping
them at the same time informed of events in the international
world; they had also translated many books on various subjects
as well as on socialism, anarchism, etc., topics heretofore
unheard of. In fact, monthly lectures on these special subjects
were already being held by the Waseda Social Studies Association (*Waseda Shakai Gakkai*) which was founded in November
1903; some of these lectures were published in such periodicals
as the *Commoners' News* (*Heimin Shinbun*).[12]

In the meantime, a student from Hupei, Chang Chi, who
studied at Waseda University (called then the Tokyo Specialist
School) and was actively involved in the publication activities of

his fellow-students, had in 1903 translated a book on anarchism which had earlier been published by Waseda's publication department. Chang Chi had been one of the students who helped to administrate the Students' Clubhouse, and his membership in the radical Tokyo Youth Club caused him to become involved later in the revolutionary attempt of Huang Hsing in Hunan.

One of the remarkable aspects of the students engaged in the publishing enterprise was their radicalism. Some were members of the radical Youth Club, or had close ties with it, others already belonged to a radical group before arriving in Japan, as in the case of the monthly, *Tides of Chekiang*, which name in fact implied "the revolutionary tide sweeping over Chekiang", a name chosen by the radical editors, Sun Chiang-tung and Chiang Po-li, in contradiction to the more common sounding name preferred by the moderates.[13]

Against this background of radicalism, Ch'iu Chin soon found herself swept up in the rising tide of the revolutionaries. Free from family duties and uninhibited by the cumbersome ethical norms of her home society, she was able to participate in many activities of the students including those of the Mutual Love Society. Her literal fluency, a talent for which she had been noted since her youth, soon placed her on the forefront of the society, next to Ch'en Chieh-fen, the chairwoman of Mutual Love Society. Ch'en and her father, Ch'en Fan, owner of the revolutionary paper *Su Pao* in Shanghai, eluded arrest and escaped to Japan in the summer of 1903 after the paper was banned for having published anti-Manchu propaganda. While in Shanghai, Ch'en Chieh-fen had published under the auspices of the *Su Pao*, the *Women Journal* (*Nü pao*). By way of introduction, the *Women Journal* was distributed to the readers of the *Su Pao* free of charge; its contents called on women to develop and educate themselves in order to become conscious of their rights and tasks with respect to the nation. In other words, the rationale was: to become emancipated, with the objective of being a patriotic member of the nation in words and deeds.

Here then was the basis for the genesis of women emancipation, which had been rendered acceptable in face of the urgent need for patriotism not only of men, but also of women, i.e., an equal share of the duty towards the country. But an equal share of duty implied equal rights as well. In this respect, even before the turn of the century, Liang Ch'i-ch'ao had already pointed out the discrepancy between the development of Chinese men and women in comparison to societies of the West and that of Japan, where education was compulsory for the young without any discrimination between males and females.

It was in Shanghai, where the atmosphere was teeming with calls for reform, that the seeds of women emancipation came to sprout under the nurturing care of a group of reform-minded intellectuals around Ts'ai Yüan-p'ei, which took the initiative to open a school for women in 1902 called the Patriotic School for Women (*Ai-kuo nü-hsüeh*). As the name indicated, "patriotism" was the spirit, and, as worded in an interview by Ts'ai Yüan-p'ei, who was head of the school in 1903, the aim was "to develop women *not* along the traditional line of a good wife and wise mother (*hsien-ch'i liang-mu*), but instead to breed a nihilist type of women; consequently, lectures were given not only on common knowledge, but also centered on the history of the French Revolution, nihilism in Russia, etc., with special emphasis on chemistry".[14] In the meantime, however, the action base of equal participation together with men for women came to be broadened into one that necessitated "individual independent action" (of revolutionary terrorists), compatible with the contemporary slogans of the radicals for "terrorist actions" and "assassinations". The agitation of 1903 in Tokyo around the Russian moves had precipitated the establishment of connections with revolutionaries on the mainland, and had set into motion the machinations of underground activities involving mainly the groups from Chekiang/Shanghai, Hunan/Hupei and Canton. By the time the National Military Education Society was set up in Tokyo, a direct connecting line existed with its counterpart at Shanghai, the Patriotic Study Society (*Ai-kuo hsüeh-she*), a school closely related to the Patriotic School for Women, forming together the training centers for revolutionaries, where military-style exercises and specific training for terrorist actions and assassinations became part and parcel of the curricula. In view of the fact that women were considered appropriate for the task of assassination, "the seeds to this end were sowed at the Patriotic School for Women", Ts'ai Yüan-p'ei revealed later. The relationship of the schools with the revolutionary journal *Su Pao* became all the more closer, when the teaching staff of the Patriotic Study Society undertook part of the editing in exchange for the financial support given by the journal to the school.

This background setting was undoubtedly of significance in helping to determine the further course of Ch'iu Chin's life. The urgent calls for patriotism, the resolute radicalism of the Tokyo Youth Club and associates "to save the nation", and the valorous war-sphere incited vis-à-vis Russia were not lost on her. Soon she availed herself of the opportunities both in the written and spoken media to further the cause of women emancipation and patriotism.

A regular participant of the speech and debating sessions held at the Students' Clubhouse, Ch'iu Chin was often seen to mount the rostrum to address the audience. Topics of discussion at these sessions were published in the *Vernacular Journal* (*Pai-hua pao*). Her first address entitled: "The advantage of public speaking", was published in the first issue of the journal of September 1904.

Employing the vernacular, Ch'iu Chin explained to the audience the reason why Chinese students in Japan were prac-tising the art of public speaking. Unlike newspapers for the understanding of which a certain degree of literacy was re-quired, public speaking offered the following advantages: firstly, a speech could be delivered at any time and at any place; secondly, because no costs were involved, many would come to listen; thirdly, every one could understand what was being said, even those who were illiterate such as women and children; fourthly, no other efforts were needed except for the fluency of the tongue; and lastly, the audience could be informed of world events. Being aware of the importance of public speaking, the Chinese students in Japan therefore started to practise it at the sessions held and they published the speeches made, so that others could learn from it and thus could help develop their countrymen.[15]

In another address published in the second issue of the same journal of October 1904, entitled: "A call on two hundred million Chinese women", Ch'iu Chin said the greatest injustice in the world was to be, as two hundred million others, a woman in China; first, to have to suffer the painful experience of foot-binding as a young girl, and later to be married off according to the will of the parents, then, in case of an unhappy marriage, to have to undergo the whims of the husband's character. Thereafter, when she became a widow, a mourning of three years was compulsory, after which remarriage was out of the question, whereas a widower could attach some pleated blue threads in his garment as a token of mourning if he chose to do so, and he could welcome a new bride as he preferred even during the first days of his widowerhood. What an injustice, considering the fact that men and women were born equal, Ch'iu Chin pointed out and wondered why women had been rendered to such an inferior state and were being treated as slaves from Africa, in such an extreme state of human injustice.

The answer to the problem lay with the women themselves, she explained further, in the face of such nonsensical Confucian sayings applicable to women as "The virtue of no talent", "Men are superior and women inferior", and "The will of the husband constitutes the rules for the wife". Women of determination should call on other women to rise up in protest instead of submissively and complacently remaining uneducated and thus becoming a class of slaves! In the end Ch'iu Chin called on all women, young and old, to wake up to the present realities, not only to educate themselves, but at the same time to encourage their husbands, sons and daughters to develop themselves for the benefit of the general public, especially so now that the country was faced with the threat of disintegration.

Chinese Women Monthly 1907

The Chinese student world in Japan underwent great commotion in November 1905 when the Japanese Ministry of Education announced new regulations for the Chinese students, restricting their activities and prohibiting their participation in political issues. The students responded by staging a strike while calling on the Chinese minister to urge for revision of these regulations by the Japanese authorities. Meanwhile, the situation climaxed when Ch'en T'ien-hua, a student from Hunan, committed suicide in protest. Ch'en, a radical who had written many anti-Manchu articles, was one of the editors of the revolutionary journal, *Twentieth Century China (Erh-shih shih-chi chi-na)*.[16] Thereupon the radicals agitated for a total exit of the students from Japan. During this episode Ch'iu Chin was one of the leading figures; the action caused many to return, including Ch'iu herself, who arrived in Shanghai at the beginning of 1906; she helped to establish there the *Chun-kuo Kung-hsüeh*, a school to accommodate the students from Japan and at which, in the words of Hu Shih,[17] "many teachers and students were revolutionaries".

From then on Ch'iu Chin moved about in the educational field functioning as a teacher while maintaining contacts with comrade revolutionaries, staging schemes for uprisings as well as fabricating explosives, which she had learned in Yokohama. But she had not neglected her main task, to promote the struggle for women emancipation. In January 1907 she published the *Chinese Women Monthly (Chung-kuo Nü-pao)* with the objective of popularizing and advocating women education, next to enhance friendly relations among them so as to forge a unity which would serve as a basis for a future Chinese women's association. The contents were meant for all who wanted to broaden their knowledge field, and hence keeping them informed of all beneficial matters.[18]

In the opening article Ch'iu Chin called on women to climb out of the "darkness" surrounding them, the darkness of ignorance, non-seeing, non-hearing, in short, a life in darkness devoid of all thinking and action which should have been normal in the human world. Therefore, she had published the monthly in order to lead women "as a magic lantern" towards a brighter world.

In another article in the same issue, she described the backward state of women and the problem of illiteracy. She urged them not to revert to the excuse of a so-called "fate"; instead, they should abandon the position of slavery and start to develop themselves in order to achieve a foundation for their independence, and build up an own basis of livelihood. In doing so they would win the respect from men and reap the bliss of liberty.

The *Women Monthly* was written in the vernacular because, as Ch'iu Chin explained, it would then be easily understood by women, many of whom were illiterate. In spite of shortage of funds, two issues of the monthly were published, but the third never appeared, for her life ended by execution on 15 July 1907. By then she had paved the first steps for the struggle of Chinese women emancipation and mapped out the blueprints for their future actions. Her experiences and the knowledge she had acquired in China and Japan had not only transformed her into the first woman revolutionary, but more important still, a forerunner of feminism in China.

NOTES

1. Arthur W. Hummel (ed.), *Eminent Chinese of the Ch'ing Period (1644-1912)*, Taipei, 1970, pp. 169-171.
2. Pao Chia Lin, *Readings in the Chinese Woman History*, Taipei, 1979, p. 373.
3. "Records on Students Activities: Get-together of Hupei Students", *Hu-pei hsüeh-sheng chieh* (*Hupei Students' Circle*), reprint, No. 2, Taipei: Chung-yang wen-wu kung-ying she, 1968, pp. 287-290.
4. Kokuryū Club (ed.), *Kokushi Uchida Ryōhei den* ("Biography of the patriot Uchida Ryōhei"), Tōkyō: Hara Shobō, 1967, pp. 179-180.
5. Sanetō Keishū, *Chūgoku ryūgakusei shidan* ("Recollections of the Chinese students in Japan"), Tōkyō: Daiichi Shobō, 1981, pp. 50-54.
6. Henry DeWitt Smith II, *Japan's First Student Radicals*, Cambridge (Mass.): Harvard University Press, 1972, pp. 22-24.
7. Katherine P.K. Whitaker (transl.), *Chinese Students in Japan in the Late Ch'ing Period*, Tōkyō: The Centre for East Asian Cultural Studies, 1982, pp. 202-209.
8. Pao, *Woman History*, p. 281.
9. *Hupei Students' Circle*, No. 4, p. 575.
10. *San ch'ung*: "the three dependencies": on the father, the husband and the son. *Szu te*: "the four virtues": right behaviour, proper speech, proper demeanour, proper employment.
11. Pao, *Woman History*, p. 352.
12. DeWitt Smith, *Student Radicals*, p. 27.
13. Hsü Shou-shang, *Reminiscence on Impressions of Deceased Friend Lu Xun* (*Wang-yu Lu Xun ying-xiang chi*), Peking, 1953, p. 13. See also, Mary Backus Rankin, "The Revolutionary Movement in Chekiang: A Study in the Tenacity of Tradition", in Mary C. Wright, *China in Revolution: The First Phase 1900-1913*, New Haven: Yale University Press, 1968, pp. 330-331.
14. Ts'ai Yüan-p'ei, *Ts'ai Yüan-p'ei's own narrative*, Taipei: Biographical Literature Publishing Society, 1967 (*Biographical series* 22), p. 39.
15. *Vernacular Journal* (*Pai-hua pao*), September, 1904, in *Ch'iu*

Chin chi ("Collected Works of Ch'iu Chin"), Shanghai: Shanghai Classics Publishers, 1979, pp. 3-4.

16. The *Twentieth Century China* was renamed *Min-pao* and became the organ of the T'ung-meng hui in 1905.

17. Yang Ch'eng-shan, *Hu Shih te cheng-chih shih-hsiang* ("Political ideas of Hu Shih"), Taipei: Commercial Press Taiwan, 1967, p. 3.

18. *Collected Works*, pp. 10-11.

"BODHISATTVA NEVER DESPISE":
CHAPTER 20 OF THE LOTUS SUTRA IN THE SŎKPO-SANGJŎL AND THE WŎRIN SŎKPO

A.M. Olof

In contrast:

"Aan den Staten-Bijbel is, door een kollege van zes overzetters en dubbel zooveel herzieners, gearbeid van 1626 tot 1637."

"Het provincialisme, in den Staat zulk eene voorname aanleiding tot verdeeldheid en naijver, bleef vreemd aan dit werk der Kerk. Uit alle oorden des lands zonder onderscheid waren de beste krachten te hulp geroepen."

"In elk geval levert, omdat de vertalers geen letterkundigen waren van beroep, bij het beoordelen van den standaard van beschaving, waartoe zij en hunne calvinistische gemeenten destijds zich opgewerkt hadden, hun arbeid een des te geschikter maatstaf."

(C. Busken Huet, *Het land van Rembrand*, Haarlem, 1924[5], II, I pp. 99-103.)

I Preface

The *Saddharmapuṇḍarīkasūtra* or *Lotus Sutra*, one of the most important scriptures of Mahāyāna Buddhism, still exists in its original Sanskrit form. Between the 3rd and 7th century, individuals and groups of a very international character in China translated this at least six times. Thus it became also accessible to the Chinese-educated upper classes of the neighbouring countries around the Celestial Empire.

Probably it was one of the sutras presented by king Sŏngmyŏng of Paekche to king Kimmei of Yamato in the winter of A.D. 552, the earliest canonical works to reach Japanese soil. It certainly was discussed by prince Shōtoku and his Koguryŏ teacher Hyeja around A.D. 600. It was recited at the time the whole Koryŏ woodblock *Tripitaka* was being burned by the Mongols, then recarved on Kanghwa Island, until 1258 the splendid refuge of king Kojong.

With the rise of the Yi dynasty the status of Buddhism in Korea and the reciting of its canon was on a decline, accompanied however by a small but strong countercurrent that would bring it closer to the people who could not or barely grasp the Chinese script. This current was enhanced with the invention of the *han'gŭl* alphabet that was promulgated in 1446. The research and development of *han'gŭl* was intended to bring Chinese (Confucian) rules and examples closer to the people, at least closer to the lower functionaries; but soon it became the tool for "Koreanizing" important Buddhist works.

Already in 1447 prince Suyang could present to his father king Sejong (r. 1418-1450) the *Sŏkpo-sangjŏl*, the first *han'gŭl* prosework, which includes a translation of the *Lotus Sutra*. The king versified this into the *Wŏrinch'ŏn'gangjigok* (1449), which was joined to the *Sŏkpo-sangjŏl* to form the *Wŏrin Sŏkpo* (1459) after the prince had seized the throne as king Sejo (r. 1455-1468).

This compilation by Sejo, as this paper will show, has not been a pure and simple one. Phrase for phrase, even word for word, the *Sŏkpo-sangjŏl* has been revised by the compilers, among whom the official Kim Suon (1409-1481) and his brother, the monk Sinmi, are note-worthy. Twelve years before they had assisted with the editing of the *Sŏkpo-sangjŏl*.

In 1461 king Sejo established the "National Sutra Institute" (Kangyŏng togam) that would turn out in the ten years of its existence the Korean translation (*ŏnhae*) of the main sutras, among which in 1463 the *Lotus Sutra: Pŏphwagyŏng-ŏnhae*. This translation has been compared in this paper with that of the *Sŏkpo-sangjŏl* and *Wŏrin Sŏkpo*, it being the most literal one.[1]

The Chinese phrases in the *Pŏphwagyŏng-ŏnhae* (hereafter *Ŏnhae*) form the full translation by Kumārajīva (fl. in the early 5th century) of A.D. 406.[2] At the beginning of every volume in the *ŏnhae* the name of a commentator, the Chinese monk Chieh Huan,[3] is given, alongside the editor I Ju. Chieh Huan's commentary in the *ŏnhae* is also partly reproduced in volume 17 of the (earlier) *Wŏrin Sŏkpo*,[4] which also contains a full Middle

Korean (hereafter M.K.) translation of the Sutra, while the text in volume 19 of the *Sōkpo-sangjōl* lacks phrases.[5]

This paper deals primarily with a comparison of the M.K. texts. For both the *Sōkpo-sangjōl* (hereafter *S.s.*) and the *Wŏrin Sōkpo* (*W.S.*) the facsimiles of a first edition have been used.[6] For translation or explanations of most of the Sanskrit terms I wish to refer to Kern, Katō and Hurvitz.[7]

The theme of chapter 20, the bodhisattva revering plain people as Buddhas, is not limited to the scriptures. Followers of the monk Hsin-hsing in sixth to seventh century China revered not just common people in the streets, but even prostrated themselves before animals.[8] The same idea is expressed in a hymn of Ćantideva (fl. during the reign of Ćila in 7th century India), as rendered by R. Grousset: "Que ceux qui me calomnient, me nuisent, me raillent, ainsi que tous les autres, obtiennent la Bodhi!" "Cette parcelle insigne qui fait lever en nous les vertus d'un Bouddha, elle est présente dans toutes les créatures, et c'est en raison de cette Présence que toutes les créatures doivent être honorées."[9]

Some notes on the transcription

The McCune-Reischauer transcription has been used with a few addenda for M.K. phonemes /ă,z,W/ and some exceptions to the rules of consonant changes for morphophonemic reasons. Also the "tone" (pitch) marks are indicated, partly to show the M.K. syllable structure: zero for level pitch, . for the high and : for the rising pitch.

/st/ and other consonant clusters are transcribed: tt, etc.[10]

/psk/ : pkk.[11] /S/ the connective particle : S.

/ng/ in final position following the /r/ indicates preglottalization and is therefore transcribed as the double of the following consonant.[12]

Chinese characters are given in their modern Sino-Korean pronunciation between [ ], since their M.K. *han'gŭl* readings are so complex as to defy transcription (exceptions are indicated by a preceding *). They provide no clue to a Korean pronunciation of those days but to the "ideal pronunciation" and "graphic harmony" in the theories of the official linguists. The diplogrammatic initials (kk,tt etc.) of characters in early texts disappeared before the end of the 15th century.[13] Also in 1447 the linguists adopted as a new rule, probably to enhance the "pattern" model, that syllables had a terminal, even if this was an insipid and empty one; thus we see the grapheme /o/ under all Sino-Korean syllables lacking another final consonant.[14]

II Translations

Wŏrin Sŏkpo 17

poem 313 of the Wŏrinch'ŏn'gangjigok (p.75b)[15]
The length of Formal Law of King Majestic Voice,
Tathāgata, in number is like Four Worlds' finest dust.
(p.76a) The monk Never Despise, of despite was deprived,
so ever and ever he made his bows to all Four the Groups.

poem 314
Thus were his words: "O you who follow bodhisattva's path,
you will for sure be Buddhas!"
(p.76b) "This monk," the rude folks said,
"this idle prophet is lacking in wisdom!"

poem 315
Insults he even suffered, but of anger did not think
and once again he spoke.
They beat him even with whips, but he ran far away
(p.77a) and spoke with steadfast voice.

poem 316
Never Despise they despised, and for a thousand kalpas
were locked away in Avīci hell.
They met again Never Despise, and were converted by him;
in this Great Congregation they flock together now.

poem 317 (p.77b)
Can this monk Never Despise be anybody else?
He is today's World-honoured One.
The Lotus Sutra he received from King Majestic Voice,
Tathāgata; thus he became the Buddha of our day.

Sökpo-sangjöl 19

(p.26a) At that time the Buddha spoke to (1)[16] the *bodhisattva-mahāsattva* Mahāsthāma: "Know this (2)! Of the monks, nuns, male or female devotees (3), whosoever (4-) scolds and derides with harsh mouth someone (-4) who preserves the *Lotus Sutra* (p.26b), he will incur the stern retribution for sin as has been said before (5); and also the obtained merits will be as said before (6), and he will be (7) pure of eye, ear, nose, tongue, body and mind. O Mahāsthāmaprāpta (8)! Innumerable immeasurable unimaginable *asaṃkhyeya* kalpas ago (9) there was a Buddha whose name was King Majestic Voice, Thus Come, Worthy of (p.27a) Worship, Omniscient, Perfect in Knowledge and Conduct, Well Departed, Understander of the World, Peerless Nobleman, Regulator of Men of Stature, Teacher of Devas and Men, Buddha, World-honoured One. His kalpa was (10) named "Free of Deterioration", and his land "Great Completion". This Buddha King Majestic Voice in that world (11) was expounding the Law for the benefit of (12) devas, humans and asuras: he spoke of the Four Noble Truths (p.27b) for the benefit of those who strive (13) to be śrāvakas, made them come over (14) birth, old age, illness and death, and enter the ultimate nirvana; and he spoke of the Law (15) of Twelve Links in one's existence for the benefit of those who strive (13) to be pratyekabuddhas, and he spoke of the Law (17) of Six Pāramitās based upon his unexcelled enlightenment for the benefit of the bodhisattvas (16), and guided them (18) to the ultimate Buddha-wisdom. (p.28a) O Mahāsthāmaprāpta! (8) The life of this Buddha King Majestic Voice lasted (19) kalpas as many as the sands of forty myriads *nayutas* of Ganges rivers and the stay of the correct Law in the world was in number of kalpas as many as the atoms in a Jambudvīpa world (20) and the stay of the formal Law in the world was in number of kalpas as many as the atoms in the four quarters of the world (21). After that Buddha had entered nirvana (22) and (p.28b) the correct Law and the formal Law all had disappeared (23), another Buddha was born in this world who also was called (24) King Majestic Voice, Thus Come (etc), World-honoured One. In this way (25) there followed in order two myriads of Buddhas who all had (p.29a) the same name (26).

After the very first King Majestic Voice Tathāgata had entered nirvana and the correct Law had disappeared (27), in the time of the formal Law the self-conceited monks were in great strength. At that time there was a boddhisattva monk named (28) Never Despise. O Mahāsthāmaprāpta! For what reason had they called (29) him "Never Despise"? When this monk (p.29b) (that is the monk Never Despise) (30) saw a monk, a nun, a male or female devotee, everytime he bowed for everyone (31), and praised (32) them with the words: "I revere you deeply (33) and do not look down on you (34)! If you might wonder why this is so, it is because you all follow the guiding rules of the bodhisattva and for sure will become Buddhas." (35) This monk did not (p.30a) give all primacy to the reading and reciting of the canonical books (36) ([chŏnju] means "to put absolutely first") (37) but only bowed to the people (38), and even when he saw the four groups from afar he went on purpose and bowed to them (39), and praised them saying: "I really do not look down on you. You (40) all for sure will become (41) Buddhas." Those in the four groups who became angry reviled him with harsh mouth (42), saying: "Whence (p.30b) does this monk who lacks knowledge and wisdom come ? (43) He is predicting our future Buddhahood saying (44): 'for sure you will be Buddhas'. This kind of idle predictions are really worthless to us !" (45) For years he endured in this way uninterrupted scolding but no anger grew in him (46) and always he said: "For sure you will become Buddhas!" So (47) when he was speaking (48) thus all (p.31a) the people (49) attacked (50-) him with sticks and tiles and stones. So he got chased away then, ran, but at a distance stood still and yet called in a loud voice (50): "I do not look down on you (34)! You will all for sure become Buddhas (51)." Because (52) he always spoke thus the self-conceited monks, nuns, male and female devotees gave him the name (53) "Never Despise". (p.31b) When the time to die had come for this monk he heard all the twenty thousand myriads of *gāthās* of the *Lotus Sutra* that once had been spoken by the Buddha King Majestic Voice in the empty space (54), ably received and kept them all and directly as has been described above (55) his faculty of the eye was pure and his faculties of ear, nose, tongue, body and mind were pure (56-); he obtained the pureness of the six faculties (-56); (p.32a) and he lived again for two hundred myriads of *nayutas* of years more and widely spoke for the people of this *Lotus Sutra* (57). Then (58) the self-conceited monks, nuns, male and female devotees, those who had slighted this man and had called him "Despise Not" (59) saw how he had acquired great supernatural powers, the power of joy in preaching and the great power of virtuous tranquility (60) (p.32b), heard the words he spoke and all submitted in belief and followed him ([pok] means "to surrender") (61). This bodhisattva (that is the bodhisattva Never Despise) (62) converted also thousand myriads of people (63) and brought them to stay in the perfect Buddha wisdom (64), and after he had died he met two billion Buddhas (65); they were all called "Sun-moon-lanternshine", (p.33a) and during their Law he spoke of this Lotus Sutra. Therefore (66) he met again two billion Buddhas (65), who uniformly were called "King Lantern Sovereign of Clouds". Thanks to his receiving, keeping, reading and reciting during the Law of these Buddhas (67) and his speaking of this book on behalf of the four groups (68) his ordinary sight became pure and his faculties of ear, nose, tongue, body and mind (p.33b) became pure (69), and among the four groups he preached the Law, and in his heart was no fear (70). O Mahāsthāma ! This bodhisattva-mahāsattva Never Despise made offerings to such numerous Buddhas (71), he revered, honoured and praised them and planted various roots of good- ness (72). Then afterwards he also met thousand myriads of Buddhas (p.34a) and again he spoke of this Book during the Law of various Buddhas and his merits were established (73); deser- vedly he would become (74) a Buddha. O Mahāsthāma! What do you think hereof (75)? Could the bodhisattva Never Despise of that time be somebody else (76)? I myself was he. If I had not received, kept, read and recited and spoken to others of this Sutra in earlier times, I would not have obtained the perfect Buddha wisdom (p.34b) quickly (77) (78). O Mahāsthāma! Because the monks, nuns, male and female devotees of that period (79) treated me rudely in their anger (80), they could not meet once a Buddha for two hundred million *kalpas*, nor hear the Law or see a *sangha* (81), and for a thousand (82) kalpas they suffered severely (83) in the hell Avīci, (p.35a) but when this crime had expired they too were converted by the perfect Buddha wisdom of the bodhisattva Never Despise. O Mahāsthāma! What do you think hereof (75)? Could the four groups who treated this bodhisattva of that time rudely be somebody else (84)? The five hundred bodhisattvas, starting with Bhadrapāla, and the five hundred monks and nuns (85), starting with Simhacandrā (Lion Moon), (p.35b) and the five hundred male and female devotees (86), starting with Thoughtful of the Buddha, who are at this congregation (87), all people who do not retreat (88) from the perfect Buddha wisdom, were those people. O Mahāsthāma! Know this! (89) This *Lotus Sutra* benefits the *bodhisattva-mahāsattvas* abundantly (90) and ably makes them arrive (91) at the perfect Buddha wisdom, (p.36a) so the *bodhisattva-mahāsattvas* should, after the Tathāgata has entered nirvana (92), always receive, keep, read and recite, interpret, speak of and copy this Sutra (93)."

Here ends the chapter of the Bodhisattva Never Despise (94). It tells how (100) an earlier incarnation of Śākya (95) kept at the time (96) of King Majestic Voice the Wonderful Law in a subtle way (97), widely made offerings (98) and gave guidance in a profitable manner (99). He did not just read and recite (101) but kept the Sutra of formlessness[17] and firmly endured rebuke and humiliation (102) and (p.36b) kept the way (103) of non-ego[18]. "Formlessness" and "non-ego" mean he kept it in a subtle way (104). He spoke widely of this Sutra in a myriad ages (105), converted a myriad beings and made (106) them abide in the correct way, and made people who were self-conceited submit in belief and follow him (107),and people whose crimes had expired he made again obtain the fruits of the Way. This means he profited them widely (108). Keeping (109-) the Sutra previously brings five kinds of merit; however perfect[19] it may be, it cannot be subtle (-109); obtaining (110-) profits previously provides six thousand virtues; however victorious it may be, it cannot be expansive (-110). That is because there are the shadows in the outer world of men's *dharmas*[20] (111). Necessarily (112-) one strives to rise to the wonderful that is formless and ego- less; one does not think of concentrating on reading and reciting or of forgetting it again (-112); (p.37a) one does not think of paying respect to the four groups, or of despising them (113). Only after the wonderful practice comes out (114) in full and the million masses are converted spontaneously, only after feelings of respect and pride, crime and happiness (115), all things that are called the shadows in the outer world of men's *dharmas* have reached the sphere of universality (116), will there be subtlety and expansiveness (117). This is the Supreme Way of keeping the Sutra in truth (118). ([yŏn] is [inyŏn] "the causes" and [yŏng] is "shadow")[21] (119).

*III Comparison of the texts of Sŏkpo-sangjŏl 19 and Wŏrin
Sŏkpo 17*

(1)   -.kküi; *W.S.* p.78a: -tă.ryŏ.
(2)   ara.ra; *W.S.*: .ije pan.dăgi :al.la.
(3)   [pigu piguni uba*säing]; *W.S.*: [pigu]Iŏ.na [piguni]ŏ.na
       [uba*sük]; as for the different *reading, *W.S.* is correct.[22]
(4)   :sară.măl :amoe.na :modin .ibŭ.ro ku.jijŏ :piu.zŭ.myŏn; *W.S.*:
       :sară.măl .hăda.ga :mo.din .ibŭ.ro ku.jidŭ.myŏ :piu.zŭmyŏn.
       This translation leaves it an open question whether "the
       monks, etc." are syntactically related to "whosoever" or to
       "a person", as the *S.s.* and *W.S.* texts also are ambiguous.
       Because later in this chapter the monks, etc. are those
       who "scold and deride", the *S.s.* and *W.S.* may express in
       this sentence the same situation. This is more clearly the
       interpretation of the *ŏnhae* (6, pp.72a-b), that assumes
       [cha] to mean "persons" and not "the fact": [yak pigu(...)]I
       [chi *Pŏphwagyŏng* cha]răl [yak yu ak ku]ro (...).
       However, Yi seems to regard the monks, etc. as the object
       (...rosŏ) of the scolding,[23] and Katō runs: "(...) if bhikshus
       (...) keep the (...) Sutra, and if anyone curses, abuses, and
       slanders them (...)."[24] Hurvitz confirms this interpreta-
       tion;[25] and Kern (from the Sanskrit): "(...) he who rejects
       such a (discourse on the law), who abuses monks, nuns
       (...), keeping this Sutra, insults them, (...).[26]
(5)   monjyŏ nirü.tät hă.myŏ; *W.S.* p.78b: :al.p'äi nirä.tät hă.myŏ.
(6)   aek.ka; *W.S.*: monjyŏ.
(7)   hă.ri.ni; *W.S.*: hă.ri.ra, and continues: "The sin of deriding
       and slandering is as told at the end of the chapter
       'Parable ([yu])' and the chapter 'A Teacher of the Law
       ([pŏpsa])', and the fortune of hearing[27] and keeping it is
       as told in the chapter 'The Merits of the Preacher ([Pŏpsa
       kongdŏk])'. That he kept up[28] and spoke (of the Sutra)
       before, in order to disclose[29] the keeping (of the Sutra)
       in a subtle way in the future, (explains why)[30] he ad-
       monished the masses and made them understand that the
       retribution for keeping (the Sutra) and for slandering is
       not undone, and made them believe deeply[31] (p.79a) in
       (his)[32] keeping hereof in a subtle way and (his) profiting
       (others) widely. Tük-tae-se is Tae-se-ji[33]."
(8)   [Tŭktaese].yŏ; *W.S.* p.79a: --.ya; thus at all corresponding
       places.

(9)   :nye [muryang ...kŏp] :ti:nae.ya; *W.S.*: :ti.nagŏn :nye [muryang...gŏp] :ti.na.

(10)   .irŏ.ra; *W.S.* p.79b: .irŏ.ni, and continues: "In a far bygone olden time he served[34] a billion Buddhas, and the formlessness and egolessness, the keeping in a subtle way and profiting widely was endowed with the great might of the Law's Power. If not, he would not be qualified for its tasks; so[35] therefore he speaks (now) to the bodhisattva Mahāsthāmaprāpta. The King Majestic Voice filled with his loud voice the worlds and became a *Sarvadharmarāja*[36] and was fearless (p.80a) in his preaching of the Law. Thus Never Despise obtained the Way and preached aptly for masses of people, but his mind was devoid of fear. The kalpa's name 'Free of Deterioration' means the period and the Way[37] rise in mutual interaction. The name of the land 'Great Completion' means that the correct conversion has no deficiencies."

(11)   .tyŏ :nwiye.syŏ; *W.S.*: .tyŏ [se chung].e.

(12)   :wi.hă.ya; *W.S.*: [wi].hă.sya.

(13)   [ku]hă.ri :wi.hăsyan[38]; *W.S.*: [ku]hăls :sarăm [wi].hă.sya.

(14)   :kŏt.na.a (...).k'e .hăsi.go ; *W.S.* p.80b: [tosŏl].hă.sya (...).k'e .hăsi.myŏ.[39]

(15)   [pŏp].ŭl nirŭ.si.myŏ; *W.S.*: [pŏp] niră.si.myŏ.

(16)   [posal].tăl :wi.hăsyan; *W.S.*: [che posal wi].hă.sya.

(17)   [pŏp].ŭl niră.sya; cf. (15); *W.S.*: [pŏp].ăl niră.sya.

(18)   [hye].k'e .hă.dŏsi.ni; *W.S.* p.81a: [.].k'e .hă.sini.ra, and adds the note: "Here he says that Majestic Voice spoke also of the Three Vehicles." (This is only part of the note in *Ŏnhae* pp.75a-b).

(19)   .isi.go; *W.S.*: .i.rŏsi.ni.

(20)   [chŏng pŏp].i [se kan].ae i.syo.măn [kŏp su]I hăn [Yŏmbuje mijin].man hă.go; *W.S.*: [chŏng pŏp chu se kŏp su].nŭn hăn [Yŏmbuje].i .kăt.ko.

(21)   [sang pŏp].i [se kan].ae i.syo.măn [kŏp su]I [sa ch'ŏn ha mijin].man .hădŏ.ni; *W.S.*: [sang pŏp chu se kŏp su](p.81b).nŭn [sa ch'ŏn ha mijin].i kăttŏ.ra.

(22)   kŭ pu:t'ye [myŏl to].hăsi.go; *W.S.*: kŭ pu:t'ye [chung saeng].ăl [yo ik].ke .hăsin [hu].e.za [myŏl to].k'ŏsi.năl ("Only after that Buddha had abundantly profited all creatures, he entered nirvana, so ...").

(23)   [chŏng pŏp sang pŏp].i :ta :ŏpsŭn [hu].e; *W.S.*: [chŏng pŏp sang pŏp].i [myŏl chin]hăn [hu].e.

(24) .tto [ho].răl (...).i.rösi.ni; *W.S.*: .tto ir.hu.mi (...) (p.82a) .i.rösi.ni.

(25) .i :ya.ngă.ro; *W.S.* p.82a: .i .kăt'i.

(26) (...) pu:t'ye :kyösya.tăe :ta hăn'ga.jit [ho]I.rösi.da(?); *W.S.*: (...)[Pul].i :ta hăn'ga.ji.ro hăn [ho]I.rösi.ni; and continues with the note: "This is the same as with the twenty thousand *Candrasūrya-pradīpas* [Tŭng myŏng][40] who from beginning to end had the same name. That is because the Way is the same. Speaking of many Buddhas clarifies that Śākya(muni)'s deeper primary causes of earlier times are (very) distant."

(27) (...)[Yŏrae myŏl to].hă.sya [chŏng pŏp]:öpsŭn [hu]; *W.S.* p.82b: [Yŏrae] hă.ma [myŏl to].hă.sya [chŏng pŏp].i [myŏl]hăn [hu].e.

(28) .irŏ.ra; *W.S.*: .irŏ.ni.

(29) ir.hu.mŭl [Sang pul kyŏng].i.ra .hăya.nyo; cf. (24); *W.S.*: ir.hu.mi [Sang pul kyŏng].ko (interrogat. < .in'go).

(30) *W.S.* lacks this note.

(31) .i [pigu].I [pigu]I.na [piguni].na (...) po.ni :mada :ta .chŏl hă.go; *W.S.*: .i [pigu]I (p.83a) mŭrŭit .po.non [pigu]Iŏ.na [piguni]ŏ.na (...) :ta .chŏl .hă.ya (so /mŭrŭit/ 'all', h.l. "always" corresponds with /:mada/ in *S.s.*).

(32) [ch'ant'an]; *W.S.*: see glossary.

(33) kă.jang; *W.S.*: ki.p'i.

(34) :öp.sio.täl a.ni. hăno.ni; *W.S.*: :öp.siu.di a.ni .hăno.ni.

(35) nŏhŭi.dăr.hi :ta [posal]S[torihaeng] .hă.ya tangdangi put'yŏ tăoe.ril.ssăini.ra (id. *W.S.* p.83b-7: /put'yŏ/ lacks the subj. marker). *W.S.*: nŏhŭi.dăr.hi :ta [posal to].răl [haeng].hănă.ni tangdangi pu:t'ye tăoe.ri.ra; and adds the note: "Here (p.83b) he predicts for all the four groups, based on the truth of the Buddha-nature. The achievements of the four groups are not of one kind, but since the Buddha-nature of Despise Not was universal he bowed to all and revered them deeply, considering: 'They all follow the path of the bodhisattva, so for sure they will become Buddhas.' The Buddha-nature of all living beings is by its nature perfect and the karmic deeds of the whole world are all in accord with the Correct Law, so when he aptly sees that all actions are the way of the bodhisattva and knows that all people will becomeBuddhas, how could there be any despising?"

(36) .i [pigu]I [kyŏngjŏn] nil.gŏ oe.o.mäl [chŏnju].hǎ.ya a.ni
      hǎ.go; *W.S.*: .i [pigu]I [kyŏngjŏn].ül [chŏn].hi [tok
      song](p.84a).t'i a.ni hǎ.go.

(37) *W.S.* p.84a lacks of course, in view of its text, this note.

(38) o.jik .chŏl hǎ.gi.räl .hǎ.ya; *W.S.*: o.jik .chŏl .hǎ.ya.

(39) [sa chung].ül mŏ.ri.syŏ po.go.do .tto pu.rŏ .ka .chŏl hǎ.go;
      W.S.: mŏ.ri.syŏ [sa chung] :po.mae ni.rü.rŏ.do .tto pu.rŏ .ka
      .chŏl .hǎ.ya.

(40) nŏhüi.dǎr.hǎl; nŏhüi.dǎr.hi; *W.S.*: nŏhüi.räl; nŏ:hüi(!)

(41) tǎoe.ri.ra .hǎdŏ.ni; *W.S.*: tǎoe.ri.ra; and adds the note: "Thus
      was his keeping of the formless Sutra ([musanggyŏng]) and
      his following of the formless Practice ([musanghaeng])."

(42) [sa chung]S [chung].e [no] hän mǎzǎm :naen :sarǎ.mi :modin
      .ibü.ro ku.jijŏ; *W.S.*: [sa chung chung].e [chine] :nae.ya
      mǎzǎm .chot'i :mot hǎn :sarǎ.mi :mo.din .ibü.ro ku-(p.84b)
      .ji.jŏ; cf. (4): "Those (...) who flew into a passion and
      were of an impure heart (...)."

(43) *W.S.* p.84b gives then, as does the *Ŏnhae*: :che nir.o.däe
      .nae nŏ.rül :öp.siu.di a.ni hǎno.ra hǎ.go: "he says: ..."; cf.
      (34).

(44) (...) .hǎnǎ.ni; *W.S.*: id.

(45) .uri.dǎr.hi .irŏ.t'üt hǎn [mangnyang].aet [sugi].za .ssü.di a.ni
      .hori.ra .hǎdŏ.ni; *W.S.*: .uri.dǎr.hi .i.rŏn [hömang].aet
      [sugi].räl .ssü.di a.ni .hori.ra.

(46) .i :ya.ngǎ.ro yŏ.rŏ .hǎi.räl syang.nye kujirŏm tü.ro.däe⁴¹
      [no]hän .ttü.dül a.ni :nae.ya; *W.S.*: .i .kät'i [tanyŏn].ül
      :ti:nae.ya syang.nye kujira.mäl tü.ro-(p.85a).däe⁴² [chine].räl
      :nae.di a.ni .hǎ.ya.

(47) .hǎgö.dün; not in *W.S.* p.85a.

(48) nirüls [sijöl].e; *W.S.*: nirälch chŏ.güi.

(49) mo.dän :sarǎ.mi; *W.S.*: han :sarǎ.mi.

(50) .t'yŏ.dün cho.ch'iyŏ tǎ.ra mŏ.ri .ka.syŏ.a.syŏ sǎn.jäi
      [kosŏng].ü.ro nir.o.däe; *W.S.*: .t'yŏ.dän [p'i].hǎ.ya tǎ.ra mŏ.ri
      .ka [chu].hǎya.syŏ sǎn.jäe no.p'än so.ri.ro nir.o.däe.

(51) nŏhüi.dǎr.hi :ta tangdangi pu:t'ye tǎoe.ri.ra .hǎdŏ.ra. *W.S.*:
      nŏ:hüi :ta tangdangi pu:t'ye tǎoe.ri.ra .hǎdŏ.ni. For /nŏhüi-/
      cf. (40); for /hǎdŏ-/ cf. (41), (44). *W.S.* then adds in a
      note: "For many years they scolded him (p.85b) but he did
      not fly into a passion; this is in truth the non-ego. All
      living beings were deluded and confused and unable to
      believe, so they said: 'He is just passing on predictions at
      will.' But a bodhisattva is of a great compassion, discards

nothing, saves and releases, so when he fled away, still he
showed himself straightforward."

(52) .hănon chyŏn.ch'ă.ro; *W.S.* p.85b: hăl.ssăe.

(53) [ho].răl chi.ho.dăe; *W.S.*: ir.hum chi.ho.dăe; cf. (24), (29).

(54) .i [pigu]I chu.gŭls [sijŏl].e [hŏgong chung].e [Wiŭm wang
Pul].i :a.rae nirŭ.sidŏn [Pŏphwagyŏng].et (...) :ta tŭt.chăp.ko;
W.S.:   .i [pigu](p.86a)I hă.ma [myŏngjong] hălch che
[hŏgong].ae [Wiŭm wang Pul]s monjyŏ nară.syan
[Pŏphwagyŏng](...) :ta tŭtchă.Wa.

(55) :ta [nŭng].hi pa.da ti.nyŏ .chŭkcha.hi u.hŭi nir.on :yang
.kăt'i; *W.S.* p.86a: :ta [su chi].hăzăWa .chŭkchae ut
yang.jă.ro.

(56) [ch'ŏngjŏng].hă.ya [yukkŭn ch'ŏngjŏng].ŭl [tŭk] hă.go; *W.S.*:
[ch'ŏngjŏng].ho.măl   [tŭk]   hă.ni   .i   [yukkŭn](p.86b)
[ch'ŏngjŏng].ŭl [tŭk] hă.go.

(57) ta.si mok:su.mi (...)[nayut'a].hăi.răl tŏ sa.ra nŏ.bi :sарăm
:wi.hă.ya .i [(..)kyŏng].ŭl nirŭ.dŏ.ni; *W.S.* p.86b: ta.si
mok:su.mi tŏ.ŏ (...)[nayut'a se].răl nŏ.bi :saram wi.hă.ya .i
[(..)kyŏng] nără.dŏ.ni; then adds as a note: "At first he did
not specially read and recite, but in the end he heard and
kept[43] many *gāthās*, had his life a million ten thousand
times extended and spoke widely on behalf of the people;
this means he was form- and ego-less, without any shadow
in the outerworld, therefore bright with the truth of spiritual wisdom, and his life of wisdom did not end prema-
turely and its deep responsiveness[44] was like this. Majestic (p.87a) Voice had disappeared; however, the voice of
the Law had not disappeared, so he could hear all of the
Sutra that had been expounded in the past. But by hearing
it in empty space he showed that only after forgetting
active and passive ideas and cutting off the phenomena[45]
could he be in full possession of this Law. That is how he
obtained the 20.000 myriads of *gāthās*. Since the active
and passive ideas were forgotten and the phenomena were
cut off[46] he soon obtained the powers of the six purified
faculties. He raised[47] the powers of the six faculties
before, and clarified the Law that he had been witness of.
Thereafter he took up (the name of) Despise Not and
showed a man who had been an able witness."

(58) kŭ chŏ.gŭi (...)[pigu]; *W.S.* p.87a: kŭ che (...)[sa(p.87b)chung
pigu].

(59)   :sарăm müdŏ.ni nŏ.gyŏ [pulgyŏng].i.ra ir.hum chihă.ni.dăr.hi;
       W.S. p.87b: :sарăm :öpsi.wŏ [pulgyŏng].i.ra ir.hum chihăn
       :sara.mi.

(60)   .k'ün [sint'ŏngnyŏk].kwa [yosŏl pyŏnnyŏk].kwa [taesŏn
       chŏngnyŏk].ül [tŭk].hă.yaennon .ko.tăl po.myŏ; *W.S.*: k'ün
       [sint'ongnyŏk yosŏl pyŏnnyŏk taesŏn chŏngnyŏk tŭk].ho.măl
       po.myŏ.

(61)   nirü.non :ma.răl tŭt.ko :ta [sin pok].hă.ya cho.ch'äni.ra
       ([pok].ăn [hang pok] hăl.ssi.ra); *W.S.*: nir.o.măl tŭt.ko :ta
       [sin].hă.ya [hang pok].hă.ya chot.tŏ.ni.

(62)   *W.S.* lacks this note.

(63)   (...):sară.măl [hwa].hă.ya; *W.S.* p.88a: (...)[chung].ül
       [kyohwa].hă.ya.

(64)   (...).ye [chu].k'e hă.go; *W.S.*: (...).ye [chu].k'e hă.ni.ra; then
       adds the note: "That the four groups saw and heard him,
       then submitted in belief and followed him, means that
       their profound acts came out in full and the innumerable
       masses were converted spontaneously. The great super-
       natural powers refer to respectfully hearing all and ex-
       tending his life, the power of joy in preaching refers to
       speaking widely for a million years, and the great power
       in virtuous tranquility refers to the true and eternal
       powers of the six purified faculties." See (60) for "great
       supernatural powers" and "power of joy of in preaching".

(65)   put'yŏ.rül; *W.S.*: [Pul].ül.

(66)   nir.on chyŏn.ch'ä.ro; *W.S.* p.88b: niră.dŏ.ni .i [inyŏn].ŭ.ro.

(67)   .i [che pul]S [pŏp chung].e pa.da ti.nyŏ nil.gü.myŏ oe.wa
       (cf. p.34a: [che pul] without /S/); *W.S.*: .i [che pul pŏp
       chung].e [su chi tok song].hă.ya.

(68)   [sa chung]:wi.hă.ya .i [kyŏngjön] nirü.dŏn chyŏn.ch'ä.ro;
       W.S.: [sa chung](p.89a).däl .wi.hă.ya .i [kyŏngjön].ül
       niră.dŏ.ni kü.röl.ssäe.

(69)   [ch'ŏngjŏng] hă.myŏ; *W.S.* p.89a: [ch'ŏngjŏng].ho.măl
       [tŭk].hă.ya.

(70)   chŏp'ün .ko.di :öpsü.ni; *W.S.*: chŏ.p'um :öptŏ.ni.

(71)   .irö.t'üt hän [che pul].ül; *W.S.*: .i .käthän (p.89b)[yakkan che
       pul].ül.

(72)   :tyohän [kün wŏn].ül simü.go; *W.S.* p.89b: [sŏn kün].äl
       sim.gŏ.

(73)   *[:hhow].e (...)[kongdŏk].i i.rŏ; *W.S.*: *[:hhuw].e (...)
       [kongdŏk].ül ir.wŏ. (The /o/ in */:hhow/ is inconsistent
       with the *S.s.* orthography.)

(74) tăoe.rirŏ.ra; *W.S.*: tăoe.ri.ra; *Ŏnhae* p.86a: tăoe.rirŏ.ni.ra; *W.S.*
adds the note: "The purpose of introducing[48] King Majes-
tic Voice, Sun-moon-lanternshine and Sovereign of Clouds
is (p.90a) that it clarifies how far off the sources are of
Despise Not's accumulating of virtues, his realizing of the
Way and his unfolding of the Law's Flower. Necessarily
when one speaks of this Sutra, one is like King Majestic
Voice and obtains great fearlessness[49], when he clarifies
this Way he is like Sun-moon-lanternshine and endlessly
succeeds one another[50], when one bestows this benefit
one is like Sovereign of Clouds and endlessly covers all
with moisture[51]. To keep (the Sutra) in a subtle way and
profit (others) widely begins necessarily here."

(75) ne ttŭ.den :ŏt.tye nŏ.ginăn.da; *W.S.* p.90a: ne ttŭ.de
:ŏttŏ.nyo.

(76) tarăn :sară.miri.yŏ; *W.S.*: :ŏt.tye tarăn :sară.miri.o.

(77) .nae (...)pa.da ti.nyŏ nil.gŭ.myŏ oe.o.myŏ .năm tă.ryŏ nirŭ.di
a.ni .hădŏ.dŭn (...):mot hă.ri.rŏni.ra; *W.S.* p.90b: .hăda.ga .nae
(...)[su chi tok song].hă.ya .năm [wi].hă.ya niră.di a.ni
hă.myŏn [nŭng].hi (...):mot hă.ri.ra (*Ŏnhae* p.87a: same verb
ending).

(78) *S.s.* has omitted here a sentence of the Sutra which is
present in *W.S.* (p.90b) and *Ŏnhae*: "Because under Buddhas
of earlier times I received, kept, read and recited this
Sutra and for other people spoke thereof, I (so) soon
obtained the perfect Buddha wisdom."

(79) .tyŏ [sijŏl]S[pigu]; *W.S.* p.91a: .tyŏ .pkkŭit [sa chung][pigu].

(80) [no]hăn .ttŭdŭ.ro :nal mŭdŏ.ni nŏ.gidŏn chyŏn.ch'ă.ro; *W.S.*:
[chine]hăn .ttŭdŭ.ro :na.răl :ŏpsi.un chyŏn.ch'ă.ro; cf. (46).

(81) put'yŏ.rŭl :mot manna.myŏ [pŏp].ŭl :mot tŭrŭ.myŏ :chyu.ngŭl
:mot .po.a; *W.S.*: put'yŏ manna.di :mot hă.myŏ [pŏp] tŭt.ti
:mot .hă.myŏ :chyung po.di :mot .hă.ya.

(82) chŭmŭn [kŏp].ŭl; *W.S.*: [ch'ŏn kŏp].ŭl.

(83) kă.jang [sugo].hăda.ga; *W.S.* p.91b: .k'ŭn [konoe].răl
[su].hăda.ga.

(84) kŭ .pkkŭit .i [posal] mŭdŏ.ni nŏ.gidŏn[52] [sa chung].ŭn tarăn
:sară.miri.yŏ; cf. (76); *W.S.*: kŭ chet [sa chung].i syang.nye
.i [posal] :ŏpsi.udŏ.nin[53] :ŏt.tye tarăn :sară.miri.o ; *Ŏnhae*
p.88b: [Sang kyŏng si posal cha] năn [ki i'in ho] Irio.

(85) [o paek pigu piguni].wa; *W.S.* p.92a: [o paek pigu].wa
[ni].wa ([ni] is an abbreviation for [piguni]; *Ŏnhae*: as
W.S.; the canonical text K-116 p.785b has: [o paek piguni];

Hurvitz: "five hundred nuns";[54] Yi: [o paek pigu.wa piguni.wa ...][55]).

(86) [ubasae ubai]; *W.S.*: [ubasük] (thus, as in the *Ŏnhae*, omitting the "female devotees"; Yi[56] as *W.S.*; Hurvitz: *upāsakas* (i.e. male devotees);[57] id.: "The Skt. has *upāsikās*, which must surely be correct."[58] Kern supposes some words (in the Skt. text) have been omitted).[59] See (3) on the transcription.

(87) .i [hoe].yet; *W.S.* p.91b: o.näl.nal(p.92a) [hoe chung].e.

(88) mürü.di a.ni.hänän :sarä.mi :küi.ra; *W.S.*: [t'oejŏn] a.ni.hänä.ni :küi.ra.

(89) a.ra.ra; *W.S.*: pan.tägi :al.la; cf. (2).

(90) [posal mahasal]tär.häl kä.jang [yo'ik].hä.ya; *W.S.*: [che posal mahasal].äl kä.jang [yo'ik] hä.myŏ; cf. (16).

(91) ni.rür.üi häl.ssäe; *W.S.*: ni.rür.e .hänä.ni .iröl.ssäe.

(92) [posal](...).tär.hi [Yŏrae myŏl to] hän [hu].e; *W.S.*: [che posal](...).i [Yŏrae myŏl] [hu].e.

(93) pa.da ti.ni.myŏ nil.gü.myŏ oe.o.myŏ sa.gyŏ nirü.myŏ ssü.myŏ .hä.ya.za hä.ri.ra; *W.S.*: [su chi tok song] hä.myŏ [haesŏl sösa].holt (p.93a).tini.ra.

(94) *W.S.* (p.93a) has as a final note: "This concludes with and discloses the act of widely profiting (others) and exhorts to keep it in a subtle way. Here ends the chapter 'the Bodhisattva Never Despise', next comes the chapter 'The powers of the Tathāgata.'" Then follows the introduction to the next chapter.
      Both in *S.s.* and *W.S.* the *gāthās* repeating the chapter have been omitted; the *Ŏnhae* however continues with these verses, which are different from those in the *Wŏrinch'ŏn'gangjigok*.
      The *S.s.* postscript, starting from this (94), is the preface in the *W.S.* (pp.74a-75b) and *Ŏnhae* (pp.70b-71b).

(95) [Sŏkka chŏn sin].i; *W.S.* p.74b: [Sŏkka chŏn sin].e.

(96) [sijŏl].e; *W.S.*: [si].e.

(97) [chŏngmi].hi; *W.S.*: [chŏng].hi.

(98) [p'osi].häya; *W.S.*: [si].hä.sya.

(99) [i'ik].ke; *W.S.*: [i].hi.

(100) .häsyan :iri.ra; *W.S.*: .hä.syan cha.ch'oe.ra; then adds: "They called him 'Despise not' since he gave predictions to all the four groups, in the spirit of Buddha-nature ([Pul sŏng üi])[60], paid his respects to all that was good, did not feel

offended   on   meeting   offence   and   revered   all   living
beings."
(101) hăngat nil.gŏ oe.ol :ppun a.ni.hă.sya; *W.S.*: [chŏn].hi [tok
song].t'i a.ni .hă.sya.
(102) ku.jinnăn [yok].ăl kudi .ch'ămă.sya; *W.S.*: ku.ji.jŏ [yok]
pa.t'yo.măl ku.di .ch'ămă.sya.
(103) [haeng].ăl; *W.S.*: [haeng].ül.
(104) [musang].gwa [mu'a].wae :küi [chŏngmi]hi; *W.S.*: [musang
mu'a].hăsya.mi [chŏng].hi.
(105) [se]; *W.S.*: [se] (see glossary).
(106) (...).hă.sya; *W.S.* p.75a: (...).hă.ya.
(107) [chŭngsangman].hănăn :sară.mi [sin pok].hă.ya chot.küi
.hăsi.go; *W.S.*: [sangman] hăls :sară.mi [sin].hă.ya [hang
pok].hă.ya chotchă.Wă.myŏ.
(108) [tük]küi .hăsi.ni :küi nŏbi [i].k'e .hă.syamira; *W.S.*: [tük].ke
.hăsya.mi nŏ.bi [i].hă.syami.ra.
(109) .mon.jye [kyŏng] ti.nyu.mi tasăt ka.jit [kong].i kă.ja pi.rok
[wŏn] .hăya.do [chŏng].t'i :mot hă.go; *W.S.*: al.p'ăet [chi
kyŏng].ŭn [o chung kong].i kă.ja pi.rok [wŏn].k'o.do
[chŏng].t'i :mot hă.myŏ.
(110) mon.jye [i'ik] :ŏdu.mi [yukch'ŏn tŏk].ŭl [tük].hă.ya pi.rok
[süng] .hăya.do nŏp.ti :mot hă.ni; *W.S.*: al.p'aet [i]
nipsă.Wo.măn [yukch'ŏn tŏk].ŭl :ŏ.dŏ pi.rok [süng].k'o.do
nŏp.ti :mot hă.ni.
(111) [inbŏp yŏnyŏng]; *W.S.*: [inbŏp].üi [yŏnyŏng] (cf. *W.S.* p.75b:
without /-üi/).
(112) mo.ro.mae [musang mu'a] hăn [myo] ae naza:gamăl
[ku].hă.ya nil.gŭ.myŏ oe.o.mae [chŏnju]. holch chul
mo.ră.myŏ ni.julch (unclear).chul mo.ră.myŏ ([ku]; cf. *Ŏnhae*
6, p.70b: [ki]); *W.S.*: mo.ro.mae [musang mu'a]S[myo].ae
na.ja.ga [tok song].ae [chŏn].hi .ho.măl :a.di :mot hă.myŏ
ni.jo.măl :a.di :mot hă.myŏ.
(113) [sa chung].e [konggyŏng].holch.chul mo.ră.myŏ
:ŏpsi.ulch.chul :mol.la; *W.S.*: [sa chung].üige
[konggyŏng].ho.măl :a.di :mot hă.myŏ :op.siu.măl :a.di
:mot.hă.ya.
(114) na.da .na.a; *W.S.*: na.da.
(115) [konggyŏng] hă.myŏ [kyoman] hăn măzăm.gwa [ch'oe].wa
[pok].kwat :iri.myŏ; *W.S.* p.75b: [kyŏng man] măzăm.gwa
[ch'oe pok] cha.ch'oe; cf. (100).
(116) (...)[kyŏnggye].ye ma.jăn [hu].e.za; *W.S.*: (...) hăn :kă.zae
ŏ.urŏ[61].za ("have joined with the banks of...").

(117) [chŏng] hă.myŏ nŏ.bu.mi tăoe.ri.ni; *W.S.*: [chŏng].k'o [kwang].ho.mi tăoenă.ni.

(118) .i [chinsil]S[chi kyŏng].ho.maet [chigŭk] hăn [to]I.ra; *W.S.*: .i [sil].lo [chi kyŏng].ŭi tadărăn [to]I.ra. "This is truly (?) the way to arrive at (truly?) keeping the Sutra."

(119) Instead of this note *W.S.* has: kŭ.rŏl.ssăe ti.nyum [kwŏn].hăsya.mi .i [p'um].e mă.ch'ăni.ra "This being so, the encouragement to keep (the Sutra) comes with this chapter to an end."

IV Conclusions

From the comparison we can deduce that the *W.S.* carries the more correct, complete translation of the two. It has also a great part of the comments by Chieh Huan: (7), (10), (18), (26), (35), (41), (51), (57), (64), (74), (94), (100) and (119) in M.K. translation, while *S.s.* has a few simple notes: (30), (37), (62), (119) to help a more average reader. As the *W.S.* is closer to the original Sutra text (like the *Ŏnhae*), it has sometimes more words in a sentence than *S.s.*: (9), (27), (54), (58), (69), (71), (79), (84), sometimes less: (85), (86), (97), (98), (99), but even then the *S.s.* incidentally seems to be more close to the Chinese text: (47), (55), (60), (112).

W.S. carries strikingly more *hanja*, where the *S.s.* gives M.K. words or less *hanja*: (11), (12)[a], (13)[a], (14), (16)*[b], (23)[c], (26)[d], (27)[c], (36)[e], (46), (50), (54), (55), (57)*, (63), (65)[d], (66), (67)[e], (68)[a], (77)*[e], (82), (88), (90)[b], (92)[b], (93)[e], (101)[e], (109)[e], (112)[e], (117). *) means there are more *hanja* in *W.S.* than indicated here. [a]) wi; [b]) che; [c]) myŏl; [d]) pul; [e]) suji, toksong, or all four; but there are exceptions where the opposite is true: (24)[f], (35), (36), (48)[g], (50), (53)[f], (54)[g], (55), (79)[g], (92), (96)[g], (110), (112), (115), (116), (118). [f]) ho; [g]) sijŏl). Apparently [sijŏl] was a colloquial word when the *S.s.* was compiled, but it's Chinese characters were not forgotten. On the other hand a word like [yangja] is treated as a pure Korean word, see (55).

As *W.S.* has more *hanja*, *S,s.* has more (M.K.) suffices: (15), (16), (20), (21), (39), (51), (57), (60), (81), (104), but also here are exceptions: (3), (27), (35), (68), (111).

Also the *W.S.* seems to use more honorific forms: (12), (98), but cf. (106) or humble forms: (54), (55), but the *Ŏnhae* probably is "the most honorific".

Next we may note some differences in spelling, c.q. pronunciation: e.g. *S.s.* /nirŭ-/ vs. *W.S.* /nirä-/ (15), (57), (68), (77), but also an example of /nirä-/ in *S.s.*: (17); from the 15th century on /ŭ/ starts to replace /ä/;[62] but see (17): *S.s.* /-ŭl/ vs. *W.S.* /-äl/ ! *S.s.* /kujirŏm/ vs. *W.S.* /kujiram/ (46); *S.s.* /-äl/ vs. *W.S.* /-ŭl/ (103) (see Yi Kimun,[63] note above), where the *W.S.* form is exceptional, as most -i-(composite) vowels are followed by /-äl,-räl or -l/, e.g. *Wŏrinch'ŏngangjigok* ki 182: /-äl/.

The opposition *S.s.* /-kŭi/ vs. *W.S.* /-ke/ (108) confirms the analysis of Ko Yŏnggŭn, who speaks of a "free fluctuation"[64]; and *S.s.* /-ŭi/ vs. *W.S.* /-e/ (91); after [pan] (14), [*hhyuye] (18), [chu] (64), (106) both have /-k'e/, and *S.s.* sticks to /-ke/ after [*ngyŏk] (99) and [i] (108), putting /-kŭi/ after /chot-/ (107).

Also we find the opposition *S.s.* /-e/ vs. *W.S.* /-ŭige/ (113), cited by Ko, who claims /-ŭige/ to be a form of the period after 1460.[65]

In the opposition *S.s.* /-kkŭi/ vs. *W.S.* /-täryŏ/ (1) *S.s.* uses the honorific form and *W.S.* the more condescending form;[66] in (77) *S.s.* /-täryŏ/ is replaced by *W.S.* /-wi häya/.

And about the forms /chŭkchahi/-/chŭkchae/ (55) Ko gives the information that *S.s.* (i.e. vols. 6, 9, 11, 13, 19) only has /chŭkchahi/, and *W.S.* 17 only /chŭkchae/.[67]

We noted already the occurence of examples with more *hanja* in *S.s.* than in *W.S.*; an example is /sijŏl/, where *W.S.* has: /chŏk/ (48), /che/ (54), /pkkŭi/ (79), /[si]/ (96), but *S.s.* also uses /chŏk/ vs. *W.S.* /che/ (58), /pkkŭi/ vs. *W.S.* /che/ (84), or both have /pkkŭi/ (*S.s.* p.34a, *W.S.* p.90a).

Neither is the parallelism very strong with the following (putting the *S.s.* examples first): /monjyŏ/-/alp'äe/[chŏn] (5), /monjye/-/alp'äe/ (109), (110), /aekka/-/monjyŏ/[hyang](6), /arae/-/monjyŏ/[sŏn]/ (54); /käjang/-/kip'i/ (33), /käjang//k'ŭn/ (83), /käjang/-/id./ (90); /chyŏnch'äro/-/...ssäe/ (52), /chyŏnch'äro/-/i [inyŏn]ŭro/ (66), /chyŏnch'äro/-/kŭrŏlssäe/ (68), both: /chyŏnch'äro/ (80), both: /...ssäe/ (91), only *W.S.*: /...ssäe/ (119).There are more comparisons to be made, e.g. the final endings /-ni/-/-ra/ (7), (10), (18), (21), (28), (44), (51), (61), which are hard to explain. They may point to individual differences of the writer-translators and editors of these works, or to developments in their (standard?) language in sound (e.g. the shift from /-ä-/ to /-ŭ-/), grammar and vocabulary; developments wherein the written form of M.K. itself, still so young, may have influenced the inventors of *han'gŭl* and other users of the spoken language to some degree.

NOTES

1. *Pŏphwagyŏng-ŏnhae*, facs. ed., Seoul: Taejegak, 1977, chapter VI has been used.
2. No. K 116 in the *Koryŏ Taejanggyŏng*.
3. Fl. under the Sung, 12th century. His commentaries are still used in the *Sŏn* schools of Korea; see Yukio Sakamoto (ed.), *The Lotus Sutra and Chinese Buddhism*, Kyoto, 1972, pp. 13-14.
4. See *IV Conclusions*.
5. See *III Comparison of the texts*: (22), (42), (43), (78). This statement at least holds true for chapter 20 of the Sutra.
6. *Sŏkpo-sangjŏl*, facs. of 1st ed., Seoul: Han'gŭl hakhoe, 1973, vols. 6, 9, 13, 19 and *Wŏrin Sŏkpo*, facs. of 1st ed., Seoul: Yŏnse taehakkyo, 1957, vols. 17, 18.
7. H. Kern, *Saddharma-puṇḍarīka or the Lotus of the True Law*, Oxford, 1884; Bunnō Katō, Y. Tamura et al., *The Threefold Lotus Sutra*, New York/Tōkyō, 1978, 3d ed.; L.N. Hurvitz, *Scripture of the Lotus Blossom of the Fine Dharma: translated from the Chinese of Kumārajīva*, New York, 1976.
8. See K. Ch'en, *Buddhism in China: A historical survey*, Princeton University Press, 1964, p. 299.
9. R. Grousset, *Sur les traces du Bouddha*, Paris, 1929, pp. 309, 312.
10. Cf. G.K. Ledyard, *The Korean language reform of 1446: the origin, background, and early history of the Korean alphabet*, Berkeley: University of California, 1966 (unpubl. Ph.D.dissertation), p. 183: they "can only have served to represent the reinforced consonants". See also S. Rosén, *A study on tones and tonemarks in Middle Korean*, Stockholm, 1974, pp. 111-112.
11. See Ledyard, *The Korean language reform of 1446*, p. 214.
12. *Ibid.*, p. 173: "/hăl?-kŏt/ is sometimes written in the same text as /hăl-kkŏt/."
13. *Ibid.*, pp. 176, 180 and Rosén, *A study on tones and tonemarks*, p. 110.
14. Ledyard, *The Korean language reform of 1446*, pp. 214-215.

15. The pages refer to the *Wŏrin Sŏkpo* facs. ed., see note 6.
16. The numbers between ( ) refer to *III Comparison of the texts* or the page numbers of the *Sŏkpo-sangjŏl* facs.ed., see note 6. As with for example comparison (4), I use the symbols (4-) (-4) to delimit some compared phrases.
17. [musang]: Skt. *animatta*.
18. [mu'a- *(anātman)*haeng].
19. [wŏn].
20. [inbŏp yŏnyŏng]; [yŏnyŏng] is a term of the idealistic school.
21. Note that in contrast with the other notes, this one is not within but at the end of the text.
22. See An Pyŏnghŭi, "*Sŏkpo-sangjŏr*.ŭi kyojŏng.e taehayŏ", *Kugŏhak* II (Seoul: Kugŏhakhoe, 1974), pp. 25-26.
23. Yi Tongnim (tr.), "*Wŏrinch'ŏn'gangjigok*", in: *Han'guk sasang taejŏnjip* VII, Seoul, 1972, pp. 253-256 (this text is based on *W.S.*, not on *S.s.*), p. 254a. Yi also wrote *Chuhae Sŏkpo sangjŏl*, Seoul: Tongguk taehakkyo ch'ulp'anbu, 1959. From p. 180 Yi offers the *Sŏkpo sangjŏl* text in a fairly carefully done copying; but every page carries a few *pangjŏm*-errors, and on p. 183 (*S.s.* p. 30a) 13 syllables are omitted. Ten misspellings were discovered and one wrong character (on p. 186, second line: [ho] "after" in stead of "name").
    The wrong spelling */:hhow/, see (73), is corrected by Yi to /:hhuw/. In the last part in small *han'gŭl* the original seems to carry more *pangjŏm*-omissions (bad photocopying?) than Yi's copying.
    Ledyard, *The Korean language reform of 1446*, p. 284, p. 431, note 53, comments on Yi's reconstruction (as appendix) of the *Tongguk chŏnggŭm* from the remaining fragments of the *S.s.*: "His references are precise and accurate, and I greatly appreciate his efforts to maintain the 15th century written style".
24. Katō, *The Threefold Lotus Sutra*, p. 289.
25. Hurvitz, *Scripture of the Lotus Blossom*, p. 279.
26. Kern, *Saddharma-puṇḍarīka*, p. 354; see his note 3, p. 6 for "(discourse on the law)".
27. tŭ.rŏ < tŭl- ([kŏ]"raise") or tŭt- ([mun-]"hear"); *Ŏnhae* 6, p.72b: [mun-].
28. tŭ.rŏ; *Ŏnhae* id.: [kŏ].

29. na.t'o.syari.ra; *Ŏnhae* id.: [chang hyŏn]. Cf. Yi Sung-nyŏng, *Chungse kugŏ munpŏp: 15 segi'ŏ-rŭl chu-ro hayŏ*, Seoul: Ŭryu munhwasa, 1975[7], p. 336-C: only examples from *Yongbiŏch'ŏn'ga*.

30. *Ŏnhae* id.: [so i].

31. .ho.măl ki.p'i (/ki-/ is unreadable; I rely on the *Ŏnhae*) [sin].k'e .hă.sini.ra.

32. *Ŏnhae* p.73a: hăsya.măl ki.p'i [sin].k'e (...).

33. I.e. Mahāsthāma.

34. syŏm.giză.Wa; *Ŏnhae* p.74a: syŏm.gi.sya.

35. [soim].ŭl :mot i.güiril.ssăi; *Ŏnhae* p.73b: [nan sŭng ki im]; 74a: kŭ .chi.mŭl i.güi.di o.ryŏ.usil.ssăi (note the honorific, and [chim]).

36. [che pŏp wang].

37. [se to].

38. /-n/ seems to be the topicative particle, not a participial ending.

39. See Ledyard's remark on the spelling of /:kŏt.na-/, Ledyard, *The Korean language reform of 1446*, p. 216.

40. I.e. [Il wŏl tŭng myŏng Pul] (*Lotus Sutra*, chapter I).

41. *Ŏnhae* p.80a: [p'i mae].

42. *Ibid.* p.80b: kujira.măl .ni.bu.dăe.

43. *Ŏnhae* p.82b: [nŭng mun chi].

44. Id.: [myŏnggye].

45. [nŭng so].răl ni.jă.myŏ [yŏng sang].ăl kŭ.ch'ŭn [hu].e.

46. [nŭng so]I ni.jă.myŏ [yŏng sang].i kŭch'ŭl.ssăe; *Ŏnhae* p.83b: [nŭng so].răl nijă.si.myŏ [yŏng sang].ăl kŭch'ŭ.sil.ssăe.

47. Id.: [kŏ].

48. .hhyŏsyan .ttŭ.dŭn; *Ŏnhae* p.86a: [in] (...)năn [ŭi].

49. Cf. *Ŏnhae* pp.86a-b: "King Majestic Voice's obtaining ..."

50. Id.: "Sun-moon-lanternshine's endless succeeding ..."

51. "Sovereign of Clouds' endless covering ..."

52. Cf. (80).

53. Id.

54. Hurvitz, *Scripture of the Lotus Blossom*, p. 282.

55. Yi, "*Wŏrinch'ŏn'gangjigok*", p. 256a.

56. Id.

57. Hurvitz, *Scripture of the Lotus Blossom*, p.282.

58. *Ibid.*, p. 398, note 5.

59. Kern, *Saddharma-puṇḍarīka*, p. 360, note 1.

60. I.e. the bodhisattva knows all beings have the Buddha-nature.

61. *ŏnhae*: [hol](= hap).
62. See Yi Kimun, *Kugŏ ŭmunsa yŏn'gu*, Seoul, 1977, p. 118.
63. Id.
64. Ko Yŏnggŭn, "*Sŏkpo-sangjŏl*.gwa *Wŏrin Sŏkpo*.wa.ŭi han pigyo", *Han'gŭl* 128 (1961), pp. 141-149, p. 144.
65. *Ibid.*, p. 145, § 3.52; p.144.
66. Yi, *Chungse kugŏ munbŏp*, p. 151, §§ 198-199.
67. Ko, "Sŏkpo-sangjŏl..", p. 146 and p. 147, § 4.51: example.

SELECTED GLOSSARY

ak ku (4)	惡口
cha (4)	者
chang hyŏn n. 29	將顯
ch'ant'an (32)	讚嘆
in W.S.: (passim)	讚歎
che n. 36 (67) Conclusions	諸
chi (4) n. 43 (67) (77) (109) (118)	持
chim n. 35	荷
chin (23)	盡
chine (42) ff.	瞋恚
chŏn(ju) (36) (101) (112)	專(主)
chŏng (20) (23)	正
hŏng(mi) (97) (104) (109)	精(微)
ch'ŏngjŏng (56) (69)	清淨
chŏngnyŏk (60)	寂力
chu (20) (21) (64)	住
chung (11) (54) (67)	中
chung(saeng) (22) (58) (63) (68)	衆(生)
chŭngsangman (107)	增上慢
hang (61) (107)	降
hap (116)	合
hol (116)	溜
hŏmang (45)	虛妄
hwa (63)	化
hye (18)	慧
in n. 48	引
inbŏp yŏnyŏng (111)	人法緣影

se n. 37 (105)   世

se (105): *W.S.*   歲

sijöl (48) (96)   時節

sin n. 31, 32 (61) (107)   信

so i n. 30   所以

soim n. 35   所任

song (36) (67) (77)   誦

söng ŭi (100)   性義

su (83)   受

su (20)   數

sugi (44)   授記

to n. 37 (118)   道

to (22) (92)   度

t'oejŏn (88)   退轉

tok (36) (67) (77)   讀

tori (35)   道理

tŭk (60) (108) (110)   得

ubasaeng(/sŭk) (3)   優婆塞

ŭi n. 48   意

wi (12) (16) Conclusions   為

wiŭm (54)   威音

wŏn (109)   圓

yak(kan) (4) (71)   若(干)

yangja (55)   樣子

yo ik (22)   饒益

Yŏmbuje (20)   閻浮提

yŏn (119)   緣

yŏng (57) (119)   影

yosŏl (60) 樂説

yu (4) 有

yu (7) 喩

RELIGIE IN JAPAN

C. Ouwehand

Religie in Japan, zo luidt de korte, misschien té korte, maar niettemin met voorbedachten rade gekozen titel van dit opstel. Waarom die titel?

In 1972 gaf het Bureau voor Cultuur (Bunkachō) van het Japanse Ministerie van Onderwijs (religie wordt in Japan ook ambtelijk tot de cultuur gerekend en een Ministerie van Religie heeft dus nooit bestaan) een Engelstalig boek uit met de titel *Japanese religion*. Al eerder, in 1959, had hetzelfde Bureau een dergelijk boek, maar toen met titel *Religions in Japan*, het licht doen zien. Op de omslag van het genoemde boek uit 1972 lezen we het volgende: "This book consists of a description of the religions of Japan, a survey of the major religious organizations with particular reference to their present circumstances, and a presentation of statistical and other essential data." We stoten hier op een discrepantie die in de tegenoverstelling van Japanse religie (enkelvoud) en Japanse religies (meervoud) tot uiting komt, een discrepantie die we hier door de titel "Religie in Japan" voorlopig uit de weg willen gaan.

Zoals de Japanse cultuur een "complexe" cultuur genoemd moet worden, is ook de religie als een der belangrijkste cultuur-aspecten een "complexe" aangelegenheid. Beginnen we met een blik te werpen op de statistiek (zie Bijlage I). Welk beeld levert ons die statistiek? Ook dit is een complex, ten dele verwarrend beeld.

Het totaal aantal gelovigen (aanhangers van religie) overtreft in 1970 het bevolkingstotaal met ca. 57, in 1985 zelfs met 75,5 miljoen. Welke redenen kunnen we nu voor deze opvallende afwijking aangeven?

De cijfers zijn geen censuscijfers, ze berusten niet op officiële gegevens van een volkstelling, maar op een enquête bij de krachtens de wet van 3 april 1951 toegelaten en geregistreer-de religieuze rechtspersonen, de zgn. religieuze corporaties. Anders dan wij, die de gelovigen misschien indelen in leden of lidmaten van een kerk of kerkgenootschap en in aanhangers van een bepaald geloof, kent men in Japan meerdere, vaag onderscheiden en elkaar overlappende categorieën zoals bv. *shinto, shinja* - gelovigen, *ujiko* - parochianen, *kai'in* - leden, *danto* - aanhangers, *sūkeisha* - aanbidders, *kyūdōsha* - zoekers, *dōshi* - genoten, gelijkgezinden, *dōnin* - meelopers, *dōjin* - volgers van de "weg". En welke kwalificatie een bepaalde persoon nu zou moeten bezitten, werd grotendeels aan het oordeel van de bevraagde corporatie overgelaten.

Een tweede reden is wel deze dat het in Japan nog altijd traditie is de families als "huis"-eenheden (als *ie*) te betrachten en dat men automatisch aanneemt dat de leden van zo'n familie - of ze nu bloedverwanten zijn of niet en permanent in het huis wonen of niet - dezelfde religie aanhangen als het hoofd van deze familie, als de *koshu* van het huis.

Belangrijker is echter de wijdverbreide praktijk dat de Japanner zich tegelijk tot twee of drie religies kan bekennen en dus ook door twee of drie religieuze corporaties geregistreerd wordt.

Een tweede blik op de statistiek toont ons hoe de twee grote, geïnstitutionaliseerde religies Shintō en Boeddhisme onderverdeeld worden. Shintō wordt in Schrijn-Shintō en Sekten-Shintō (het traditionele *kyōha* Shintō, ten dele al vroeg in de 19de eeuw ontstaan en tussen 1900 en 1945 officieel erkend en, na 1945, de nieuwe sekten, het *shinkyōha* Shintō) onderscheiden.

Bij de traditionele boeddhistische sekten neemt de *Sōka Gakkai* een bijzondere plaats in. Deze in 1930 gestichte, maar tijdens de oorlog vervolgde en verboden "Studievereniging voor creatieve waarden", zoals men de naam letterlijk zou kunnen vertalen, beschouwt zichzelf als deel van de traditionele Nichiren Shōshū sekte en werd na 1945 niet als zogenaamde "nieuwe religie" geregistreerd. Maar beschouwen we de Sōka Gakkai wél als zodanig - en daar zijn goede redenen voor - dan zien we hoe *in 1970* de getallen voor de aanhangers van Schrijn-Shintō en die voor traditioneel Boeddhisme (en dus minus de Sōka Gakkai) *ongeveer gelijk* zijn en het ligt voor de hand om aan te nemen dat de numerieke gelijkwaardigheid van beide grote religies erop zou kunnen wijzen dat de Japanner zich zowel als Shintoïst als ook als Boeddhist beschouwt of zich tenminste zo laat registreren.

En tellen we nu, wederom voor het jaar 1970, het gemiddelde aantal aanhangers van Schrijn-Shintō + traditioneel Boeddhisme, nl. 63,5 miljoen, op bij de 34 miljoen aanhangers van Sekten-Shintō, Sōka Gakkai, Christenen en andere, dan komen we heel aardig in de buurt van het totale bevolkingsaantal.

Voor 1985 gaat deze berekening niet meer in gelijke mate op. Vergeleken bij de toch aanzienlijke bevolkingstoename, is het aantal Boeddhisten niet noemenswaardig gestegen. Wat echter bijzonder in het oog springt is het buiten alle proporties en ten koste van Sekten-Shintō en Boeddhisme gestegen aantal aanhangers van Schrijn-Shintō. We kunnen op dit verschijnsel hier helaas niet dieper ingaan, maar dat de reden vermoedelijk gezocht moet worden in een toename van nationalistische gevoelens ná 1970, zou ook aan de hand van andere verschijnselen kunnen worden aangetoond.

Intussen geldt zowel voor 1970 als voor 1985 dat ongeveer *een derde* van de bevolking zich bekent tot de genoemde Shintō-Sekten, Sōka-Gakkai, Christendom en andere religieuze groeperingen (dit zijn nieuwe en nieuwste, meestal op Shintō-basis gestichte religies als Tenri, P.L. Kyōdan, Seichō no Ie en andere).

Welnu, tegen de achtergrond van deze gegevens is het misschien niet toevallig dat een in 1981 in het gehele land op basis van *individuele* bevraging doorgevoerde enquête van de N.H.K. (Nippon Hōsō Kyōkai) tot resultaat had dat slechts 33% van de bevraagden zich tot een bepaalde, georganiseerde vorm van religie bekende.[1]

Betekent nu het resultaat der enquête: 33% of één derde der bevraagden bekent zich tot een georganiseerde religie, dat twéé derde der bevraagden - en men mag aannemen dat zij representatief zijn voor de gehele Japanse bevolking - als *areligieus* beschouwd moet worden? Nee, het betekent veeleer dat deze twee derde meerderheid zich kennelijk niet tot een van de grote, geïnstitutionaliseerde religieuze tradities kan bekennen en wel omdat die tradities, juist als instituties, de bevraagden voor de religieuze praktijk van hun dagelijks leven ver en vreemd gebleven zijn.

In deze context ontstaat het dilemma van de Japanner die op zijn reis door Europa door ons naar zijn religie wordt gevraagd. In vele gevallen zal hij verlegen lachen en na enig twijfelen waarschijnlijk antwoorden dat hij Boeddhist is. Hij weet namelijk dat de Europeaan het Boeddhisme als wereldreligie en als ethisch-filosofisch systeem kan waarderen. Hij weet bovendien dat hij na zijn dood op een boeddhistische begraafplaats zal worden bijgezet en dat hij de gestorvenen uit zijn familie op het Boeddha-altaar in zijn eigen huis de nodige offergaven brengt. En thuis, in Japan, hoeft hij er zich niet voor te schamen dat hij in de meeste gevallen niet weet tot welke boeddhistische sekte en tot welke huistempel hij eigenlijk behoort of dat hij thuis nog een tweede, shintoïstisch altaar bezit, waar hij op bepaalde tijden zijn voorouders de nodige eerbied bewijst.

En toch worden in de meeste handboeken over Japanse religies bijna uitsluitend juist deze geïnstitutionaliseerde religies behandeld, religies dus die theoretisch-doctrinaire systemen ontwikkeld hebben, hun eigen geschriften bezitten, één of meer stichters aanwijzen kunnen en die - dit moet men eigenlijk toevoegen - een gemeente, een geloofsgemeenschap vormen. Dit laatste punt is belangrijk. De beroemde Franse godsdienstsocioloog Emile Durkheim heeft er op gewezen, hoezeer de sociale component van een geloofs*gemeenschap* de eigenlijk beslissende component is, waardoor religie zich bijvoorbeeld van filosofie onderscheidt.[2] Voor Japan is dit punt bijzonder belangrijk, want het impliceert de vraag naar boeddhistische of shintoïstische geloofsgemeenschappen. Bestaan die in Japan of hebben ze bestaan? Het antwoord moet wel luiden dat, afgezien van boeddhistische of shintoïstische sektengemeenschappen (zoals de Sōka Gakkai of de "oude" Shintō-sekten), boeddhistische kloostergemeenschappen, of de nieuwe en nieuwste, op Shintō gebaseerde religies, zulke geloofsgemeenschappen in Japan niet bestaan. Zelfs in een tijd (1900-1945), toen Shintō staatsreligie was en iedere Japanner bij wijze van spreken gedwongen was, zich Shintoïst te noemen, is van een shintoïstische geloofsgemeenschap nooit sprake geweest.

Maar wanneer men de vraag stelt of de Japanners dan - en wederom afgezien van de in de statistiek verwerkte getallen van leden van bepaalde religieuze corporaties die ongeveer een derde van de bevolking omvatten - helemaal geen geloofsgemeenschappen kennen, dan moet ook die vraag ontkennend worden beantwoord. Want binnen een sociaal bestel als dat van de familie of familieverband, van het gehucht, het dorp, het stadskwartier, zelfs in de grote steden, vinden Japanners hun geloofsgemeenschap op basis van de *volksreligie*.

De in 1974 helaas te vroeg gestorven, grote kenner van die volksreligie en hoogleraar aan de Universiteit van Tōkyō, Hori Ichirō, heeft de volksreligie "de eigenlijke religie van Japan" genoemd en Takeda Chōshū, Professor voor Volkskunde aan de Dōshisha Universiteit in Kyōto, zelf eens priester van een Zen-sekte en voormalig dorpspriester in de buurt van Kyōto, sprak van "dé religie van het Japanse volk".

Buiten Japan werd de Japanse volksreligie lange tijd niet waargenomen of gebagatelliseerd. Zo spreekt Wilhelm Gundert over "Vulgärreligion und Aberglauben".[3] En zelfs W.M. Creemers schrijft over de volksreligie: "It is true ... that Shinto elements survive in Japan, not necessarily as conscious religious practices, but as *a sort of folklore*, comparable to many so-called Christian practices ..... which have no direct connection anymore with Christianity as a faith."[4] Ook hier is, zo lijkt het, de gering-schattende toon niet mis te verstaan. Alleen de Amerikaanse godsdiensthistoricus H. Byron Earhart heeft zich duidelijk tot de volksreligie als "the living fabric of the everyday practice of religion in traditional Japan" bekend.[5] Maar ook hij hield zich aan een historische benadering en moest zich zodoende vooral tot de "grote traditie" der geïnstitutionaliseerde religies beper-ken.

Nu is het zeker waar dat, hoewel de volksreligie in haar uitingen vaak bijzonder systematisch is, theorieën en doctrines haar vreemd zijn, dat ze in plaats van geschreven bronnen in de meeste gevallen alleen de mondelinge overlevering en de dage-lijks geleefde religieuze praktijk kent, zodat men naar het volk zelf moet gaan om deze religie te leren kennen. Het niet beschikken over schriftelijke bronnen of over duidelijke stich-terfiguren en een coherente leer betekent intussen geenszins dat de volksreligie op een lagere trap zou staan en bij het zoge-naamd primitieve, ja bij het pre-religieuze gebleven is. Natuur-lijk vinden we er veel oorspronkelijks in - de volksreligie kenmerkt zich bijna altijd als hoedster van het "verzonken cultuurgoed" - maar anderzijds overleefde zij als levende religie honderden van jaren en veranderde zij zich in een voortdurend proces van aanpassing aan en overname van vreemde elementen. Men kan hier spreken van een proces van *interactie*, waarbij de volksreligie elementen uit de grote religies opnam en tegelijk ook harerzijds die grote religies kon beïnvloeden. Zo speelt zij ook nu nog een grote rol in de Japanse maatschappij en kan zij - vooral dank zij het *socio-religieuze kernstuk der doden- en voorouderverering* - inderdaad als *de* religie van een grote meerderheid van het Japanse volk worden beschouwd.

Vóórdat we nu op dit "kernstuk" nader ingaan, keren we nog een ogenblik terug naar de voorheen genoemde N.H.K.-enquête en Jan Swijngedouws artikel.[6] Die enquête vroeg niet alleen naar het behoren tot een bepaalde religieuze groepering of beweging, maar ook naar wat men geloofde en bepaalde geloofspraktijken.

Het is nu interessant om te zien (Bijlage II) hoe de percentages voor het huiselijk bezit van een Shintō-altaar (*kamidana*) en een Boeddha-altaar (*butsudan*) vrijwel aan elkaar gelijk zijn en ook nauw samenhangen met het geloof aan en de verering van tot *kami* geworden voorouders enerzijds en de *hotoke*, de meestal tot 33 jaar na de dood vereerde en verzorgde zielen der doden anderzijds. Er zijn, zoals uit de grafiek in Bijlage II blijkt, betrekkelijk weinig families met alleen *kamidana* of alleen *butsudan*, terwijl eigenlijk alleen jonge of jongere, meestal in de stad woonachtige gezinnen die nog geen doden te betreuren hadden over geen van beide beschikken.

Hoog ligt het percentage voor het regelmatige grafbezoek tijdens het grote "Allerzielen"-feest (het Bon-feest) in midzomer (midden juli/augustus) en tijdens de lente- en herfst-equinox (*higan*). Voor velen buiten Japan onbekend en ook niet iedere Japanner duidelijk bewust is het feit dat het *hatsumōde*, het eerste bezoek aan tempels en schrijnen in het nieuwe jaar, eveneens in het kader der verering van dodenzielen en voorouders gezien mag worden.

Het is dit kernstuk van religie in Japan dat de laatste jaren ook in het Westen vermeerd belangstelling gevonden heeft. Men kan hier denken aan de studie van Robert Smith[7] en vooral ook aan het onlangs verschenen boek van Herman Ooms.[8]

Het is helaas niet mogelijk dit onderwerp uitvoerig uit de doeken te doen, maar op enkele punten willen we graag de aandacht vestigen. Belangrijk is dat in het ogenschijnlijk zo vanzelfsprekende naast en met elkaar van doden- en voorouderverering boeddhistische en pre-boeddhistische elementen zich vermengden en op elkaar inwerkten, om dan later - vooral op het sociaal-politieke vlak - met confucianistisch beïnvloede Shintō-ideeën verbonden te worden. Het is dus een mooi voorbeeld van de hierboven genoemde interactie van verschillende tradities.

Men neemt aan dat het in een van oorsprong en tot in onze tijd toe agrarische cultuur als de Japanse, waarin de zo belangrijke, arbeidsintensieve natte rijstbouw alleen al bij de openlegging en irrigatie der rijstvelden een nauwe band met de bodem schiep en waarbij het arbeidsproces een menselijke gemeenschap als gesloten verwantschappelijke of territoriale groep noodzakelijk maakte, de voorouderverering van het begin af aan een grote rol speelde. Zo laat zich de ontwikkeling van vereerde voorvader van een bepaalde familie of groep van families tot beschermgodheid van een heel dorp ook nu nog aan de hand van vele voorbeelden illustreren. En zo komt het ook dat een meerderheid der huidige dorpsschrijnen schrijnen van zulke dorpsbeschermgoden zijn en dat de bewoners van een dorp, ja zelfs die van een stadswijk in Tōkyō (zoals de Engelse socioloog R.P. Dore heeft aangetoond)[9] zich in de eerste plaats als parochianen (*ujiko*) van zo'n beschermgodheid voelen. In deze schrijnen wordt ook de moderne, ontwikkelde Japanner als kind aan de godheid opgedragen en bewijst hij op feestdagen zijn eerbied.

Daarnaast blijven de voorouders der eigen familie natuurlijk een belangrijke rol spelen. Zij zijn het die (meestal) vanaf het 33ste jaar na de dood, dat wil zeggen nadat de gestorvene in de herinnering der levenden verbleekt of verdwenen is en tot het collectief der voorouders (*senzo daidai*) gaat behoren, in de huiselijke schrijn en op bepaalde feestdagen vereerd worden. Vóór die tijd is een constante, zij het ook met het voortschrijden van de tijd in intensiteit afnemende, zorg voor de zielen der gestorvenen (*shirei*) noodzakelijk. Hoe sterk de band tussen de levenden en doden is, blijkt ook uit de N.H.K.-enquête, waarbij 95% der bevraagden te kennen gaf dat hun betrekking tot de gestorvenen en de voorouders op de een of andere manier voor hen het allerbelangrijkste was.

Als regel worden de gestorvenen tot de 7de dag na de dood drie maal per dag met wierook en voedsel ritueel herdacht. Daarna vind de herdenking tot de 49ste dag wekelijks plaats en vervolgens met grotere tussenpozen: de 100ste dag, het eerste, derde, zevende en dertiende jaar. Het 25st en 33ste jaar vormen dan weer belangrijke fasen in het rijpingsproces van de dodenziel; de herdenking neemt algemeen een feestelijk karakter aan met vele bezoekers en een groot aantal offerspijzen.

Ooms heeft deze herdenkingsfasen met het bijbehorende ritueel vergeleken met de overgangsriten (rites de passage) in het socialisatieproces van de levende mens en spreekt daarbij van een "double domestic life cycle".[10] Zo zijn de eerste 49 dagen niet alleen voor de pas geboren baby maar ook voor de dodenziel een kritische tijd; in het 25st/33ste jaar is de dodenziel tot voorouderziel (*sorei*) gerijpt en staat de levende mens aan het begin van zijn meest productieve levensperiode. Het Japanse woord voor *geboren worden*, *umareru*, betekent, als *maryōrun*, in het dialect van het eiland Hateruma (Z. Ryūkyū) *sterven*, dat wil zeggen in feite een opnieuw geboren worden.

Meyer Fortes drukt het als volgt uit: "It is as if the dead are nurtured into full ancestorhood by stages that mirror the normal maturation process of the living through childhood to reproductive adulthood and finally to a second symbolic death ....".[11]

Het herdenkingsritueel, de zorg voor de zielen der doden vindt op het huiselijke Boeddha-altaar (de *butsudan*) plaats en het is op de hoofdeilanden van Japan veelal gebruikelijk dat de *butsudan* zich naast of in de buurt van het voorouderaltaar (*kamidana*) bevindt en men kan zeggen dat de boeddhistische invloed zich het sterkst bij het dodenritueel heeft doorgezet. Het Boeddhisme richt zich - ook in zijn oorspronkelijke vorm- op het zieleheil van het individu en niet op een collectief van voorouders. En zo lijkt het niet overdreven, wanneer men poneert dat het Boeddhisme in zijn Japanse uitingen juist daarom zo levend gebleven is, omdat het bij begrafenis- en dodenriten nog altijd een centrale plaats inneemt. Zo gezien is het huidige Japanse Boeddhisme in zijn traditionele gestalte als het ware eerder een religie voor de doden dan voor de levenden.

De boeddhistische invloed komt ook in de gebruikte terminologie tot uiting. Het woord *hotoke* (de benaming voor de dodenziel ná het eerste op de dood volgende Bonfeest) wordt met het schriftteken voor Boeddha (*butsu*) geschreven en ook de afkorting Bon als benaming voor het grote midzomerse "Allerzielen"-feest gaat via *Urabon* en het Chinese equivalent *Yü lan p'en* als fonetische weergave terug op het Sanskrit-woord *Ullambhana*, zoals in *Ullambhana Sutra*, d.w.z. de Sutra voor de zielen die "omgekeerd hangen", met andere woorden de zielen die in nood zijn, bevrijd moeten worden en daarom met bepaalde offers gespijsd worden.

De grote pionier op het gebied van de Japanse volkscultuur en volksreligie, Yanagita Kunio (1875-1962), heeft deze boeddhistische invloed geenszins ontkend, maar er terecht op gewezen dat het schriftteken voor het woord Bon ook wordt gebruikt in een oud Japans woord *hotoki* of *hotogi* in de betekenis van een uit grof aardewerk of hout gemaakte bak of schaal, waarin de offergaven naar het graf werden gedragen. Bovendien is hij van mening dat het woord *hotoke* op dit *hotoki* teruggaat en in feite dus niets met een "Boeddha" te maken heeft. In de loop van de tijd zou dan dit woord voor de bak met offers voor de doden-zielen ook voor die zielen zelf in gebruik zijn gekomen.

Het grote Bonfeest werd in de loop der geschiedenis sterk boeddhistisch beïnvloed en is nu in de eerste plaats een feest voor *alle* dodenzielen ("Allerzielen") geworden. Het is daarom ook een van de weinige Japanse feesten, waarbij boeddhistische priesters welkom zijn.

Dat is niet altijd zo geweest en is ook nu niet overal in Japan zo. In feite blijft de dood en daarmee ook de latente vrees voor schadelijke invloeden van de, vooral gedurende het eerste jaar na de dood, nog niet gepurifieerde ziel van de gestorvene met veel taboes omgeven en laat zich de verering van zulke dodenzielen met Bon eigenlijk niet goed verenigen met de vreugdevolle viering der gerijpte voorouderzielen. Zo komt het dat men in bepaalde streken niet van *shinbotoke* ("nieuwe" *hotoke*, de benaming voor de dodenziel vóór het eerste Bon-feest), maar van *aramitama* spreekt, waarbij dit *ara-* dan wel opgevat wordt als "nieuw", zoals in het woord *arata ni* (op-nieuw). We zien dan echter dat men zulke *aramitama* - in tegenstelling tot de *shinbotoke* elders - juist *niet* graag naar huis uitnodigt, maar aan het graf met offergaven gunstig wil stemmen en met Bon-dansen als het ware exorciseert. Het lijkt dan ook waarschijnlijk dat men hier van "getaboeïseerde" zielen moet spreken en dat het *ara-* van *aramitama* veeleer met het *ara-* van *ara-imi* (strikt taboe) samenhangt. In zulke streken heeft het Bonfeest nog veel van zijn oorspronkelijke betekenis als feest der voorouderzielen behouden. Daarmee hangt ook samen dat men thuis aparte Bon-altaren (*bondana*) inricht en de *butsudan* van de eigen familie leeg blijft of leeg wordt gemaakt, zodat de dodenzielen niet met die van de voorouders in beroe-ring kunnen komen. Op het eiland Hateruma wordt de scheiding tussen dodenzielen en voorouderzielen bovendien tot stand gebracht door *alle* dodenherdenkingen zoveel mogelijk in de drie "lege" zomermaanden te verleggen, d.w.z. in die maanden, waarin geen met de voorouders verbonden landbouwrituelen plaatsvinden.

We raken daarmee een voor de voorouderverering belangrijk punt, nl. dat van de gang der landbouw (rijstbouw) seizoenen en de daarmee verbonden feesten. Het begint met nieuwjaar dat volgens de in vele streken van Japan nog gebruikte maankalender niet noodzakelijkerwijze op 1 januari valt en met de tijd voor het uitzaaien van de rijst in verband kan worden gebracht. De lente-equinox staat voor het omplanten van de rijstzaailingen zoals de herfst-equinox met de rijstoogst pleegt samen te vallen. In beide gevallen spreekt men van *higan-e*, een boeddhistische benaming met de betekenis van "feesten van de andere oever" (d.w.z. de andere oever in het Westelijke Paradijs over de zee, waarheen naar boeddhistisch geloof de zielen der gestorvenen gaan). Het zijn feesten die met grafbezoek gepaard gaan, maar aan het keizerlijk hof werden deze dagen tot belangrijke shintoïstische voorouderfeesten en zelfs tot nationale feestdagen. Op het land - en wel in heel Japan - zijn ze nog altijd sterk verbonden met het heen en weer trekken van de godheid die in de lente uit de bergen naar de dalen heet te komen om dan na de oogst, in de herfst, weer naar de bergen terug te keren. En dat deze berg-veldgodheid oorspronkelijk met heen en weer trekkende, mobiele voorouder-beschermgodheden te maken had, behoeft in dit verband wel nauwelijks vermelding.

Tussen lente- en herfst-equinox ligt de zomer met het grote Bonfeest. In de hete zomermaanden rijpt de rijst. Het is een kritische tijd voor mens en gewas; er kunnen ziekten en epidemieën heersen, een insektenplaag kan de oogst in gevaar brengen. Dat zulke schadelijke invloeden dan vooral met schadelijke, kwaadwillende dodenzielen in verband worden gebracht, behoeft geen betoog en zo diende het midzomerse Bonfeest aanvankelijk ook om dergelijke invloeden tegen te gaan en af te weren.

Tenslotte nieuwjaar als tegenstuk van het Bonfeest, als feest van een nieuw begin, tegenwoordig vooral gevierd met eten en drinken, met bezoek en tegenbezoek, geschenken en tegengeschenken. Maar bij nader toezien bezit het nieuwjaarsfeest ook nu nog tal van elementen, waarin we het oorspronkelijke karakter van het voorouderfeest terug kunnen vinden. In een stad als Kyōto, maar ook in de oudere woonwijken van Tōkyō, kunnen we met nieuwjaar nog altijd de pijnboompjes of pijnboomtakken, de *kadomatsu*, voor de ingang van het huis zien staan. Boven de ingang hangt dan vaak het kunstig geknoopte en gevlochten touw uit rijststro, de *shimenawa*. De *kadomatsu* dienen als imaginaire, symbolische zetel, als *yorishiro*, waarop de voorouderzielen of de nieuwjaarsgodheid kunnen neerdalen om tijdens de feestdagen bij de betrokken familie te verblijven. De *shimenawa* dient - zoals ook bij andere, shintoïstische, gelegenheden - om het huis af te schermen, te omperken, om het zo, tijdelijk, tot een soort van geheiligde plaats te maken. De familie is, zoals het heet, "binnen de pijnbomen" (*matsu no uchi*), d.w.z. afgeschermd, op zich gesteld en vormt nu, samen met de voorouders, als het ware een "heilige familie", ofschoon men zich daarvan meestal niet meer bewust is. Een andere aanduiding voor het oorspronkelijke karakter van nieuwjaar als voorouderfeest ligt in het feit dat de eerste nieuwjaarsdag zeer rustig en zonder bijzondere evenementen wordt doorgebracht. Die eerste dag is aan de familie en de voorouders, aan graf- en schrijnbezoek gewijd. Pas op de tweede dag beginnen de activiteiten. Dan werkt men weer, vindt het eerste schrijven in het nieuwe jaar plaats, neemt men het eerste bad, dan wordt de eerste nieuwe droom geduid en krijgt zelfs de eerste copulatie in het nieuwe jaar (de *himehajime*) een symbolische betekenis. Ook wanneer dit alles tot louter gewoonte zonder bewuste inhoud geworden is, blijkt toch uit het vasthouden aan die gewoonte dat men nieuwjaar als feest voor een nieuw begin én nieuwjaar als stille herdenking van de voorouders ergens uit elkaar wilde houden. Over de nieuwjaarsviering als herdenkingsfeest der voorouders zou, vooral met betrekking tot de gebruiken op het land en uit historisch perspectief, zeer veel meer te zeggen zijn. We moeten het echter hierbij laten.

Religie in Japan is een complexe, maar ook fascinerende aangelegenheid. Het was de bedoeling van dit opstel zowel het complexe als het fascinerende met enkele voorbeelden te verduidelijken en te illustreren.

BIJLAGE I

Statistiek per 31.12.1970

Totaal bevolking   103.720.000
Totaal gelovigen   160.640.000

I   *Shintō*   70.322.000

Schrijn-Shintō	61.631.000
Sekten-Shintō (trad.)	6.854.000
Sekten-Shintō (nieuw)	1.837.000
	70.322.000

II   *Boeddhisme*   81.320.000

Tendai	4.655.000
Shingon	11.177.000
Jōdo	20.942.000
Zen	10.150.000
Nichiren	31.887.000
(= >Sōka Gakkai 16.223.000)	
Nara	2.262.000
Andere	237.000
	81.320.000

III   *Christenen*   742.000

IV   *Andere*   8.257.000

       Totaal: 160.640.000

Statistiek per 31.12.1985 (uit: *Asahi nenkan* 1988)

Totaal bevolking	121.049.000	
Totaal gelovigen	196.548.000	

I	*Shintō*	99.568.000

Schrijn-Shintō	92.624.000
Sekten-Shintō	
(trad.)	5.355.000
Sekten-Shintō	
(nieuw)	1.589.000

	99.568.000

II	*Boeddhisme*	85.208.000

Tendai	3.122.000
Shingon	15.420.000
Jōdo	20.060.000
Zen	9.367.000
Nichiren	34.727.000
(= >Sōka Gakkai	
17.297.000)	
Nara	2.434.000
Andere	78.000

	85.208.000

III	*Christenen*	1.201.000

IV	*Andere*	10.571.000

	Totaal:	196.548.000

BIJLAGE II

Bezit van een { *kamidana* 60%
{
{ *butsudan* 61%

alleen *kamidana*   15% | 45%   *kamidana* + *butsudan*
                        |
   totaal 100%   -------------------
                        |
geen van beide   24% | 16%   alleen *butsudan*
  (25-40 jaar)

Min of meer regelmatige verering van { *kamidana* 53%
{
{ *butsudan* 57%

Regelmatig grafbezoek (*obon - higan*)   89%

Hatsumōde (Nieuwjaarsbezoek aan schrijnen en tempels)   81%

NOTEN

1. De uitkomsten van de enquête werden in 1984 in *Nihonjin no shūkyō ishiki* (Het religieuze bewustzijn der Japanners) gepubliceerd. Jan Swijngedouw, Professor aan het Instituut voor religie en cultuur der Nanzan Universiteit in Nagoya, verwerkte ze in een artikel: "Religion in contemporary Japanese society", *The Japan Foundation Newsletter* (January 1986), pp. 1-14.

2. Emile Durkheim, *Les formes élémentaires de la vie religieuse*, 1912 (1e druk).

3. Wilhelm Gundert, *Japanische Religionsgeschichte*, Stuttgart, 1943, pp. 139-144.

4. W.M. Creemers, *Shrine Shinto after World War II*, 1968, p. XVI.

5. H. Byron Earhart, *Japanese religion: unity and diversity*, 1974 (2e druk).

6. Zie noot 1.

7. Robert Smith, *Ancestor worship in contemporary Japan*, Stanford (California), 1974.

8. Herman Ooms, *Sosen sūhai no shimborizumu* (Symbolisme der voorouderverering), Tōkyō, 1987.

9. R.P. Dore, *City life in Japan - Life in a Tokyo ward*, London, 1958.

10. Herman Ooms, "A structural analysis of Japanese ancestor rites and beliefs", in W.H. Newell (ed.), *Ancestors*, Den Haag/Parijs, 1976, pp. 71-73.

11. Zie in zijn inleiding van *Ancestors*, pp. 7, 8.

SHUDŌSHO: ZEAMI'S INSTRUCTIONS FOR HARMONIOUS TEAMWORK

Erika de Poorter

Of the twenty-one known writings of Zeami Motokiyo (1363?-1443?) the *Shudōsho* ("Book for Acquiring the Art") is the only one dedicated to the members of the company. Zeami dedicated several of his other treatises on Nō to one specific person, a son, brother or other member of the family, accompanied by the exhortation to transmit it to following generations under conditions of the greatest secrecy.[1] The *Shudōsho*, however, a short tract about the duties and tasks of actors and musicians in achieving harmonious teamwork during the performance, ends with the following sentence: "I write this down for the members of the troupe." Therefore, the *Shudōsho* is not a real *hidensho*, a writing secretly transmitted from father to son or teacher to pupil. Probably several actors had it in their possession. It is very probable that Zeami's son Motoyoshi, the compiler of the *Sarugaku dangi* ("Talks on Sarugaku"), also had this text at his disposal.[2]

From the conclusion it appears that the *Shudōsho* was completed in 1430, a few months before the *Sarugaku dangi*. From Zeami's biography we can infer that this must have been a very difficult time for the old Nō actor and his sons. One year earlier Ashikaga Yoshinori (1393-1441) had become shōgun. Like his father Yoshimitsu (1358-1408), Zeami's great benefactor and patron, Yoshinori was a fervent lover of the art of Sarugaku, and even before his accession he already supported the son of Zeami's younger brother, Saburō Motoshige, usually called On'ami (1398-1467). After becoming shōgun, Yoshinori continued to favour Zeami's nephew On'ami, a fact which not long afterwards had extremely unpleasant consequences for Zeami. In 1429 the shōgun prohibited Zeami and his son Motomasa (d. 1432) from giving performances in the ex-Emperor's palace. There are indications that in this year there must already have been a rift between Zeami and his successor Motomasa on the one hand, and On'ami on the other hand, and that they stood at the head of two rival troupes. In 1430 through the good offices of the shōgun, On'ami was appointed as *gakutō*, an important function given to the principal actor of a group, for the Sarugaku performances in the Daigoji temple at Kyōto. Zeami himself had obtained this post six years earlier. For the following years there are many references to On'ami's performances in the sources, while the names of Zeami and his son are seldom mentioned any more in connection with important performances.[3]

Now we might suppose that under these circumstances unrest or dissension could have broken out in Zeami's own troupe too. There may have been troubles between the leader (Zeami or Motomasa) and the other actors. This then could explain why Zeami wrote this short treatise for the members of the troupe. Its tenor is unmistakable: the leader plays the main role and all other players have to assist him as well as they can. Only the leader has the general direction of the performance.

The *Shudōsho* was the first of Zeami's writings to be printed. In 1772 the 15th Kanze head Motoaki (1722-1774) published an annotated text of the *Shudōsho*, which he gave to members of his company.[4] Still this writing too remained almost unknown until 1909, when it was among the collection of sixteen of Zeami's texts discovered and published by Yoshida Tōgo.[5]

Of the *Shudōsho* two manuscripts are known about today.[6] The eldest one (the so-called *Yoshida-bon*) formed part of the collection of sixteen of Zeami's texts just mentioned. One suspects that these were copies made in the first half of the 17th century. They belonged to the Matsunoya bunko which was burned in 1923. The text of this manuscript is preserved in Yoshida's publication of 1909. A second, more recent copy (the so-called *Kanze-bon*) is kept in the library of the head of the Kanze school. Only this manuscript has the title *Shudōsho*. Still we may assume that this must have been the original title, because it is to be found in the *Sarugaku dangi* (1430).[7] Of the 1772 edition only three copies are known. My translation is based on the text edition by Omote Akira who took the *Yoshida-bon* as basic text.[8]

The *Shudōsho* consists of seven sections. The first is very general: co-operation and harmony of all players is essential for a successful performance. The following five sections contain separate instructions for each category of players: the leading performer, the supporting actor and other players, the drum players, the flute player and the Kyōgen actor. The text ends with a section about problems concerning the composition of the programme.

The leading part played by the leader of the troupe forms the centre of the performance, and therefore its success depends completely on him. Important passages of the Nō play have to be sung by him alone. If he is unable to do this, he is not a real main performer (*shite*). In certain plays a main performer may sometimes come onto the stage with another actor, but when he is meant to be appearing alone, he may on no account be accompanied by anyone else. In the parts where the main performer has to sing alone, all the other actors have to remain silent. As the play goes on more actors appear on the stage, but the *shite* must continue to lead.

The supporting actor (*waki no shite*, nowadays *waki*) has an important task at the beginning of the play: he sings the opening song, announces the theme and prepares the audience for the performance. After that he has to take a back seat and assist the main performer. Even when the *shite* proves to be incompetent, the supporting actor has to remain in the background. The section closes with instructions for the other supporting actors (*sono hoka no waki no ninju*). They may not be too numerous and they must sing harmoniously. Moreover, Zeami disapproves of their appearing in ordinary dress. It is not quite clear which kind of players are meant here: the companions (now called *tsure*) who sing with *shite* or *waki no shite*, or the members of a chorus.

In the following two sections Zeami gives instructions for the instruments: *tsuzumi* (hand-drum), *taiko* (drum) and *fue* (flute). Before the main performer enters, the drum players are free to play as they like. Afterwards, however, they have to adapt themselves to the main performer and to support the dancing and singing.

The flute player has to get the audience into the right mood before the performance starts. After that he has to lead the singing. In normal cases an actor has to sing according to the tone of the flute. But Zeami is of the opinion that the flute should make concessions to the voice of the singer and should deviate slightly from its own tone, when there is a danger of disharmony. In the parts between dancing and singing the flute has then to revert imperceptibly to the right tone. All this is illustrated by an anecdote about the great flute player Meishō.

The next section is one of the very rare passages in Zeami dealing with Kyōgen. Zeami distinguishes two functions of the Kyōgen actor: his comic acting in the Kyōgen and his appearing in the serious Nō plays themselves, as is still the case today. A Kyōgen actor has to avoid vulgarity, his main aim being to make the people smile. As in Nō his aesthetic ideal should be *yūgen* (elegant beauty).[9]

The last section deals with the problems of composing the programme. Usually a programme is built up according to the principle of *jo-ha-kyū*, a sequence of three parts with gradually increasing tension. This is best achieved with five plays: one for the introduction (*jo*), three for the middle part *ha* (breakthrough, development) and one for the climax (presto, *kyū*). When the actors perform for the nobility, however, they are often commanded on the spot to give more plays than planned. In that case they should extend the middle part *ha*.

The *Shudōsho* is not a purely theoretical treatise. The subject is very concrete and exactly circumscribed: the problem of coordination between the playing of the different kinds of actors and musicians. This is still one of the problems in the Nō performances of today, as the actors specialised in main roles (*shite-kata*), the actors specialised in supporting roles (*waki-kata*), the Kyōgen actors (*Kyōgen-kata*) and the musicians (*hayashi-kata*) belong to different schools with their own traditions and techniques. Only on the occasion of a performance do they come together and then they play without any previous rehearsals. The *Shudōsho* gives us some idea of the casting and some practical aspects of the performance in Zeami's time. As far as we can see these seem to have been identical with Nō as it is now. However, we have to be very careful in interpreting the data. For instance, it is not clear from the text if there was really a separate chorus like there is today, nor exactly how the supporting actors and companions functioned. Neither does the text tell us much about the composition of a troupe.

Finally one general remark: in Zeami's writings the art itself is not yet called Nō but Sarugaku. The term *nō* still has the general meaning of performance, acting, play-script. In the *Shudōsho* Zeami even uses the combination *shin no nō no Sarugaku sanban*, lit. "three items of Sarugaku of real nō", as opposed to *Kyōgen niban*, "two items of Kyōgen".

Before we come to the translation, a word about the choice of the *Shudōsho* for this collection. I have been working on Zeami for some years and this text struck me as being very apposite to offer to a leading performer who has left his fellow-players after so many years. A parting professor may well wish, like Zeami, that the members of his troupe would go on playing as a harmonious team.

SHUDŌSHO
BOOK FOR ACQUIRING THE ART

The respective tasks of the people in a troupe of Sarugaku -
sequence for acquiring the art

The players[10] who give a performance of Sarugaku have all mastered their own personal style, yet in their hearts there is something about which they must be careful. The moving style[11] attained by a troupe[12] will not be according to the way, if the artistic skill of the members is not in harmony. If the co-operation of all the members is incomplete, no matter how well each of them performs his art, dancing and singing of equal level will not be realised. Therefore, one must try to perform dancing and singing in a spirit of mutual adaptability. One should not think one is going to make it alone. Taking as an example the art acquired by the leader[13] of the troupe, one must perform the arts according to his instruction. Paragraphs about that [follow].

The task of the leading performer[14]

Having arrived at the actual performance, he appears from the dressing-room, stands still on the bridge, starts the *issei*,[15] then comes out on the stage, and the singing from the *sashigoto* until the end of one part of the music,[16] is the task of the main performer alone. His voice may be insufficient, but when he does not perform the *issei*, he cannot be the main performer. If, according to the subject of the play, there is a couple, and an old man and an old woman[17] appear together and perform, it will be allowed. Yet, in places where he has to appear alone, it will not be [according to] the way that the main performer,

saying that his artistic skill is insufficient, or that his voice is
not strong enough, takes along a superfluous person and performs in the style of a beginner. To repeat, to send people [on
stage],[18] saying that [the main performer] is unable to cope
with the style of a song for him alone, and what makes matters
worse, to sing with him from the lower seat,[19] will definitely
not be [according to] the way. In all [performing] arts somebody
becomes leading performer in the stage in which he is recog-
nised as an expert. A direct proof of that stage is that, even if
his voice is insufficient, he [can] perform on the spot, but if he
does not have that capacity, it is difficult to call him an expert.
Somebody is called an expert in something, if he does things
that seem impossible; so he must be called a performer who
mastered the way.

Well, after that,[20] the supporting actor is already standing
[on the stage], and in order that the people of the troupe
perform *mondō*[21] and *join*[22] uniformly, [the main performer]
sings with the others, and through the piece as a whole he must
try to give a performance [successful] when seen and heard.
This is the way of the leader. In addition to this, the main
performer alone is responsible for the first tones of the transi-
tions in the *rongi*.[23]

Paragraphs about what the supporting actor should know

First of all, he appears at the beginning, and from the *kaikō*[24]
onwards he tells clearly about the subject [of the play] and
prepares the performance. This is the task of the supporting
actor alone. As the *kaikō* especially forms the opening sentences
of that day, and is a congratulatory song[25] seen and heard by
everybody, it should be studied very well. After that,[26] aiming
at equal co-operation of the troupe, he must keep in mind the
basic beat prescribed by the leader and perform the music in
co-operation and the same mood.

Now, in the heart of the supporting actor there is something
in particular which he must know. As he follows the guidance of
the leader, he is called "side actor" (*waki no shite*). Even if the
leader is inadequate, the supporting actor in particular should
follow the head who leads the troupe, accepting it as unavoidable that he is the main performer. If a skillful supporting actor
performs in a different mood, saying that the leader is inade-

quate, the troupe[27] will be lacking in uniformity and the
performance will be confused. The supporting actor has to follow
[the leader] whether he is good or bad. This is supreme co-
operation. If there is no co-operation, the general impression of
the performance will not be serene. To perform [the art of] the
troupe[28] while knowing this principle very well, must be called
the way of the supporting actor.

And, the other supporting people have to study [the rules of]
shortening and spreading in the basic beat of the music prescribed by the troupe very well, and have to perform with one
accord, carefully and uniformly. This must be the way of the
supporting people. As a rule, the [number of] people appearing
[on the stage] in a performance, should not exceed four or five.
So, in ancient times, although they used to play with many
performers, they performed plays in which two persons or so
were sufficient, with one or two persons. A great number [of
actors] sitting in a row and chanting in unison in ordinary dress
with *eboshi*[29] and *suō*,[30] saying that there should be many
people, will definitely not be [according to] the way. It is very
wrong. Over these last years one comes across this style. It is
unacceptable.

What the players of the hand-drum should know

As they have charge of [the passage] after having started
beating [the prelude] and before the main performer starts
singing the *issei* and *sashigoto*, they must by all means just as
they like, take great pains over the music, and play. But, having
arrived gradually at the two elements dancing and singing, and
imitation,[31] they should not play as they like [any more]. After
having understood the mind of the main performer, and based on
the two elements, they must perform. This must be the way of
the hand-drums of Sarugaku.

[The player of] the drum too, must have the same mental
attitude. Generally speaking, no matter of what kind the drum
[music] be, when he starts beating, it must be *ranjō*.[32]

Concerning the player of the flute

He has the very important task of giving the key during the introduction, development and climax of the performance.[33] Before Sarugaku starts, he has the task of playing for some time to calm [the people] down, and to create the right mood in which to start the performance. Having arrived at dancing and singing, while listening to and in accordance with the voice of the main performer, he has to give the key and to colour his voice.

Here there is something which the player of the flute must know above all else. Now, as the flute is the instrument for the tone, it is normal to consider the flute as being the basis, but the fact that it is responsible for the success of the troupe,[34] is another important thing. Flutes of Gagaku players have rules that must be different. As for the rules of the Sarugaku flute, of itself the voice of a performer will be high-pitched or low-pitched as the tone rises or drops a bit. But, if one goes on carelessly playing in the original tone, saying that the flute must be leading, the voice of the performer and the tone of the flute will be inharmonious. And so, the music at that moment will sound uninteresting. Therefore, if he only knows the tone, and colours the key a little bit according to the changes of the voice of the performer, the tone of the troupe[35] will not sound irregular. It will only sound as serene music.

And, when the tone of a performer rises or drops a bit, this does not mean he is so inadequate. Even in Buddhist chanting[36] and banquet music[37] too the tone rises or drops a bit. As for Sarugaku, as there are various kinds of voices such as in the case of all imitation,[38] of congratulatory [music], [music of] grief, [music of] love, [music of] sorrow, [music of] regret, [music of] anger, and of dancing and actions, the tone rises and drops before one realises. The flute-player too, knowing this principle, has to follow the voice of the main performer and to choose the tone according to these rules. And then, in the pauses between dancing and singing he has to mix it with the original tone, and without the people being aware of it, he has to link the key. This must be the way of the Sarugaku flute. (This is because it is the flute for Sarugaku.)[39]

As in Sarugaku the voice changes into all kinds of music according to the changes of the mood [in the different kinds] of imitation, it certainly does not mean, when the tone rises or drops a bit, that a performer is inadequate.

In ancient times, in Yamato Sarugaku, there was an expert in the flute called Meishō.[40] He was so skillful with the flute that lay monk Lord Kyōgoku no Dōyo[41] (called the magistrate of Sado) said full of admiration: "It is bad when Sarugaku drags on and on, but when I listen to the flute of this Meishō, I forget how the time is passing."

Once, at a performance of Sarugaku during religious services, when a leader as main performer and a lad were singing the *rongi*,[42] the [original] tone at that moment was *rankei*.[43] The young voice was still the voice of a lad, and went on rising to *banshiki*. The voice of the main performer was *rankei*. But, as they went on singing the *rongi*, the tone of both was inharmonious, and it was about to become uninteresting. Nevertheless, Meishō, although he played on the flute in the tone of *rankei* as before, carefully gave a flavour of *banshiki* to the tone for the young voice and played in the original tone of *rankei* for the main performer, and so the music by each one sounded serene, and that performance was interesting. Now then, there was nobody in the troupe[44] who understood that he played like that, but when the main performer afterwards addressed himself to Meishō and praised him with the words: "The flute today was really divine work!", Meishō said: "As you have heard the difference, I will tell you. I did my very best [to adjust] the tones of the *rongi* of an old voice and a young tone."

As he changed and coloured the tone for the old and the young [voice], the tone of the old and the young [voice] was combined into one, and serene music was realised. This corresponds to "the voice in a world of good order" and will probably be the voice "that is quiet and joyful".[45] So, in this way, skillful players of old realised immediate success by only basing [their performance] on the feeling of the performers of the troupe.[46] Should not that be an example even to this generation? In the Introduction to the Book of Poetry it is said: "The music in a world of good order is quiet and joyful."[47]

Concerning the actor of Kyōgen

[This role is] a means for humour,[48] and he performs taking as material either a witty remark,[49] or funny things from old novels. And when assisting in real nō, he should not try to make [the people] laugh. He has only to explain the subject [of the play] or to tell serious circumstances to the audience.[50]

Now, when many people immediately burst out laughing, it must be a vulgar style of comic acting. "To bear pleasure in the smile," they say. This is an emotion of delight and joy. If the spectators sharing that feeling, smile and enjoy themselves, it is interesting and it will be comic acting of the high level of elegant beauty.[51] This is called being skillful in comic acting. Master Tsuchi[52] of ancient times had a style belonging to this level in Kyōgen.

In this connection, to be gifted with charms that make him beloved by many people, must be good luck for an artiste. He should not perform with vulgar words and acting, and be careful with jokes and funny stories familiar to the nobles and the people of the upper class. To repeat, [to perform] with very vulgar words and acting, saying that it is a comic play, is absolutely forbidden. He should know this.

Concerning the number of plays of Sarugaku

In ancient times there were no more than four or five plays [on the programme]. Nowadays too, during religious services or subscription [performances],[53] there are three Sarugaku plays of real nō, and two Kyōgen plays, five plays altogether. These last years, when performing before nobles we augment the number of plays considerably, and perform at command seven or eight plays, or even ten plays, but it is not of our own free will. Now, as far as [the build-up according to the principle of] introduction, development and climax of a performance is concerned, the opening play is the introduction. The second, third and fourth plays are the development, and after finishing that, the fifth play is the climax. So introduction, development and climax are realised, and it is a performance of successful theatrical entertainment, but when unexpectedly the number of plays increases, the introduction, development and climax too change, and the order of the plays gets mixed up. To repeat, this is a very serious thing for the artistes. Nevertheless, as it has been commanded, it is something unavoidable.

In this connection, knowing the performance,[54] one should pause at the place where the development changes into climax, be sparing with one's gestures, make the play last out and think of means of keeping one's last resources in the style of the performance. The artistic skill of a talented master will probably be revealed at such a moment. One should in advance think very carefully of means of prolonging the introduction, development and climax of a performance.

Acquiring the art for a performance of Sarugaku is like this.

A day in the third month of the second year of Eikyō.[55]

I write this down for the members of the troupe.

NOTES

1. See Erika de Poorter, *Zeami's Talks on Sarugaku: An Annotated Translation of the Sarugaku dangi with an Introduction on Zeami Motokiyo*, Amsterdam, 1986 (*Japonica Neerlandica* 2), pp. 45-46.
2. *Ibidem*, p. 73.
3. *Ibidem*, pp. 39-40.
4. Several years earlier this leader also had Nō texts printed. On that occasion he even seems to have consulted Kamo Mabuchi (1697-1769). See Kawase Kazuma, *Tōchū Zeami nijūsanbu-shū*, Tōkyō: Nōgakusha, 1945, pp. 42-43 and Konishi Jinichi (comp.), *Zeami-shū*, Tōkyō: Chikuma shobō, 1970 (*Nihon no shisō* 8), p. 344.
5. Yoshida Tōgo, *Nōgaku koten Zeami jūrokubu-shū*, Tōkyō: Nōgakkai, 1909.
6. For this section frequent use has been made of Omote Akira and Katō Shūichi, *Zeami Zenchiku* [hereafter *ZZ*], Tōkyō: Iwanami shoten, 1979[5] (*Nihon shisō taikei* 24), pp. 567-568.
7. See De Poorter, *Zeami's Talks on Sarugaku*, p. 119 (Section 157).
8. Omote, *ZZ*, pp. 234-240. Omote compared the *Yoshida-bon* with the *Kanze-bon*. According to him the 1772 edition was based on the *Kanze-bon*. *Ibidem*, p. 568. The text of the *Shudōsho* can also be found in Nonomura Kaizō (comp.), *Kōchū Zeami jūrokubu-shū*, Tōkyō: Shunyōdō, 1926, pp. 223-234, Nose Asaji, *Zeami jūrokubu-shū hyōshaku*, 2 vols., Tōkyō: Iwanami shoten, 1979[17] and 1979[14] (1st ed. 1940 and 1944), II, pp. 241-281, Kawase, *Tōchū Zeami nijūsanbu-shū*, pp. 241-250 and Konishi, *Zeami-shū*, pp. 344-357. The

Shudōsho was translated into modern Japanese by Nose, side by side with the text in his edition just mentioned, Yamazaki Masakazu in *Zeami*, Tōkyō: Chūō kōronsha, 1969 (*Nihon no meicho* 10), pp. 269-278 and Konishi, under the original text in *Zeami-shū*. A full German translation has appeared in Hermann Bohner, *Seami (Zeami), Shū-dōsho, Kyakurai-kwa, Schriften der dritten Schrifttumsperiode des Meisters*, Tōkyō, 1961 (*Mitteilungen der Deutschen Gesellschaft für Natur- und Völkerkunde Ostasiens* XLI, C), pp. 1-28. In 1984 Thomas Rimer and Yamazaki Masakazu published an English translation (*On the Art of the Nō Drama: The Major Treatises of Zeami*, Princeton, 1984, pp. 163-171), which in my opinion is quite unsatisfactory. Cf. my review in *Bulletin of the School of Oriental and African Studies* (1985), pp. 591-592.

9.   This term of Zeami's is considered briefly in De Poorter, *Zeami's Talks on Sarugaku*, pp. 55-56.

10. *yakunin*, all participants of a performance, including the musicians.

11. *kanpū*, a style that impresses the spectators.

12. *ichiza jōju* could also be translated as "[The moving style] of a successful performance". From the context we can deduce that Zeami must have used the term *ichiza* in more than one sense in his writings: not only "a troupe", but also "a performance" or "the audience". In many cases Omote even suggests the interpretation "at that moment" (*tōza*) or "on the spot" (*sokuza*). See Omote, *ZZ*, pp. 488-489, added note 139.

13. *tōryō*, lit. "the ridge and cross-beams" (of the roof of a house), somebody with an onerous duty, the leading person, the boss. The leader of a troupe was also called *tayū*.

14. *tōryō no shite*. In Zeami's time the word *shite* was used for an actor in general, as well as for the main performer. In this section *shite* is the main performer.

15. Short song of the leading part (usually when coming on) in which he describes the landscape or his feelings.

16. After the *sashigoto* (or *sashigoe*, nowadays *sashi*), the song following immediately after the *issei*, the main performer also sings the important songs called *sageuta* (sung in a low key) and *ageuta* (sung in a high key). See the fragments of plays preserved in Zeami's writing *Goon* ("The Five Melodies"), Omote, *ZZ*, p. 205ff.

17. This kind of role is played nowadays by the companion (*tsure*).
18. I.e. in order to sing with the main performer.
19. *geza*. In the *Sarugaku dangi* [hereafter *SD*] we learn that a large group of actors (probably the chorus, possibly also the supporting actor and companions) were sitting on a lower part of the stage. See De Poorter, *Zeami's Talks on Sarugaku*, p. 114 (Section 137).
20. I.e. after the main performer entered the stage.
21. Spoken dialogue between the leading part and the supporting part.
22. The singing of one or more actors with the main performer or the supporting actor.
23. Long duet between the main performer and the supporting actor, or between the main performer and the chorus. In Zeami's time sung or spoken, nowadays only sung.
24. Short song at the beginning of the first play of the performance, sung by the supporting actor of the first play. It contained a congratulatory address for the ruler (*shūgen*, congratulatory song) and was specially composed for each occasion.
25. *shūgen*, see preceding note.
26. I.e. after the *kaikō*.
27. *ichiza* could also be translated as "the performance" or "at once".
28. For *ichiza o nasu* Omote suggests "to aim at the success of the performance as a whole". Omote, *ZZ*, p. 236, note.
29. Headdress of an adult man.
30. Wide robe and long *hakama* usually of the same colour in hemp cloth, in Zeami's time everyday wear of the samurai.
31. I.e. the depiction of a character. For a concise discussion of the term *monomane* see De Poorter, *Zeami's Talks on Sarugaku*, pp. 55-56.
32. Now called *raijo*: musical accompaniment when an imposing figure (e.g. sovereign, god, goblin) enters or leaves the stage.
33. I.e. during the whole performance, from the beginning until the end.
34. *ichiza no jōju* could also be translated as "the success of the performance".
35. Omote: "at that moment".

36. *shōmyō*, chants based on sacred Buddhist texts, see William P. Malm, *Japanese Music and Musical Instruments*, Rutland and Tōkyō: Charles E. Tuttle Company, 1978[8], p. 64ff.
37. *sōga* or *sōka*, songs which were very popular among noblemen and monks in the 14th and early 15th century and which were mainly sung during banquets. See James T. Araki, *The Ballad-Drama of Medieval Japan*, Berkeley & Los Angeles, 1964, pp. 56-57.
38. *issai no monomane*, i.e. the depicting of all the various characters.
39. Does not appear in the *Yoshida-bon*.
40. Data unknown. From this anecdote we understand that he must have been a contemporary of Zeami's father Kan'ami Kiyotsugu (1333-1384).
41. Dōyo is the Buddhist name of Sasaki Takauji (1306-1373), a retainer of Ashikaga Takauji. He lived in Shijō Kyōgoku in Kyōto. "Sado *hangan*" was his official title.
42. In the *SD* we learn that this main performer and child actor were Zeami's father Kan'ami and Zeami himself as a child, and that they were performing the play *Shōshō* ("The General"). See De Poorter, *Zeami's Talks on Sarugaku*, p. 119 (Section 157).
43. The ninth tone of the twelve Japanese tones, corresponds to the note A sharp. *banshiki* is half a tone higher, the note B. See Malm, *Japanese Music*, p. 101, fig. 9.
44. Omote: "at that moment".
45. See note 47.
46. Omote: "at that moment".
47. Quotation from the Great Preface of the Book of Poetry (*Shih-ching*). See James Legge, *The Chinese Classics* IV, part I, Hongkong-London, 1871, p. 34, 3.
48. *okashi*, lit. "comicality", "pleasantry", in Sarugaku also "comic acting", "comic play", as well as "comic actor".
49. The meaning of the word *zashikishiku* is unclear. For a concise survey of the different interpretations, see Omote, *ZZ*, p. 492, added note.
50. Omote: "at that moment".
51. *yūgen*, see note 9.
52. Probably the same as Tsuchi dayū mentioned in the *SD*. See De Poorter, *Zeami's Talks on Sarugaku*, p. 115 (Section 138) and Section 138, note 8.

53. *kanjin*, lit. "to raise funds for pious purposes", large-scale performance to raise funds.
54. The *Yoshida-bon* only says *ichiza kokoroete*. This gives the translation: "[the actors of] the troupe should carefully ...".
55. Between March 24th and April 22nd of 1430.

CHARACTER LIST

*: appears in the original text; (   ) the original text only gives *kana*

ageuta	上歌
Ashikaga Takauji	足利尊氏
Ashikaga Yoshinori	足利義教
*banshiki**	盤式〔＝盤渉〕
*eboshi**	（烏帽子）
Eikyō*	永亨
*fue**	笛
gakutō	楽頭
*geza**	下座
Goon	五音
hakama	袴
hayashi-kata	囃子方
hidensho	秘伝書
*ichiza jōju**	一座成就
*ichiza kokoroete**	一座心（得）て
*ichiza o nasu**	一座を（成）す
*issai no monomane**	一切の物（真似）
*issei**	一声
*jo-ha-kyū**	序破急
*join**	助印〔＝助音〕
*kaikō**	開口
Kamo Mabuchi	賀茂真淵
Kan'ami Kiyotsugu	観阿弥清次
*kanjin**	勧進
*kanpū**	感風

Kanze Motoaki	観世元章
Kanze-bon	観世本
*Kyōgen niban**	（狂言）二番
Kyōgen-kata	狂言方
Kyōgoku no Dōyo*	京極の道与
Matsunoya bunko	松廼舎文庫
Meishō*	名生
*mondō**	問答
*monomane**	物（真似）
Motomasa	元雅
Motoyoshi	元能
*okashi**	をかし
On'ami	音阿弥
raijo	来序
*ranjō**	（乱声）
*rankei**	（鶯鏡）
*rongi**	論義 or 論議 ［now ロンギ］
Saburō Motoshige	三郎元重
Sado *hangan**	佐渡判官
sageuta	下歌
Sarugaku*	申楽［or 猿楽］
Sarugaku dangi	申楽談儀
Sasaki Takauji	佐佐木高氏
sashi	サシ
sashigoe	指声
*sashigoto**	（指）事
Shih-ching	詩経
*shin no nō no Sarugaku sanban**	信の能の（申楽）三番

*shite**	為手[now シテ]
shite-kata	為手方
*shōmyō**	(声明)
Shōshō	少将
Shudōsho*	習道書
*shūgen**	祝言
sōga or *sōka**	(早歌)
*sokuza**	即座
*sono hoka no waki no ninju**	その外の(脇)の人数
*suō**	(素襖)
*taiko**	大(鼓)
tayū	大夫 or 太夫
*tōryō**	棟梁
*tōza**	当座
Tsuchi dayū*	(槌)太夫
tsure	連[now ツレ]
*tsuzumi**	鼓
*waki**	脇[now ワキ]
waki-kata	脇方
*yakunin**	役人
Yoshida Tōgo	吉田東伍
Yoshida-bon	吉田本
Yoshimitsu	義満
*yūgen**	(幽玄)
*zashikishiku**	ざしきしく
Zeami Motokiyo	世阿弥元清

"DE JONKER" EN "DE BLAAUWE RUITER": RANGAKU EN NEDERLANDSE LITERATUUR

Jack Scholten

Inleiding

Gedurende lange tijd, van 1639 tot 1854, is Nederland de enige Westerse natie geweest die betrekkingen onderhield met Japan. Vanaf de tweede helft van de achttiende eeuw tot enige jaren na de opening van het land, legden vele Japanners zich daarom toe op het Nederlands, om zodoende op de hoogte te komen van de politieke, wetenschappelijke en technische ontwikkelingen in het buitenland. Dit duidt men aan met de term "Rangaku", dat wil zeggen "Hollandologie". Op die manier heeft ons land belangrijke bijdragen kunnen leveren aan de ontwikkeling van diverse wetenschappen in Japan, zoals geneeskunde, astronomie, natuur- en scheikunde, krijgskunde en zelfs sociale wetenschappen. Ook op het gebied van de beeldende kunst of in de Japanse taal is er Nederlandse invloed merkbaar.

Bovenstaande feiten zijn alle genoegzaam bekend, maar zelden of nooit leest men in dit verband iets over literatuur. Haast als vanzelf rijst dan de vraag of die eeuwenoude betrekkingen tussen beide landen, met name de intensieve studie van de Nederlandse taal in Japan, destijds ook geleid hebben tot verspreiding van kennis omtrent de Nederlandse literatuur. In zijn algemeenheid moet deze vraag echter ontkennend beantwoord worden. Alleen al het feit dat tussen de meer dan tienduizend Nederlandse boeken die door het shogunaat verzameld zijn, zich slechts enkele deeltjes van literaire aard bevinden, illustreert al dat de studie van de schone letteren niet bepaald als één der eerste prioriteiten beschouwd werd.[1] De weinige staaltjes van Nederlands literair proza of poëzie die desondanks in vertaling of anderszins tot in Japan zijn doorgedrongen, zijn over het algemeen te fragmentarisch en te anekdotisch om van veel betekenis genoemd te kunnen worden.[2]

Van de weinige teksten met noemenswaardige omvang en inhoud vallen de meeste strikt genomen al weer buiten het kader van dit artikel, enerzijds omdat het geen oorspronkelijk Nederlands werk betreft, anderzijds omdat het niet meer onder het hoofdstuk Rangaku te schikken is. Zo zijn er bijvoorbeeld op 20 oktober 1820, ter gelegenheid van het afscheid van de gouverneur van Nagasaki, Tsutsui Masanori (1778-1859), door de Nederlanders op Deshima een aantal toneelstukjes opgevoerd, te weten *De Twee Jaagers en het Melkmeisje*[3] en *De Ongeduldige*,[4] beide uit het Frans vertaalde kluchten. Wegens overweldigend sukses bij de Japanse magistraten moest deze voorstelling twee dagen later zelfs geprolongeerd worden. Tsutsui heeft van deze twee stukken door zijn tolken een samenvatting laten maken, die een zekere bekendheid heeft gekregen.[5] Een tweede voorbeeld is het beroemde verhaal van Robinson Crusoë, dat rond 1848, in 1857 en zelfs nog zo laat als 1872 verschillende vertalingen naar de Nederlandse editie mocht beleven.[6] Nog een ander zeer kurieus geval, een grensgeval wat de Rangaku betreft, maar één dat zeker nader onderzoek verdient, is de Japanse vertaling van een Nederlandse science-fiction roman, *Anno 2065, een Blik in de Toekomst*, in 1865 geschreven door de Utrechtse dierkundige Prof. dr. Pieter Harting, onder het pseudoniem van Dr. Dioscorides. In 1868, het eerste jaar van de Meiji-periode dus, was van deze unieke roman al een vertaling gereed, gemaakt door Kondō Makoto (1831-1886) en getiteld *Shin-mirai-ki*, maar deze verscheen pas in 1878 in gedrukte vorm. Daarvoor, in 1874, had iemand anders, Kamijō Shinji (1846-1912), al een tweede vertaling van hetzelfde werk gepubliceerd onder de titel *Kōsei yume monogatari*, gebaseerd op een latere, Engelse versie.[7]

In het algemeen was de Nederlandse literatuur echt geen studieobjekt van de beoefenaars der Rangaku. De verklaring hiervoor moet gezocht worden in het feit dat zij, noodzakelijkerwijs, meer belang hadden bij natuurwetenschappelijke en technische kennis. Zeker in de eerste helft van de negentiende eeuw was dat het geval, toen met het opdringen van de Engelsen, Russen en Amerikanen de studie van techniek en krijgskunde steeds belangrijker werd. De spirituele aspekten van de Westerse kultuur lagen duidelijk nog buiten de interessesfeer.[8] Bovendien was het Christendom geheel verboden, en daarmee was Japan tegelijkertijd afgesloten voor een groot deel van de Westerse denkwereld. Ook al werd op materieel gebied de superioriteit van de "Barbaren" erkend, op geestelijk gebied werden hun zeden minderwaardig geacht aan het Confucianisme. Het meest kernachtig is deze houding samengevat door Sakuma Shōzan (1811-1864) in de slagzin "*Tōyō-dōtoku, Seiyō-geijutsu*": "Oosterse ethiek, Westerse techniek". De studie van sociale wetenschappen als Europees recht en ekonomie nam dan ook pas een aanvang na de opening van Japan in 1854. En nòg veel later, een tiental jaren na de Meiji-restauratie, was de tijd pas echt rijp voor de introduktie van literatuur en waagde men zich aan vertalingen van Shakespeare, Verne enz.

Het lijkt mij een gewaagde stelling dat de onbekendheid met Westerse literatuur in de Tokugawa-periode te wijten zou zijn aan een gebrek aan geestelijke bagage bij de bezoekende Nederlanders, zoals sommige boze tongen beweren.[9] Toegegeven, winstbejag was van meet af aan de drijfveer geweest achter de Nederlands-Japanse betrekkingen, en zelfs Donker Curtius, het laatste opperhoofd van de Nederlandse faktorij, die in de jaren vijftig van de negentiende eeuw met een gigantische boekenimport de kennis van de Nederlandse taal in Japan nog meer trachtte te verbreiden, verleende daarmee niet louter en alleen een soort kulturele ontwikkelingshulp, maar beoogde in laatste instantie ook de belangen van de Nederlandse boekhandel en de orderportefeuille van de industrie.[10] Maar degenen die naar Japan werden uitgezonden, met name de hogere funktionarissen, waren bepaald geen onbelezen lieden, zoals wel blijkt uit de lektuur die zij in hun persoonlijke bagage mee naar Deshima namen. Een aantal vrij gedetailleerde gegevens zijn daarover bewaard gebleven.

Vanwege het verbod op het Christendom werd er een scherp oog gehouden op alle boeken aan boord van de binnenlopende Nederlandse schepen. Bijbels en andere ongewenste geschriften werden in beslag genomen en soms werden er zelfs van alle boeken lijsten opgesteld. Deze lijsten dienden nog een ander doel, want ze werden namelijk opgestuurd naar Edo, waar het shogunaat nog voor het vertrek van de schepen een bod kon uitbrengen op de boeken die het dacht te kunnen gebruiken. Volgens Van Assendelft de Coningh, die in 1851 Japan bezocht en deze procedure beschrijft, waren de geboden prijzen niet te versmaden.[11] Een aantal kopieën van dergelijke lijsten uit de jaren 1845-1854, kennelijk met hetzelfde doel vervaardigd, bevindt zich in het archief van de familie Nabeshima in Takeo.[12] Ook aan Nederlandse zijde werden van 1854 tot 1856 van alle schepelingen dergelijke opgaven verlangd, die tussen de ingekomen stukken bewaard zijn gebleven.

Nu mag men zich van de romans en dichtbundels die op deze lijsten voorkomen ook weer niet een al te hoge verwachting maken, maar toch vinden we er bekende werken uit de Nederlandse literatuur op terug. Zo had Donker Curtius in 1852 bij zijn komst naar Japan ruim vijfhonderd boeken bij zich, waaronder de *Historie van den Heer Willem Leevend*, van het duo Betje Wolff en Aagje Deken, alsmede het *Leven van Jan Punt*, geschreven door Simon Stijl en een dichtbundel van Juliana Cornelia de Lannoy. Verder bezat hij natuurlijk de benodigde vakliteratuur en meer dan vierhonderd niet gespecificeerde anderstalige boeken. In het jaar daarop werden nog eens meer dan driehonderd boeken voor hem overgevaren, daarbij *De Vrouwen uit het Leycestersche tijdvak* van A.L.G. Bosboom-Toussaint (wier *Mejonkvrouwe de Mauléon* blijkbaar ook nogal geliefd was op Deshima), *Karolingische verhalen* van J.A. Alberdingk Thijm, de zestiende jaargang van *De Gids* en nog enige werkjes van minder duidelijk allooi, zoals *Invloed van Sterken Drank* en *De Vrouwen in Frankrijk*. De grootste keuze uit de wereldliteratuur vinden we in 1854 bij de assistent der eerste klasse J.A.G. Basslé. In zijn bibliotheek van zo'n zeshonderd boekdelen treffen we schrijvers aan als Tollens (*De Overwintering der Hollanders op Nova Zembla*), Schiller, Shakespeare, Sir Walter Scott (54 delen) en Alexandre Dumas (131 delen).[13]

Het was dus voor de Japanners fysiek niet onmogelijk om literaire werken in handen te krijgen, en als ze de wens daartoe te kennen hadden gegeven, dan zouden er nog veel meer aangevoerd zijn, want er werden nog wel zeldzamer voorwerpen geëist. Op deze plek raken wij het spoor echter bijster. Er moeten op deze manier, ook al in vroeger tijden, boeken uit partikulier bezit van eigenaar gewisseld zijn, getuige bijvoorbeeld de aanwezigheid van Hoofts *Nederlandsche Historiën* en een vertaling van de werken van Ovidius op Hirado[14] en verscheidene dichtbundels van Bilderdijk in Sendai.[15] Het ontbreekt ons echter aan de nodige dokumentatie, want de aanwezigheid van zulke boeken alleen hoeft nog niet eens te betekenen dat ze ook maar gelezen zijn. Uit andere bronnen is het van een enkeling bekend dat hij zich voor Nederlandse literatuur interesseerde, bijvoorbeeld van Nakano Ryūho (1760-1806), ook wel Shizuki Tadao genaamd. Van hem is zelfs de titel van een artikel bekend: *Ranshi sakuhō* ("Kompositie van Nederlandse Gedichten"), maar het artikel zelf is verloren gegaan of wellicht nooit voltooid.[16]

Als er dus al literaire kanten aan de Rangaku geweest zijn, dan begint het onderzoek daarnaar al spoedig op speurwerk in het duister te lijken. Het is daarom wel toepasselijk dat het juist twee detectiveverhalen zijn geweest die, misschien wel als enige, in de Tokugawa-periode vertaald en door een hooggeëerd publiek gelezen zijn, en, zij het later, hun sporen in de Japanse literatuur hebben achtergelaten. Het gaat hier om twee verhalen van de in eigen land geheel in het vergeetboek geraakte Jan Bastiaan Christemeijer, en de volledig titels ervan luiden *De Jonker van Roderijcke, of een dubbele moord, door den titel van een blijspel, ontdekt*, en *De Blaauwe Ruiter en zijn huisgezin, of een regtsgeding van zonderlingen zamenhang, door de eindelijke ontdekking van eene zware misdaad, opgelost*. Deze beide verhalen zijn in het Japans vertaald door Kanda Takahira en aan de geschiedenis van deze vertaling zal ik de rest van mijn artikel wijden.

Jan Bastiaan Christemeijer

Er zijn helaas niet veel biografische gegevens beschikbaar over de schrijver van onze verhalen, Jan Bastiaan Christemeijer. Hij werd in 1794 te Amsterdam geboren. In december 1813, tijdens de woelige dagen waarin ons land na de Franse overheersing zijn onafhankelijkheid herwon, trad hij als vrijwilliger in militaire dienst. Hij had gehoopt deel uit te zullen gaan maken van een garde huzaren van de Prins van Oranje, maar de plannen voor de formatie van een dergelijke garde werden nooit verwezenlijkt. Uiteindelijk kwam hij terecht bij het vierde regiment dragonders, waarin hij de rang van korporaal bereikte en op 18 juni 1815, onder aanvoering van luitenant-kolonel J.C. Renno, aan de slag bij Waterloo deelnam. Na deze vrij avontuurlijke jeugd vestigde hij zich met zijn vrouw, Anna Elizabeth Doll, in Utrecht, waar hij een veel gezapiger loopbaan begon als ambtenaar bij de provinciale griffie en als huisvader van een vijftal kinderen. Na de dood van zijn vrouw, in 1867, bracht hij de laatste jaren van zijn leven weer door in zijn geboortestad, Amsterdam, waar hij op 1 januari 1872 overleed.[17]

Als amateur-schrijver heeft Christemeijer ruim twintig werken op zijn naam staan, maar geen daarvan is bij het nageslacht bekend gebleven, overigens niet zonder reden. *Vrolijke tafereelen aan de vrienden van leven en gezelligheid toegewijd; Kleine vertellingen, anekdoten en andere verstrooide opstellen; Vedelklanken, verzamelde rijmelarij van vrolijken inhoud* en dergelijke

titels zijn al een voldoende indikatie van de middelmatige, ui-
terst simpele en soms kinderlijke inhoud, die hier en daar
duidelijk een slechte imitatie is van de destijds zo populaire, en
ook door Christemeijer bewonderde, Hendrik Tollens.

Iets interessanter en ook origineler zijn een vijftal bundels
met misdaadverhalen, waarvan de eerste twee voor ons van
belang zijn, namelijk *Belangrijke tafereelen uit de geschiedenis
der lijfstraffelijke regtspleging en bijzonderheden uit de levens
van geheime misdadigers* (Amsterdam, 1819) en *Oorkonden uit de
gedenkschriften van het strafregt en uit die der menschelijke
misstappen* (Amsterdam, 1820). In de laatstgenoemde bundel zijn
voor het eerst *De Jonker* en *De Blaauwe Ruiter* opgenomen. Deze
misdaadverhalen werden echter vaak herdrukt en zelfs in het
jaar van zijn dood, 1872, verscheen nog eens een verzameling in
vier delen.

In de inleiding heb ik de term "detectiveverhalen" gebruikt,
maar misschien is dat niet helemaal juist. De geschiedenis van
het echte detectiveverhaal laat men meestal pas beginnen in
1841, met de verschijning van *The murders in the Rue Morgue*
van Edgar Allan Poe. Aan hèm komt de eer toe in dit verhaal
voor het eerst de figuur van een detective, Auguste Dupin, te
hebben geschapen, die de bizarre moordzaak weet op te lossen
door middel van een methodische deduktie. Aan de eigenlijke
aktie laat Poe zelfs een uitgebreid exposé voorafgaan over de
analytische vermogens van het menselijk intellekt.

Bij Christemeijer vinden we nog niets van dergelijk briljant
speurwerk. De misdaden in zijn verhalen, zoals de twee onder-
havige, worden min of meer bij toeval opgelost. In *De Jonker*,
waarin op een gegeven moment het onderzoek naar de daders is
vastgelopen, wordt zelfs expliciet gesteld dat de mens vaak
tekortschiet en hulp van bovenaf noodzakelijk is om de waarheid
aan het licht te brengen:

"Als wij menschen eene zaak ten laatsten opgeven, dan
treedt er eene hoogere magt tusschen beide. Het is dan
even zoo, als of de Hemel ons, met zoo vele woorden,
wilde toeroepen: zoo ver moest het komen, tot gij,
menschenkinderen geene kans meer zaagt om te helpen.
Dit is eene les, welke velen niet ten onpas komt, die
dikwijls te veel op hunne eigene krachten stoffen. Wij
zien er tevens de waarheid in van de spreuk: Als de nood
op het hoogst is, is de redding meest nabij."[18]

Afbeelding van het gordijn bij de toneelvoorstelling op 20 oktober 1820 te Deshima. "Ars Longa Vita Brevis" was de naam die de Nederlanders aan hun toneelgezelschap hadden gegeven. Tekening vermoedelijk van Kawahara Keiga. (Collectie Nederlands Theater Instituut, Amsterdam)

Tussen de vertelling door is af en toe duidelijk een moraliserende toon te lezen: misdaad loont niet, want de gerechtigheid Gods zal zegevieren.

De opbouw van Christemeijers verhalen vertoont overigens wèl overeenkomst met de latere detectiveverhalen. De spanning wordt opgevoerd door suggestieve aankondigingen van de misdaad, er wordt bewijsmateriaal overlegd, aanvankelijk verdachte personen blijken onschuldig en uiteindelijk worden de ware schuldigen gegrepen en tot een bekentenis gedwongen. In formeel opzicht is hij er echter niet altijd in geslaagd, om zoals Poe, de verschillende getuigenverklaringen en de vaak gekompliceerde intriges vanuit een konsekwent vertelperspectief weer te geven. In *De Jonker* verschijnen hier en daar zelfs toneeldialogen, kompleet met regie-aanwijzingen, wat de eenheid in konstruktie van de vertelling ook al niet bevordert. In het algemeen moet deze tekortkoming geweten worden aan zijn al te grote vasthoudendheid aan het waarheidsgehalte van zijn werk, zijn schroom voor "verdichting", en daardoor zijn onbeholpenheid daarmee. Christemeijers verhalen zijn namelijk gebaseerd op ware gebeurtenissen die hij uit de mededelingen of aantekeningen van anderen heeft leren kennen. Zoals hij zelf toegeeft, veroorlooft hij zich slechts nu en dan een afwijking van het feitenmateriaal van zijn informanten, nota bene uit vrees dat anders "... het zwarte in dit tafereel het gevoelig hart mijner Lezeren daarvan mogt afschrikken."[19] Zodoende is hij blijven steken in een soort halfslachtigheid tussen waarheid en fiktie en heeft hij wellicht de kans gemist om zich als pionier van een nieuw genre een blijvende plaats te verwerven in de Nederlandse literatuurgeschiedenis.

Dergelijke problemen daargelaten, om een indruk te krijgen van de inhoud volgt hier een samenvatting van beide verhalen. Een zeer beknopte, weliswaar, daar elk van beide in de oorspronkelijke uitgave zo'n vijftig pagina's beslaat.

De Jonker van Roderijcke

Op het jaarlijks akademiefeest van de universiteit te G.[20] wordt door het studententoneelschap een blijspel opgevoerd, geschreven door één van de leden, de Jonker van Roderijcke. Enige tijd later, in de kerstvakantie, vangt deze onder barre weersomstandigheden op de schaats de tocht aan naar zijn ouderlijk slot. Hij wordt een eind weegs vergezeld door een medestudent, tot bij een zekere molen, alwaar ze nog een afscheidsborrel drinken. Daarna wordt er niets meer van de Jonker vernomen en men vreest dat hij verdronken is.

Inderdaad wordt drie weken later, als de dooi is ingetreden, zijn lijk uit het water opgevist. "Maar, barmhartige Hemel! ... in welk eenen toestand?!" De ongelukkige blijkt te zijn gewurgd, waarna het lijk in een mat is genaaid. Aanvankelijk worden de bewoners van een naburige pachthoeve, waar ook nogal wat rondzwervend volk pleegt te overnachten, van de roofmoord verdacht. Maar dan meldt zich bij het Gerecht een kramer, die de verdenking laadt op twee schippersgasten die hij in de molen in gesprek heeft gezien met de Jonker, en die een meer dan normale belangstelling voor de Jonker en zijn beurs aan de dag legden. De beide lieden worden gauw gevonden, maar ook hùn onschuld wordt aangetoond, waarna aan de uiteindelijke ontdekking van de daders gewanhoopt wordt.

Bijna twee jaar later, echter, volgt toch nog de onverwachte ontknoping. Een vroegere studiegenoot van de Jonker vindt in een herberg het originele manuskript van het blijspel, waar onder de titel in hetzelfde handschrift een stuk in het Latijn staat bijgeschreven, namelijk dat de maker van dat geschrift zich in handen van zijn moordenaars bevindt. De in allerijl ingeschakelde dorpsschout weet de knecht van de herberg, een notoire schurk, tot een bekentenis te verlokken, waarna ook de hoofdschuldigen, de waard en zijn vrouw, gegrepen worden.

Zij blijken uiteindelijk nog een tweede moord gepleegd te hebben. De dag voor de moord op de Jonker verblijft er in de herberg een koopman, die de vrouw op diefstal betrapt en tijdens een daarop volgend handgemeen door de waard wordt doodgeslagen. Nog voordat zij zich, vanwege de strenge vorst, van het lijk hebben kunnen ontdoen, komt de volgende avond de Jonker om onderdak verzoeken. Deze opent tijdens een nachtelijke tocht naar het "geheim gemak" een verkeerde deur en ontdekt daar het lijk van de koopman, wat hem noodlottig zou worden. Aanvankelijk alleen maar opgesloten op zijn kamer, wordt hem tenslotte door de waard voorgoed het zwijgen opgelegd: "Dien zullen de tanden niet meer wee doen." Dankzij de vingerwijzing die de Jonker op het manuskript heeft achtergelaten, ontvangen alle drie de booswichten echter alsnog hun verdiende straf.

De Blaauwe Ruiter en zijn Huisgezin

In het huis van een rijke weduwe is tijdens haar afwezigheid
een inbraak gepleegd. Op instigatie van de naburige wolkammer
Van N. en op grond van bijkomend belastend bewijsmateriaal
wordt de tapper Nicolaas D., bijgenaamd "De Blaauwe Ruiter",
achter slot en grendel gezet, en voor alle zekerheid ook maar
meteen zijn vrouw, die de vroegere meid der weduwe is, en de
twee overige leden van zijn familie. Enige dagen later verschijnt
er een houtkoper ten tonele, die vanwege verdachte betalingen
met zilvergoed zijn vermoedens uitspreekt over de betrokkenheid
van de timmerman Van E. bij deze zaak. Maar laatstgenoemde
weet de verdenking terug te kaatsen op Nicolaas D., die overigens halsstarrig blijft ontkennen. Juist als men dreigt de
duurzaamheid van deze ontkenning op de pijnbank te gaan
beproeven, wordt er een brief bezorgd volgens welke Nicolaas D.
onschuldig is. De brief heet geschreven te zijn door ene korporaal Rühler, die echter al enige weken spoorloos verdwenen is,
reden waarom aan de betrouwbaarheid van de brief getwijfeld
wordt. Bij nader onderzoek blijkt het handschrift inderdaad ver-
valst te zijn, wat averechts de verdenking van Nicolaas D. alleen
maar versterkt. Gelukkig weet een nieuwe getuige voldoende
bewijsmateriaal tegen de timmerman Van E. naar voren te
brengen om hem als de ware inbreker aan te kunnen wijzen.

Daarmee blijven echter enkele punten onopgehelderd, met
name de kwestie van de geheimzinnige brief. Uiteindelijk leidt
deze het spoor naar de bakker H., die bekent dat hij, samen met
de wolkammer Van N. en diens vrouw, Rühler heeft vermoord.
Deze misdaad is het uitvloeisel van malafide leveranties van
brood en slobkousen aan de kompagnie van Rühler. De gelijktij-
dige ontdekking van de inbraak in het huis van de weduwe
brengt hen danig in het nauw, want het te verwachten buurt-
onderzoek door de politie dreigt ook hun eigen misdrijf aan het
licht te zullen brengen. Daarom pogen ook zij met slinkse
middelen Nicolaas D. verdacht te maken en zo tijd te winnen om
het lijk te laten verdwijnen. Als dat gebeurd is laten ze door
een doofstomme weesjongen de bewuste brief schrijven om
Nicolaas D. weer vrij te pleiten en om tegelijkertijd de indruk
te wekken dat Rühler de wijk genomen heeft naar het buitenland. Al hun listen ten spijt, eindigen ook in dit geval de
schuldigen hun leven op het schavot.

Kanda Takahira

Over het leven van de vertaler van deze verhalen is meer bekend dan over dat van de oorspronkelijke auteur. Kanda Takahira, ook wel Kanda Kōhei genaamd, werd in 1830 te Iwate in de provincie Mino (de huidige prefectuur Gifu) geboren. Zijn vader was een vazal van de kasteelheer van Iwate, die op zijn beurt weer een leenman van de shōgun (*hatamoto*) was. Wegens de vroege dood van zijn vader werd hij opgevoed door zijn oom, Kanda Sanesuke (of Ryūkei), een Confucianistisch geleerde, die ook een medisch werkje op zijn naam heeft staan, *Rangaku jikken* ("Experimenten in de Rangaku", 1848). In 1846 werd Kanda Takahira door deze oom naar Kyōto gezonden voor verder onderricht in de Chinese klassieken bij Maki Zensuke (1801-1863). Vervolgens reisde hij in 1849 naar Edo en zette daar bij verschillende leermeesters zijn studie voort. Ook studeerde hij enige tijd te Kōfu, onder Nagai Naomune (1816-1891), in het jaar 1851. In datzelfde jaar stierf zijn oom, waarna hij tijdelijk naar zijn geboorteplaats terugkeerde.

In 1853 ging hij voor de tweede maal naar Edo en aange-spoord door de komst van de vloot van Perry verlegde hij zijn aandacht naar de Rangaku. Achtereenvolgens nam hij les bij befaamde Hollandologen als Sugita Seikei (1817-1859), Itō Gemboku (1800-1871) en Tezuka Ritsuzō (1822-1878). Volgens een opmerking in Kanda's biografie[21] zou hij zelfs samen met Fukuzawa Yukichi (1835-1901) in Nagasaki gestudeerd hebben. Fukuzawa zelf, die in 1854 en begin 1855 in Nagasaki was, zegt daar echter niets over en als we Kanda's aktiviteiten in deze periode bekijken, dan lijkt het ook onwaarschijnlijk dat hij in Nagasaki geweest kan zijn.

De twee kenden elkaar overigens wel. In het laatse decen-nium voor de Meiji-restauratie was het huis van Katsuragawa Hoshū (1826-1871) een trefpunt van de nieuwe intelligentsia in Edo. Het was een groepje ondernemende jonge mannen, met een brede belangstelling voor het buitenland. Overigens wisten zij zich bij tijd en wijle goed te vermaken, want er zijn ook verhalen overgeleverd over partijtjes met geisha en vrolijk ge-zang, doorspekt met Nederlandse woorden of wat daarvoor door moest gaan. Katsuragawa Hoshū zelf, een telg uit het beroemdste geslacht van beoefenaren der Rangaku, was lijfarts van de shōgun en heeft tevens de uitgave verzorgd van een omvangrijk Nederlands-Japans woordenboek, *Oranda jii* (1858), een verbeterde versie van het woordenboek van het vroegere Nederlandse opperhoofd, Hendrik Doeff.

Kanda behoorde ook tot deze salon en volgens de dochter van Katsuragawa, Mine, die als kind al deze mensen gekend had, was hij een klein, dik mannetje met een pokdalig gezicht, een kletskous, maar niettemin een mannelijk en vriendelijk type.[22] Andere vaste bezoekers waren Yanagawa Shunzō (1832-1870), een zeer veelzijdig talent, schrijver van boeken over medicijnen, wiskunde, fotografie en schaken, en Narushima Ryūhoku (1837-1884), leraar van de shōgun, tot hij het in 1863 te bont maakte met zijn satirische verzen.[23] Verder waren daar nog Mitsukuri Shūhei (1825-1886) en Fukuzawa Yukichi, die beiden deel uit maakten van de delegatie die in 1862 een bezoek bracht aan Nederland, ook aan Utrecht, waar zich tussen de nieuwsgierige toeschouwers misschien ook wel Christemeijer bevond.

Kanda werd in 1862 docent in de wiskunde en het Nederlands aan de Bansho Shirabesho, de officiële school voor Westerse studiën. Later zou hij zelfs tot direkteur van deze school benoemd worden, dan herdoopt in Kaiseisho. Onmiddellijk na de machtsovername in 1868 was hij met Yanagawa en Fukuzawa één der eersten die door de nieuwe regering ontboden werden. De andere twee weigerden, maar Kanda aanvaardde de opdracht en zou vervolgens diverse vooraanstaande posities gaan bekleden, o.a. gouverneur van de prefectuur Hyōgo (1871-1876) en lid van het Hogerhuis.

In tegenstelling tot velen die na de opening van Japan overschakelden van het Nederlands op Engels, Frans of Duits, is Kanda altijd Nederlands-georiënteerd gebleven. Behalve de verhalen van Christemeijer heeft hij nog een aantal vertalingen gemaakt van boeken over ekonomie, de Nederlandse grondwet, de provinciale wet, de gemeentewet en de rechtspraak. Ook heeft hij de uitgave verzorgd van *Seihōryaku* ("Natuurrecht", 1870), gebaseerd op de aantekeningen die Nishi Amane (1829-1897) had gemaakt toen hij bij Simon Vissering in Leiden studeerde (1863-1865).

Op grond van zijn vele verdiensten werd hij in 1898 in de adelstand verheven met de titel van "*danshaku*" (baron), maar een dag later overleed hij, op 5 juli 1898.

Scène uit het toneelstuk "De Twee Jaagers en het Melkmeisje", gespeeld op 20 oktober 1820 te Deshima. Tekening vermoedelijk van Kawahara Keiga. (Collectie Nederlands Theater Instituut, Amsterdam)

Oranda biseiroku

De vertaling van *De Jonker* en *De Blaauwe Ruiter* dateert van 1861, toen Kanda nog een leerling was van Tezuka Ritsuzō. Aan de verhalen gaf hij de titels *Yonkeru fan rodereiki ikken*, en *Seikihei narabi ni migi kazoku tomo gimmi ikken*, met als overkoepelende titel *Oranda biseiroku* ("Gedenkschriften van Wijs Bestuur in Nederland").

De tekst die hij gebruikt heeft was een gekombineerde derde druk van Christemeijers eerste twee bundels, die in 1830 verschenen was onder de titel *Belangrijke Tafereelen uit de Geschiedenis der Lijfstraffelijke Regtspleging*. Hoe hij dat boek in handen heeft gekregen is niet bekend. Op de al eerder genoemde importlijst voor het jaar 1854 vinden we in het bezit van de pakhuismeester P. Lange een boek, in *katakana* aangeduid als *"Berangureike tafereeren oito de geshikiidenisu"*, dat wel haast het bewuste werk moet zijn. Uit de toevoeging *"hanashi"* blijkt bovendien dat het geen echt geschiedenisboek, maar een verhalenbundel betreft. Toevallig klopt het jaartal precies met de theorie dat Kanda omstreeks deze tijd in Nagasaki geweest zou zijn, maar als bewijs daarvoor kan het toch niet dienen. Waarschijnlijker is dat het boek iets later via zijn leraar Tezuka, die ook aan de Bansho Shirabesho verbonden was, in zijn bezit is gekomen. Ook een ander boek dat Lange in 1854 bij zich had, vinden we in 1857 in de bibliotheek van de Bansho Shirabesho terug.

Hoe het ook zij, gelet op Kanda's interesse voor juridische zaken, moet hij zeer geboeid zijn geweest door deze ongewone geschiedenissen en de lust gevoeld hebben de beste daarvan te vertalen. Als we de originele en de vertaalde versie naast elkaar leggen, dan bekruipt ons behalve de ongewone sensatie om dergelijke Nederlandse verhalen in klassiek Japans weergegeven te zien, ook een gevoel van grote bewondering. Wat vooral opvalt is de rijke woordkeus, zoals men van een klassiek geschoold iemand als Kanda mag verwachten, en de grote precisie van zijn vertaling. Natuurlijk is die niet geheel foutloos, hij wordt een aantal keren op een dwaalspoor geleid door de dubbele betekenis van sommige woorden, maar dat mag aan de kwaliteit van het geheel niet afdoen. Een zeer fraaie vondst is de vertaling van de "Latijnse" tekst op het manuskript van het blijspel. Deze passage is in werkelijkheid gewoon in het Nederlands geschreven, maar is door Kanda geheel in het Chinees (*kanbun*) overgezet.

Het is niet bekend in hoeverre beide verhalen destijds al de ronde hebben gedaan, in ieder geval zijn ze gelezen door Narushima Ryūhoku. Deze was zo enthousiast dat hij ze liet lezen aan de shōgun, Tokugawa Iemochi. Helaas ging dat exemplaar verloren, maar gelukkig bleken er nog meer kopieën in omloop te zijn. Vijftien jaar daarna kreeg Narushima, die toen uitgever was van het literaire tijdschrift *Kagetsu shinshi*, één daarvan, alleen *De Jonker* dit keer, in handen en publiceerde dit van september 1877 tot februari 1878 als vervolgverhaal, onder de titel *Yongeru no kigoku* ("De Zonderlinge Klacht van de Jonker"). In 1886 werd het ook nog eens van illustraties voorzien in boekvorm uitgegeven, dan genaamd *Yongeru kidan* ("Het Zonderlinge Verhaal van de Jonker"). Narushima heeft het verhaal daarbij wat ingekort en Kanda's taalgebruik wat gemoderniseerd, met name de wel erg formele *sōrōbun* in de dialogen.

Heel interessant is de opmerking die Narushima tussen de tekst heeft geplaatst, waardoor we een idee krijgen hoe dit verhaal ontvangen is. Deze opmerking staat na de volgende passage waarin de vroegere studiegenoot van de Jonker vertelt van zijn ontdekking van het manuskript.

"Duizenderlei gewaarwordingen bestormden mijne ziel. Ik kon niet geregeld denken. Het bloed joeg mij met drift naar boven. Alle mijn zenuwen trilden. Ik werd beurtelings heet en koud. Snellijk als de bliksem ontstond in mijne ziel eene gedachte. Een donker voorgevoel zeide mij iets. Er zweefde mij een denkbeeld voor den geest: ik wilde het vatten ... Plotselijk ging een ontzettende lichtstraal voor mij op. Hu! nog huiver ik: eene ijskoude rilling greep mij aan. Ik doorzag het heele verschrikkelijk geheim: daar stonden de waard en zijne vrouw, als de moordenaars van den Jonker voor mijne oogen! Ik verbeeldde mij den ongelukkigen te zien in zijnen doodsangst ... met zijne moordenaars worstelende. Hier, waar ik thans zat, lag hij veelligt te stuiptrekken ... in het ledekant, nevens mij, werd hij misschien afgemaakt! ... Ik meende te bezwijken. Het geheel afschuwlijk voorval lag voor mij bloot: ik had het akelig geheim ontknoopt!"[24]

Volgens Narushima beschrijven Japanse en Chinese auteurs een dergelijke situatie nooit zo nauwgezet en is deze passage een mooi voorbeeld van de grote openhartigheid van Westerse literatuur.[25]

Uit Narushima's bewerkingen en vooral uit zijn expliciete kommentaar blijkt duidelijk dat hij oog had voor de zuiver literaire kwaliteiten van de tekst, die voor het Japan van die tijd iets geheel nieuws was. Grappig genoeg vinden we hiermee Christemeijers tweestrijd in Japan uitgekristalliseerd in twee verschillende personen, want Kanda zelf was meer getroffen door de dokumentaire waarde van het verhaal. In de inleiding van zijn eigen publikatie van beide verhalen, in het tijdschrift *Nihon no hōritsu* (1891-1892), spreekt hij zijn waardering uit voor Narushima's stijl, maar deze is toch teveel ten koste gegaan van de feiten. Zoals al blijkt uit de titel die hij aan de verhalen had meegegeven, *Oranda biseiroku*, zag hij ze meer als instruktieve voorbeelden van hoe dergelijke misdrijven door de Nederlandse politie onderzocht, en door de justitie berecht werden. Ongetwijfeld zal hij op de hoogte zijn geweest met soortgelijke verhalen uit China of Japan, bv. die over de befaamde rechter Ooka. Misschien wel om deze overeenkomst nog meer te benadrukken heeft de sinoloog Yoda Gakkai (1833-1909) een nog ongelofelijker bewerking van de vertaling van *De Jonker* gemaakt, namelijk volledig in *kanbun*.[26]

Ondanks al deze publikaties in de vorige eeuw zouden beide verhalen misschien toch vergeten zijn als ze niet, in de jaren twintig van deze eeuw, herontdekt zouden zijn door Yoshino Sakuzō (1878-1933), die er opnieuw bekendheid aan gaf.[27]

Besluit

Inmiddels zijn we echter al aardig ver in de tijd gevorderd en als we naar ons uitgangspunt, Rangaku en Nederlandse literatuur, terugkeren, dan kan niet ontkend worden dat de oogst wat schraal is. Beide verhalen hebben in de persoon van de shōgun dan wel een uitzonderlijke lezer gevonden, maar eigenlijk is alleen *De Jonker* bij een groter publiek bekend geworden, en dan niet eens meer in de Tokugawa-periode.

Toch is de publikatie van dit verhaal niet zonder belang geweest, zonder direkt van invloed op de Japanse literatuur te willen spreken. Na de Meiji-restauratie was het immers één van de eerst beschikbare literaire vertalingen, waarvan de produktie pas later goed op gang zou komen. Voor velen was het hun eerste kennismaking met buitenlandse literatuur. De beroemdste vermelding in dit verband vinden we in het eerste hoofdstuk van de roman *Gan* (1915), "De Wilde Ganzen" (of gans, zo men wil), van Mori Ōgai (1862-1922):

"... Ik herinner het me omdat ik ook een trouw lezer was van *Kagetsu shinshi*. Dat was het tijdschrift dat voor het eerst een vertaling publiceerde van een Westers verhaal. Als ik het goed heb ging het over een student, ergens op een universiteit in het Westen, die onderweg naar huis vermoord werd. Ik meen dat het Kanda Takahira was die het in gewone omgangstaal vertaald had. Dat was geloof ik de eerste keer dat ik een Westers verhaal gelezen heb."

Naast alle andere bijdragen op het wetenschappelijke, technische of culturele vlak, is er dus toch ook op het literaire een, zeer bescheiden, Nederlandse bijdrage geweest aan de overdracht van kennis omtrent het Westen in Japan.

NOTEN

1. *Edo bakufu kyūzō ransho sōgō mokuroku*, Tōkyō: Nichiran gakkai, 1980, p. 222.
2. Wat poëzie betreft, zie Nisei Rankatei Shujin (pseudoniem van Sugimoto Tsutomu), "Seiō shiika honyaku, sōsaku no ranshō", *Kokubungaku kaishaku to kanshō* XXXXV, 8 & 9 (1980).
3. Lijnslager, Philip Fredrik, *De twee Jaagers en het Melkmeisje, kluchtige opera naar het Fransch*, 1778.
4. Witsen Geijsbeek, Pieter Gerard, *De Ongeduldige, blsp. gev. n. h. Fr. van Lantier*, 1795.
5. Tekst en uitleg zijn opgenomen in Shinmura Izuru, *Kaihyō sōsho* II, Kyōto, 1928.
6. Yanagida Izumi, *Meiji shoki honyaku bungaku no kenkyū*, Tōkyō: Shunjūsha, 1961, passim.
7. Id. Ook G.B. Sansom noemt het boek, "*A Dream of the Future*", in zijn *The Western World and Japan* (1950). Geen van beiden kennen echter de schrijver.

8. Zie met name Numata Jirō, "Dutch Learning (*Rangaku*) in Japan, A Response Pattern to the Foreign Impact", *Acta Asiatica* 22 (1972).

9. Yanagida, *op. cit.*, p. 193: "... *orandajin ga bungaku kokumin de nai no ni mo yoru*", "... het komt ook omdat de Nederlanders geen letterkundig volk zijn."

10. Donker Curtius aan de G.G. van N.I., 17 aug. 1854 (geheim archief der Factorij). Id., 16 aug. 1855.

11. C.T. van Assendelft de Coningh, *Mijn verblijf in Japan*, Amsterdam, 1856. Ook geciteerd in Paul, Huibert, "De Coningh on Deshima", *Monumenta Nipponica* XXXII, 3 (1977), pp. 353-354.

12. Deze archiefstukken zijn nooit gepubliceerd, maar wel op microfilm gezet door de Takeo-shi kyōiku iinkai, die ze beheert.

13. Lijst der boeken en brochures die door den ondergeteekenden naar Japan worden medegenomen. Get. door J.A.G. Basslé, 17 juni 1854.

14. In het Matsuura shiryō hakubutsukan.

15. In de Miyagi-ken toshokan.

16. Okamura Chibiki, *Kōmō bunka-shi-wa*, Tōkyō: Sōgensha, 1953, p. 119.

17. Gegevens ontleend aan A.J. van der Aa, *Biografisch woordenboek der Nederlanden*, Amsterdam, 1969 (herdruk), bijvoegsel, waarin ook een bijna volledige bibliografie. Andere gegevens o.a. ontleend aan Christemeijers *Geschiedverhaal der merkwaardige levensredding van een Ned. onderofficier* enz., Utrecht, 1865.

18. Christemeijer, *Oorkonden* enz., pp. 22-23.

19. Id., p. 293.

20. Uit de kontekst blijkt dat het gebeurde zich in werkelijkheid in Leuven en omstreken moet hebben afgespeeld.

21. Kanda Naibu, *Kanda Takahira ryakuden*, Tōkyō, 1910.

22. Imaizumi Mine, *Nagori no yume*, Tōkyō: Heibonsha, 1963 (*Tōyō bunko* 9), p. 38. Dit boekje geeft veel vermakelijke inside-information, niet alleen over Kanda, maar vooral ook over Fukuzawa en Yanagawa.

23. Maeda Ai, *Narushima Ryūhoku*, Tōkyō: Asahi shimbunsha, 1976.

24. Christemeijer, *op. cit.*, pp. 26-27.

25. *Kagetsu shinshi* 28 (1877), p. 7.

26. "*Yongeru-goku*", *Shōnen bunshū* (april 1897), p. 315.

27. Kommentaar en vertaling van *De Jonker* zijn opgenomen in
     de *Meiji bunka zenshū* 22, Tōkyō: Nihon hyōronsha, 1927. In
     de heruitgave van dit werk (1967) is tevens de vertaling
     van *De Blaauwe Ruiter* in het bijvoegsel (*Geppō* 11) afge-
     drukt. Eerder was deze al verschenen in *Meiji bunka* V, 9
     & 10 (1929) en *Shinseinen* (april 1931). Voor de merkwaar-
     dige geschiedenis van Kanda's manuskript, dat een aantal
     keren is zoekgeraakt en weer teruggevonden, zie Yoshino
     Sakuzō, *Kandan no kandan*, Tōkyō, 1933.

SAKOKU:[1] THE FULL RANGE OF TOKUGAWA FOREIGN RELATIONS?

Miao-Ling M. Tjoa

The Dutch East India Company, the Verenigde Oost-Indische Compagnie (VOC) was left to maintain the link between Japan and Europe, after the Portugese were expelled from Japan in 1639. The English abandonded trade with Japan earlier, in 1623, and relations with the Spanish were cut off in 1624.

Of the northeast Asian countries, China was allowed to let her merchants continue to come to Nagasaki, strictly to do business with the Japanese, without any implications for diplomatic status or whatsoever.

Formal diplomatic relations were maintained with Korea and the Kingdom of Ryūkyū (Chūzan Dynasty). However, in contrast to the horizontal relationship with Korea, a strongly vertical relationship was established with the Ryūkyūs, and the Chūzan King addressed the *Shōgun* as his superior. The embassies from the Ryūkyū Kingdom were regarded as tribute missions by the *Bakufu*. The Ryūkyū Kingdom was incorporated into the Satsuma domain after it was conquered by the Shimazu clan early in the seventeenth century. Since the Ryūkyū Kingdom was simultaneously a vassal state of China and regarded as a foreign country by the Japanese, it was relegated to the unique status of being supervised by two nations, China and Japan, at the same time.

In summary, the nations which Japan dealt with during the Tokugawa period were clearly ranked in the following order:

1. With Korea, Japan's equal, official diplomatic relations were conducted.
2. With the Kingdom of Ryūkyū, Japan had a sovereign-vassal relationship, with the *Bakufu* regarding the embassies from Ryūkyū as tribute missions.
3. With Holland, Japan had private trade relations with the stipulation that each new *Kapitan* (*Opperhoofd*), the Director of the VOC at Dejima, had to pay an official visit to the *Bakufu* upon first taking office.
4. With China, Japan had private business deals with Chinese merchants who came to Nagasaki to trade.

Holland and China belong to the group of countries whose dealings with Japan were controlled directly by the *Bakufu*, but without any formal diplomatic relations.

Korea and the Kingdom of Ryūkyū belong to the group of countries whose dealings with Japan were managed by individual domains, - Korea by the Tsushima domain and the Kingdom of Rūykyū by the Satsuma domain. Formal diplomatic relations, were, of course, conducted in the name of the *Bakufu*, the central government of Japan. But all of the diplomatic machinery for administering Japan's foreign affairs resided in the individual domains to which the *Bakufu* had entrusted it. In exchange for handling the *Bakufu*'s diplomatic affairs, the domains demanded as compensation exclusive rights to trade with the particular country.

With China and Holland "inbound trade" was conducted, i.e. the foreigners came to Japan to trade. With Korea and the Kingdom of Ryūkyū "outbound trade" was conducted, i.e. the Japanese merchants conducted their trade respectively in Korea and the Ryūkyūs.

Tsushima conducted its trading, and various diplomatic negotiations at a Japanese concession, called *waegwan*[2] (*wakan* in Japanese) in Pusan, Korea. With this evidence of the Korean trade, it is clear that the Japanese did indeed make voyages outside of their own waters during the Tokugawa period.

Japanese foreign relations in the beginning of the Tokugawa period have been extensively studied by numerous scholars. However, these scholars, both western and Japanese, tend to treat the Japanese foreign relations almost exclusively with the approaching Western World.

So when the Europeans, with the exception of the Dutch, were ousted, this retreat from the Western World symbolizes for many the complete case of isolationism, while Japan's relations with Asia were considered minor and irrelevant to the system as a whole. In analyzing the entire Tokugawa period, European relations have come to play a vital part.[3]

I would like to focus this short article mainly on an examination of Japan's relations with Korea during the Tokugawa period, concentrating on the Korean embassies. In so doing, I shall corroborate that *sakoku* is, indeed, not the full range of the Tokugawa foreign relations. Time and space do not allow me to go into Japan's other Asian relations in any detail.

The relations between Korea and Japan were termed *kyorin* in Korean, - neighbourly relations or relations with a neighbouring country. This term, *kyorin*, contrasts with the Korean term *sadae*, which means "serving the Great". While the Koreans showed great deference to the Chinese Empire (*sadae*), they treated the Japanese officially and diplomatically as their equals (*kyorin*) as was mentioned earlier. Deep in their hearts, the Koreans despised the Japanese and considered them "barbarians" in certain respects, for instance in the scientific and literary fields. They also thought some of the Japanese customs barbaric. On the other hand, the Koreans also admired the beauty of Japanese women, the Japanese landscape, cities, streets, mountains etc. This attitude is illustrated by the remarks made by Kim Ingyŏm (1707-1772) in his *Iltong Changyu Ka*,[4] a narrative poem he wrote about the 1763-1764 Embassy to Japan.

There were also many significant differences in the methods and forms of communication. In Korea's approach to China, distinct ceremonial and diplomatic procedures were conducted without alterations. With Japan however, procedures were sometimes altered. While the Korean government of the Chosŏn kingdom dealt directly with the Board of Rites in Peking, Korea maintained relations with Japan mainly indirectly through the *daimyō* of Tsushima, or *Taemadoju/Toju*, Master or Lord of Tsushima, as the Koreans called him. The *daimyō* of Tsushima not only carried on his independent trade and diplomacy with the Korean Court, he also acted as intermediary between the *Shōgun* and the Korean King.

Japan's relations with Korea had involved a long-standing exchange of embassies, trade and cultural activities, only occasionally interrupted by the raids of *wakō*, Japanese pirates[5] in Korea in the fourteenth and fifteenth century. The embassies were exchanged between the Ashikaga *shōguns* in Kyōto and the Chosŏn kings in Seoul. Trade was conducted in general by *daimyōs* in western Japan. However, when the Ōuchi clan of western Honshū was destroyed in 1551, the Sō clan of Tsushima was left as the only Japanese that were permitted to trade in Korea. Consequently there remained only one single, easily identifiable entity through which negotiations could be conducted.

The Hideyoshi invasions at the end of the sixteenth century not only caused a complete rupture in the relations between Japan and Korea, but also maneuvered Japan into a position of being at war with all of East Asia. When Toyotomi Hideyoshi (1536-1598) died on the eighteenth of the ninth month of 1598, it was evident that Tokugawa Ieyasu (1542-1616) was the *primus inter pares* among the Five Elders (*go-tairō*), who emerged as the caretaker government of Japan. After Hideyoshi's demise, Ieyasu and the other Elders immediately ordered the withdrawal of Japanese troops from Korea. This was achieved in a short time, though with rather heavy losses on the Japanese side.

Hideyoshi's successor Ieyasu, the first Tokugawa *Shōgun*, sought to reestablish contact with the Chosŏn kingdom early in the seventeenth century. Ieyasu had authorized the *daimyō* of Tsushima, Sō Yoshitoshi, to start negotiations with Korea for the restoration of relations between Japan and Korea. That Korea was not yet ready to negotiate with Japan was hardly surprising. As a matter of fact, at that very time the court in Seoul was discussing reprisal raids on Tsushima.

Sō Yoshitoshi tried to negotiate with Korea at the end of 1598, but his attempt came to naught due to the fact that the Envoy he sent to Pusan never returned to Japan. By 1599, Sō Yoshitoshi was authorized by Ieyasu to sent another Envoy. The Ambassador not only brought letters from Yoshitoshi and his Chief Adviser, Yanagawa Shigenobu, but also a number of Koreans who had been taken prisoner during the seven year war, which the Hideyoshi invasions had caused.

It was essential for the agriculturally poor island of Tsushima, located between Japan and Korea, in the straits between Hakata and Pusan, to restore the relations between the two countries. The foundation of its economy had, for centuries, relied upon its position in the Japanese-Korean trade. If relations with Korea and Tsushima's right to trade in Pusan were not restored, the island would be unable to survive economically.

However, after several endeavours by the *daimyō* of Tsushima, Korea responded to his rapprochement in the mid-1600. The Korean government set the repatriation of Korean prisoners of war still in Japan as a condition for further negotiations. Korea's conceivable reluctance was due not only to continuing resentment of the damage inflicted upon them by the Japanese after the Hideyoshi invasions, and the large number of Koreans still held in Japan, but also to the presence of Ming officers in Korea, who were using their influence in delaying negotations between Japan and Korea.

The battle of Sekigahara in 1600 convinced the Koreans that Japan's concern for the near future would be domestic rather than externally orientated, hence not aggressive toward the outer world. This notion seemed to have brought the Koreans more in the mood for favorable negotiations. Due to the domestic Japanese situation however, negotiations did not get on very smoothly over the next few years, in spite of repeated supplications from Tsushima which were always accompanied by repatriated prisoners. The Korean government had sent a reconnaissance mission to Tsushima in 1602. At last, in the late fall of 1604, Korea responded to further pressure from Tsushima. Son Munik was dispatched as an aide to the prominent monk-politician Song'un, who had experience in negotiating with Japanese generals like Katō Kiyomasa.[6]

The Envoys went to Tsushima to investigate conditions in Japan, as an orientation to deciding what steps towards peace would be ensured. Since they did not bring a Letter of State from the Chosŏn King Sŏnjo to Ieyasu, it may not be regarded as an embassy of normalization. Actually Seoul did not expect the Envoys to go beyond Tsushima, hence they delivered only a letter from the Third Minister of Rites, Song Imun, to the *daimyō* of Tsushima, Sō Yoshitoshi. The letter expressed gratitude for the return of the Korean prisoners, especially for the repatriation of Kim Kwang[7], who was mentioned separately.

It is clear that the goal of the mission of Song'un and Son Munik was the normalization of relations between the two countries, since Song'un made clear that Korea was acting in consultation with the Ming government and offered to reopen both diplomatic relations and trade if Japan would demonstrate good faith. Immediately it was arranged by Yoshitoshi's chief adviser Yanagawa Shigenobu, (who was sent to Edo by Yoshitoshi), through Honda Masanobu and the Zen monk Saishō Shōtai, Ieyasu's foreign affairs advisers, that Yoshitoshi was to accompany the Korean Envoys to Kyōto to meet Ieyasu there. After Ieyasu received the Envoys in audience at Fushimi Castle on the twenty second day of the fourth month of 1605, they discussed Korean-Japanese reconciliation with the two advisers, Honda and Saishō. Since Ieyasu did not take part in the invasion of Korea, this fact was emphasized, the Japanese asked that the two countries be reconciled.

As a demonstration of good faith, which Song Imun, the Third Minister of the Rites, had sought, Ieyasu ordered that over 1300 Korean war prisoners be repatriated to Korea with Song'un.

Still Seoul was not satisfied with this gesture of good will, so in 1606 the Chosŏn court set two preconditions for the dispatch of a formal embassy: an official State Letter from Ieyasu as "King of Japan" requesting an embassy, and the extradiction of the Japanese soldiers who had desecrated the tombs of some of the former monarchs of the Chosŏn dynasty.

Tsushima was in a big dilemma. It realized that Ieyasu, as a non participant in the war, most likely would not send the letter which Seoul demanded. Such a letter would have admitted a Japanese defeat in the late war. On the other hand, Tsushima was anxious that trade, upon which its very survival depended, be resumed fully as soon as possible. And full resumption of the trade could not be realized until there was a reopening of state-to-state diplomatic relations, which in turn would not materialize until the two conditions were met. So, while a further Korean exploratory mission was in Tsushima in late 1606, Yoshitoshi, Yanagawa Shigenobu's heir Yanagawa Kagenao and Yoshitoshi's diplomatic adviser Keitetsu Genso, decided to forge a letter from the "King of Japan" to the King of Korea, which met the Korean conditions, and also sent two young criminals to Korea, to be executed as the desecrators of the royal tombs. It was obvious to the Korean court that the letter was a forgery. The letter was totally different from normal Japanese protocol. In particular the fact that the Ming calender was used and the letter was signed and sealed as if it came from the "King of Japan". And because the criminals were very young, it was clear that they could not have been soldiers in the late war. The Korean court decided nonetheless that the time was ripe to send an embassy to Edo and reopen relations with Japan.

The government in Seoul was particularly interested in restoring relations with Japan at this point because the Manchus were increasingly attacking Korea on its northern border, and the Korean government realized that it was imperative to keep the southern border peaceful. Hence the Korean government decided to send a Korean embassy supposedly in response to an invitation from Ieyasu. Ambassador Yŏ Ugil and his retinue of four hundred and sixty seven left Seoul in the first month and arrived in the fifth month of 1607.

It is noteworthy to mention that the Japanese public and even the *Bakufu*, was unaware of the Korean court's purposes,

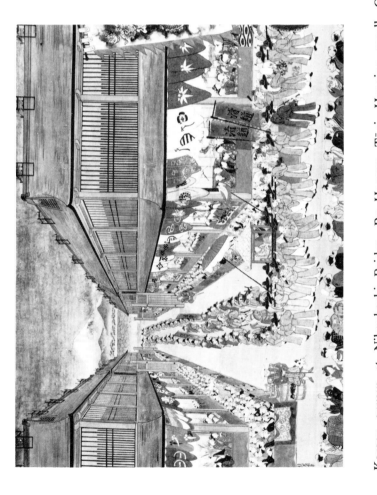

Korean envoys at Nihonbashi Bridge. By Hagawa Tōei. Hanging scroll. Colour on paper. 69.7x91.2. Kōbe Municipal Museum, Hyōgo. (From the catalogue for the exhibition "Envoys from Korea, Japan-Korean Cultural Exchange for 200 Years in Pre-Modern Period", held in the Ueno National Museum in Tōkyō from Oct. 29th-Dec. 1st 1985.)

to say nothing of the forged letter to which the Embassy was responding. Ambassador Yŏ Ugil bore with him a letter from Sŏnjo, which began: "The King of Korea, Yi Kong, offers a Response to His Majesty, the King of Japan".[8]

Thus Tsushima was forced to substitute a forgery which would not imply the existence of a prior letter from Ieyasu to Sŏnjo. The forgery was somehow accomplished by Yoshitoshi's accomplices and the letter that Ambassador Yŏ Ugil presented to the *Bakufu* on the twentieth day of the sixth month of 1607 was written as if it were a spontaneous greeting from Sŏnjo to Hidetada (1579-1632), Ieyasu's successor. The Embassy also delivered letters from Vice-Minister of Rites O Ŏngnyŏng to the *Bakufu*'s Senior Councillors and letters from Song'un to Shōtai, Hayashi Razan, and Senior Officials of the *Bakufu*. The Embassy's chief interpreter, Pak Taegŭn, delivered these to Honda Masanobu the following day.

Some of the issues which Ambassador Yŏ and his party may have discussed with *Bakufu* officials were how firmly established the *Bakufu* was, how secure the peace between the two countries would be, and the repatriation of war prisoners, which was a specific task assigned to the Embassy. By the time the Embassy left Tsushima it had gathered 1418 repatriates from all over Japan.[9]

On their way home, the Korean Embassy stopped in Sunpu, (present day Shizuoka), to pay a courtesy call on Ieyasu "in retirement". Ieyasu stressed the institutionalized nature of *Bakufu* power and the hereditary nature of the shogunal office by insisting that the Embassy present its credentials to, and conduct its formal diplomatic business with Hidetada in Edo.

So the 1607 Embassy had served to restore state-to-state diplomatic relations between Japan and Korea. From that time on, the Korean government agreed to continue sending envoys to Japan to celebrate events of great national significance each time the *Shōgun* requested it. Subsequently, eleven more Korean embassies were sent to Japan during the Tokugawa period.

Hereafter follows a chart of all the Korean embassies sent to Japan during the Tokugawa period.[10]

Year	Shōgun	Korean King	Ambassador	Number in retinue
1607	Hidetada	Sŏnjo	Yŏ Ugil	467
1617	Hidetada	Kwanghaegun	O Yun'gyŏm	428
1624	Iemitsu	Injo	Chŏng Ip	300
1636	Iemitsu	Injo	Im Kwang	475
1643	Iemitsu	Injo	Yun Sunji	462
1655	Ietsuna	Hyojong	Cho Hyŏng	488
1682	Tsunayoshi	Sukchong	Yun Chiwan	475
1711	Ienobu	Sukchong	Cho T'aeŏk	500
1719	Yoshimune	Sukchong	Hong Ch'ijung	479
1748	Ieshige	Yŏngjo	Hong Kyehŭi	475
1764	Ieharu	Yŏngjo	Cho Ŏm	472
1811	Ienari	Sunjo	Kim Igyo	336

The purpose of the respective embassies were:[11]

1607	Reconciliation; prisoner repatriation and "response".
1617	Congratulations on the victory at Ōsaka; prisoner repatriation.
1624	Congratulations on succession to office; repatriation.
1636	Congratulations on the peace.
1643	Congratulations on the birth of a shogunal heir.
1655	Congratulations on succession.
1682	Congratulations on succession.
1711	Congratulations on succession.
1719	Congratulations on succession.
1748	Congratulations on succession.
1764	Congratulations on succession.
1811	Congratulations on succession.

Up till 1763 all eleven embassies went to Edo, but the last one sent under the Tokugawa regime did not go any further than Tsushima, where it met the emissaries of the Shōgun there in 1811.

Nine of the embassies were dispatched to congratulate each new Shōgun upon his accession to power. There was one exception to this practice, no Korean embassy was sent at the accession to power of the seventh Tokugawa Shōgun, Ietsugu (1709-1716). Ietsugu became Shōgun at the age of four and died at the age of seven. On the other hand two extra embassies were sent during the lengthy rule of the third *Shōgun*, Iemitsu (1604-1651).

Incidentally, the congratulatory embassies were usually dispatched a few years, ranging from one to four years, after a *Shōgun's* accession to power, with the exception of the last embassy, which was sent twenty five years after *Shōgun* Ienari came to power in 1786! The reason for this was because the Japanese requested formalities to be postponed due to the prevailing famine in Japan and because the *Bakufu* had decided that the benefits of a Korean embassy were minimal at that moment. Several years later, after the Japanese reopened the question of sending a Korean embassy to Edo, as usual through the intermediary of the *daimyō* of Tsushima, it still took five years (1805-1810) to come to an agreement. After many years of laborious negotiations, a Korean official went to Tsushima in 1809 and met a representative of the Tokugawa *Bakufu* there who gave him a written request of *Shōgun* Ienari stating that the "*Kanpaku*", (as he is most frequently referred to in the Korean records) desires the Korean Envoy to come to Tsushima instead of to Edo.[12]

It is interesting to observe that although, as a rule, the Tokugawa shogunate received the Korean embassies in Edo, the Chosŏn court refused to allow the Japanese emissaries to go beyond Pusan since relations were resumed after the Hideyoshi invasions. So the only shogunal response to Korean embassies to date had been in the form of letters and gifts to the Korean kings, and the repatriation of Korean war prisoners.

There was one exception to this procedure. When the Manchu forces invaded Korea in early 1627 and drove quickly south from the Yalu river to Seoul, King Injo was forced to flee to Kanghwa Island. Kanghwa Island, off the coast west of the capital, was traditionally a refuge of Korean royalty in time of crisis.

After King Injo took an oath of fealty to the Manchu Ruler and capitulated to the invaders on the eighteenth of the fourth month of 1627, the Korean government immediately informed the Director of Tsushima's trading post, *waegwan*, in Pusan of the invasion for two reasons. The first reason was that the Japanese would soon find out anyway. The second reason was that the Korean government used the invasion as an excuse to terminate, or at least to suspend, the Pusan trade. Tsushima, understandably, was unwilling to do either, and Korea, with an enemy at its back, could not resist effectively. But while Tsushima was attempting to exploit Korea's weakness to expand its trading privileges, Sō Yoshinari, as a diplomatic agent of the *Bakufu*, had to inform the shogunate of the Manchu invasion of Korea. It is not clear from the records when exactly Yoshinari reported the invasion to Edo, but the following year, 1628, just before Yoshinari left Edo to return to his domain, Iemitsu summoned the *daimyō* of Tsushima to Edo Castle. He ordered the *daimyō* to send a reconnaissance mission to Seoul, and apparently told Yoshinari that if Seoul was still in military danger, he would send troops to Korea to help to resist the Manchus. But by the time Edo responded to the crisis, hostilities in Korea had long ceased.

Still, Yoshinari had received his orders, and he was not reluctant to use the opportunity to expand his own trading interests in Korea, consequently, upon his return to Tsushima, following Iemitsu's order, he started to assemble an embassy. After extended discussions in Tsushima, Yoshinari named as Ambassador Kihaku Genpō, who had been an adviser on diplomatic matters since the time of Yoshitoshi, Yoshinari's father, and Sugimura Uneme Toshihiro, an Elder of the Tsushima domain, as Vice-Ambassador. Their retinue consisted of seventeen more people, two Zen clerics and fifteen other Tsushima *samurai* experienced in Korean affairs. They crossed to Pusan on the fourth of the fourth month of 1629, representing themselves quite properly as a Shogunal Embassy, seeking to become the first Japanese Emissaries to go to Seoul since the end of the invasions of the 1590s.[13]

Earlier envoys from Tsushima had also sought to go to Seoul to negotiate, but they had all been refused, and required to remain in Pusan.

Genpō and Sugimura Uneme were greeted with considerable suspicion when they arrived in Pusan. The reason was that, although they claimed to have shogunal orders to go to Seoul, they did not bring a letter from Iemitsu to King Injo. All they had with them was a letter from Sō Yoshinari addressed to lesser Korean authorities.

Yet by pleading and persuading fervently, Genpō and Sugimura Uneme, the two Envoys, seemed to have been able to convince the Korean officials that they were indeed a bona fide mission authorized by Edo. And with the help of substantial debate by their Korean hosts, both in Pusan and Seoul, they were permitted to proceed to Seoul. This Embassy turned out to be the only Japanese mission during the Tokugawa period which was permitted to go all the way to the Korean capital.

The Korean ambassadors sent to Japan were called *tsūshinshi* by the Japanese or *t'ongsinsa* (literally "communicate letter envoy", i.e. envoy who carries letters of communication, Communication Envoy) by the Koreans. The embassies they led were large affairs, their entourage even more splendid than the embassies sent to Peking. Each ambassador was accompanied by a group of people numbering somewhere between three hundred to five hundred persons as we have seen in the chart above. And the journey from the Korean capital, Seoul, via Tsushima, to the Japanese "political" capital Edo and back to Seoul again lasted, in general, about a year. The Japanese authorities supplied the expenses and the provisions of the embassies from the moment they reached Tsushima on their way to Edo until they returned to the island.

The Finance Department of the Korean government provided for the supplies of the embassies during their travel in Korea on the condition that it was to be repaid later out of the proceeds of the gifts the embassies received in Japan.

The Chief Envoys were each granted hats, furs, shoes, linen, cotton, bolts of silk, forty bushels of rice and one hundred taels of silver for other foods; the other members of the entourage were provisioned in accordance with their rank.

In order to get an idea of what members an embassy usually consisted of, let us take a look at the following lists of the Embassy of 1763-1764, the last Embassy to go to Edo during the Tokugawa period.

Table 1[14]

Personnel of the 1763-1764 Embassy

3   Official Envoys, Chief Envoy, Auxiliary Envoy and Document Official
3   Translating Officials, first grade
2   Translating Officials, second grade
10 Translating Officials, lower rank
2   Copyists
3   Clerks[15]
1   Literary Official[16]

1   Artist[17]
1   Doctor, first grade
2   Doctors, lower grade
2   Musical Directors
12   Musicians
5   Military Attachés, two for each Envoy and one for the Document Official
2   Army Officers for the advance guard
12   Officers, skilled in archery
2   Skilled horsemen[18]
4   Swordsmen
6   Gun-bearing officers
3   Beaters of large drums
6   Drum-beaters on horse
2   Signalers
2   Assistant signalers
3   Ship Captains
3   Ship Pilots
3   Guides
1   Official in charge of gifts to the *Shōgun*
3   Officials in charge of other gifts and goods
3   Assistants in charge of gifts and goods
1   Official in charge of horses
3   Commissariat Officials
18   Trumpeters, six for each Envoy
7   Sword Carriers, two for each Envoy and one for the Head Translator
6   Handlers of private goods, three for each Envoy
3   Valets
16   Messengers, four for each Envoy, two for each Document Official and Translating Official
17   Messenger boys
49   Servants, two for each Envoy and first grade officials, one each for other ranking officials
24   Sailors
250   Soldiers
1   Butcher

Table 2[19]

Major Public Gifts exchanged between Korea and Japan, 1763-1764

Korean Envoy to *Shōgun*	*Shōgun* to Korean Envoy
50 catties of ginseng	20 pairs of gold inlaid
160 bolts of silk and linen	lacquer six-leaf screens
15 tiger skins	2 gold inlaid lacquer tables
20 leopard skins	100 rolls of flowered silk
30 black squirrel skins	20 lacquer saddles decorated
100 shark skins	with gold inlay
30 rolls of coloured paper	200 rolls of striped silk pongee
2 accoutred horses	
50 coloured brush pens	
50 ink stones	
100 catties of yellow honey	
10 jugs of refined honey	
20 falcons	
20 decorated mats	

Korean Envoy to Each of Four High Officials	Each of Four Officials to Korean Envoy
2 tiger skins	100 pieces of silver
25 bolts of linen and silk	100 bundles of raw cotton
5 flowered mats	
5 rolls of oiled paper	
1 falcon	

Korean Envoy to *Daimyō* of Tsushima	*Daimyō* of Tsushima to Korean Envoy
5 catties of ginseng	2 gold inlaid lacquer screens
2 tiger skins	2 decorated inkstone sets
3 leopard skins	2 decorated stationary boxes
25 rolls of linen and silk	
5 flowered mats	

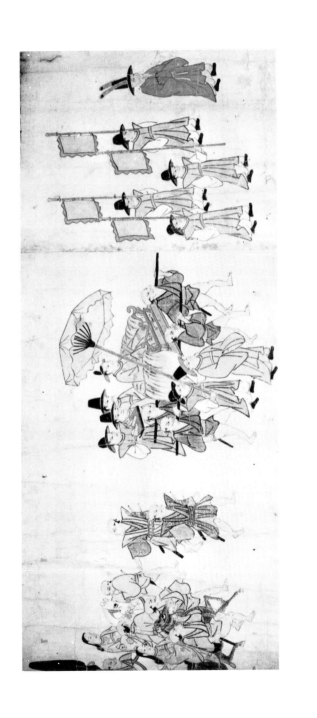

Part of the Korean Envoys of 1624 (Kan'ei 1). Handscroll. Colour on paper. 32.1x984.2. Central National Library of Korea. (From the catalogue "Envoys from Korea, Japan-Korean Cultural Exchange for 200 Years in Pre-Modern Period".)

Table 3[20]

Major Private Gifts exchanged between Korean and Japanese Officials, 1763-1764

Envoys to *Shōgun*	*Shōgun* to Envoys
10 catties of ginseng	1500 pieces of silver
5 tiger skins	900 bundles of raw cotton
10 bolts of white linen	

Envoys to Each of Four nese Officials	Each of Four Officials to Japanese Envoys
10 rolls of silk	100 pieces of silver
3 rolls of coloured paper	
10 inkstones	
20 brushes and a variety of medicinal herbs and other articles	

Table 4[21]

Summary of All Public and Private Gifts exchanged, 1763-1764

Koreans to Japanese	Japanese to Koreans
102 catties of ginseng	2840 pieces of silver (12,212 oz.)
187 bolts of white linen	
127 bolts of white silk	300 rolls of silk pongee
259 bolts of linen and silk	209 bolts of various types of decorated silk
42 tiger skins	
40 leopard skins	1430 bundles of raw cotton
32 black squirrel skins	33 pairs of gold inlaid lacquer screens
195 shark skins	
46 falcons	20 gold inlaid lacquer saddles
2 accoutred horses	
103 coloured flowered mats	1350 rolls of various paper
1096 yellow brushes	5000 rolls of coloured paper
701 inkstones and inksticks	Numerous special items, such as
150 rolls of coloured paper	copper articles, decorated

44   peacock fans
837   flat fans
Miscellaneous paper, oiled
paper, cotton, rice, fish,
fruit, medicinal products,
etc.

boxes, mirrors, umbrellas,
porcelain, dyes, pepper, etc.

The usual route taken by the embassies was, roughly, from Seoul to Pusan over land, from Pusan to Tsushima by ship stopping at other islands as well, to Akamagaseki, near Shimonoseki, sail on through the Seto Naikai, the Inland Sea, to arrive at Ōsaka at last some six months after leaving the Korean capital. Then the party moved on over land, via Kyōto and Nagoya, to Edo, their ultimate destination.

A Welcoming Official of high rank would greet the *t'ongsinsa* and his retinue outside Edo and escort them into the capital of the *Shōgun*. As a general rule the envoys did not stop for an audience with the Emperor in Kyōto, though the chief envoys dressed in official clothes when they passed through the imperial capital. This was, as we have seen above, because the *t'ongsinsa* was accredited to the *Shōgun* and not to the Japanese Emperor.

The Koreans admired the Japanese greatly for the elaborate feasts they offered the members of the embassy, especially when the *Shōgun* hosted the party, at which time, it seems, he conducted the tea-ceremony himself.

One of the important duties of the Korean ambassador was the presentation of gifts to the proper Japanese authorities and in return accept gifts from them. This was not an easy transaction, even though all the gifts were prescribed in advance. There were two kinds of gifts. The first kind was exchanged as a public gift. The ambassador acted as intermediary for the Korean Department of Rites in presenting the items to a big number of Japanese officials and accepting their gifts in return. The second kind of gifts was meant as a personal exchange of gifts between the envoys and the Japanese officials. In addition to this exchange, the Japanese *Shōgun* and some Japanese officials rewarded Korean embassy members of lower rank.

When *Shōgun* Ieyoshi (1793-1853) was inaugurated in 1837 after his predecessor, *Shōgun* Ienari, died, the question of dispatching *t'ongsinsa* was raised again. But once more, just like with the Embassy of 1811, a dispute arose as to whether the embassy should go to Edo or to Tsushima. In 1841, the responsible Japanese official arrived in Pusan to request that the precedent of the 1811 Embassy be followed, i.e. that the Korean embassy go to Tsushima. Due to disagreement over proper credentials and over the destination of the *t'ongsinsa*, (Tsushima or Edo), the plan in the end did not materialize. There were obvious reasons. Great changes had taken place upon the opening of Japan by the American Commodore Perry. And the *shōguns* succeeded each other in rapid succession after 1853. It was decided in 1864 to postpone the dispatch of an embassy for the time being, but when finally an embassy was dispatched in 1876, the old precedents were no longer applicable since the Tokugawa regime of some two hundred and sixty odd years had come to an end. And the embassy which did go in that year went in consequence of a completely new treaty. The hope of Tokugawa Ieyasu, the founder of the Tokugawa Shogunate, to be able to send envoys to Seoul again, just like it was common practice during the early Chosŏn period for the Ashikaga Shogunate to send envoys regularly to Korea to perform ceremonial obligations and engage in trade, was not fulfilled.

Conclusion

Sakoku, taken as the totality of the Tokugawa foreign relations, has been linked causally to the establishment of the Tokugawa state system. Some have regarded it as a necessary precondition to the stability of the *bakuhan* state. Others have taken the *Bakufu*'s ability to cut Japan off from the rest of the world as evidence that the Tokugawa state system was already established in the 1630s. Isolation has been considered a decisive condition, described as either a necessary precondition to, or an inevitable outgrowth of, the whole polity which it supported. Both of these views have merit in them, but neither is sufficiently specific about the nature of the causality linking premise and result. More important, both are weakened by implicitly viewing *sakoku* as the full range of Tokugawa foreign relations.

As we have seen above, foreign relations, especially Asian relations, were intrinsically and organically important to the nature of Tokugawa *Bakufu* and to Tokugawa period history in general: Japan and Asia are inextricably intertwined.[22] It is virtually impossible to remove Asia from Japanese history after 1640 by simply saying that Japan was "closed", for, as we have noted above, Japan was not closed to Asia, nor even entirely closed to Europe for that matter.

Japan rejected foreign intercourse in the 1640s to eliminate the subversive ideology of Roman Catholicism and to monopolize the profits of foreign trade in the hands of the *Bakufu*. In order to achieve those goals, the cessation of Japanese travel outside of Japan was effected. Indeed, the brakes were applied on the contacts with and travels to the *southeast* Asian countries, such as Thailand and The Philippines. This ban on travelling abroad was seen as a great discontinuity in the course of Japanese history. This view has been achieved by, expediently, ignoring Japan's *northeast* Asian relations in order to examine its relations with Europe. Actually there was less discontinuity in Japanese foreign relations in the 1640s than in the 1590s when Japan invaded Korea and found herself at war with all of East Asia.

As a matter of fact, the *Bakufu* actually promoted the trading interests of certain *daimyōs*. It authorized Satsuma to trade with the Ryūkyū Kingdom and China, and Tsushima to trade with Korea in the beginning of the seventeenth century, and those authorizations were reconfirmed by all the succeeding *Shōguns*. Furthermore, the *Bakufu*, in fact, allowed Japanese to travel abroad, mainly to Korea and the Ryūkyū Islands and permitted the repatriation of Japanese from those countries.

Indeed, the external relationships which survived 1639 were important elements in creating and maintaining stability in the Tokugawa regime. Korean and Ryukyuan diplomatic missions to the *Shōgun*'s court in Edo, which continued into the nineteenth century, were important to the structure of the *Bakufu*'s legitimacy. A study of the exchange of envoys between Japan and Korea during the Tokugawa period thus repudiates to a great extent the common notion that Japan was completely secluded. The practically continuous exchange of information and knowledge, as well as goods, between Japan and Korea was considerable. Even though the intercourse was largely conducted between Tsushima and Pusan officials, it was undoubtedly carried on with the full approval and support of the respective home governments.

In sum, the *Bakufu* never intended to isolate Japan entirely from foreign intercourse. *Sakoku* indeed, was certainly not the Full Range of Tokugawa Foreign Relations.

NOTES

1. This term meaning "closing the country", or "the closed country", as C.R.Boxer calls it in his book *The Christian Century in Japan 1549-1650*, Berkeley and Los Angeles: University of California Press, 1951, p. 362, did not exist in the seventeenth century. In fact, the word itself was, strictly speaking, even not of Japanese origin. It was a word which a Nagasaki interpreter, by the name of Shizuki Tadao (1760-1806) has "invented" to use as the title for his essay which he called *Sakokuron*. The first to identify Shizuki as the creator of the word *sakoku* (the word was formed by reversing the characters "*kuni o tozasu*") was Itazawa Takeo in his *Mukashi no nanyō to Nihon*, Tōkyō: Nihon Hōsō Shuppan Kyōkai, 1940, p. 145. The term *sakoku* which did not become a common term of historiography until after the Meiji Restoration, has come to be used to describe the policies and edicts of an era 160 years prior to its "invention". In Shizuki's translation: "Ima no Nihon-jin wa zenkoku o tozashite kokumin o shite kokuchū kokugai ni kagirazu aete iiki no hito to tsūshō sezarashi-muru jijitsu ni shoeki naru ni ataureri ya ina ya no ron", he relied on the Dutch translation: "Onderzoek, of het vanbelang is voor 't Ryk van Japan om het zelve geslooten te houden, gelyk het nu is, en aan desselfs Inwooners niet toe te laaten Koophandel te dryven met uytheemsche Natien't zy binnen of buyten 's Lands" (Engelbert Kaem-pfer, *De Beschrijving van Japan*, Amsterdam: Jan Roman de Jonge, 1733, p. 476); cf. Itazawa Takeo, *Nichiran bunka kōshō shi no kenkyū*, Tōkyō: Yoshikawa Kōbunkan, 1959, pp. 553-554) of Engelbert Kaempfer's (1651-1716) essay, entitled in English: "An Enquiry, whether it be conducive to the good of the Japanese Empire to keep it shut up as it now is, and not to suffer its inhabitants to have any Commerce with foreign nations, either at home or abroad". Shizuki's translation is an accurate rendition of the Dutch, as the Dutch is of the English on which it had been based, but the English version was not faithful to the original German text: "Beweiss, das im Japanischen Reiche aus sehr guten Gründen den Eingeborenen der Ausgang, fremden Nationen der Eingang, und alle Gemeinschaft dieses Landes mit übrigen Welt untersagt sey" (Engelbert Kaempfer, *Geschich-*

te und Beschreibung von Japan, 2 vols., Stuttgart: F.A. Brockhaus, 1964). The phrase "'t Ryk geslooten te houden" or "keep it shut up", which is the basis of Shizuki's "*kuni o tozasu*" is absent from the original German text. See R.P. Toby, "Reopening the Question of *Sakoku*: Diplomacy in the Legitimation of the Tokugawa *Bakufu*", *Journal of Japanese Studies* III, 2 (Summer 1977), pp. 323-324 and R.P. Toby, *State and Diplomacy in Early Modern Japan: Asia in the Development of the Tokugawa Bakufu*, Princeton, N.J.: Princeton University Press, 1984, pp. 12-14. Shizuki started to use this word for the first time in 1801, soon the use of the word spread and before long it was commonplace among *bakumatsu* intellectuals as the counterpart of *kaikoku*, opening the country. See Itazawa, *Nichiran bunka kōshōshi no kenkyū*, pp. 552-560.

2. The size of this Japanese concession in Pusan was 100,000 *tsubo* (1 *tsubo* = 3.305 sq. m.). This is 25 times bigger than Dejima, the Dutch factory, which has only an area of about 4000 *tsubo*. In the beginning of the fifteenth century there were settlements in three different places in Korea: in Pusanp'o, Yŏmp'o and Chep'o. In the sixteenth century the number was reduced to one, due to the fact that riots broke out among the Japanese living in those three settlements.

    Apart from the permanent trading post, a ceramics factory was maintained by the *daimyō* of Tsushima on this concession in Pusan. At times, the population of this *waegwan* reached about a thousand! In pursuit of trade, Tsushima maintained relations with Korea (Pusan) from 1611 into the Meiji period.

3. See e.g. C.R. Boxer, *Jan Compagnie in Japan, 1600-1817*, The Hague: Martinus Nijhoff, 1936; J. Feenstra Kuiper, *Japan en de Buitenwereld in de achttiende eeuw*, The Hague: Martinus Nijhoff, 1921. But on the other hand, Ronald P. Toby, Tashiro Kazui and Nakamura Hidetaka to mention a few scholars, have written several books, essays and articles focussed on Japan's foreign relations, both diplomatic and trade, with Asian countries, in particular with Korea, the Kingdom of Ryūkyū and China.

4. See *Iltong Changyu Ka. Manŏn Sa. Yŏnhaeng Ka. Pokchŏn Ka* in the series *Hanguk kojŏn munhak taegye* 10, Seoul: Kyomunsa, 1984, pp. 89, 93, 109, 135 ("barbaric"), 117, 165,

167, 169, 171, 175, 195, 197, 205, 207, 209, 213 ("admiration").

5. Japanese piracy already existed, on a smaller scale, before the fourteenth century, but due to the national chaos in the fourteenth and fifteenth century, it took on vast forms and became a serious threat to the neighbouring countries. The pirates raided the coasts of Korea and China, operating from three bases: the first base was on Tsushima and the Iki Islands, the second base on the Gotō Islands and the third base on a group of small islands off the southwest coast of Kyūshū near Kagoshima.

6. Katō Kiyomasa (1562-1611), Shimazu Yoshihiro (1535-1619) and Konishi Yukinaga (?-1600) were the Japanese field generals who immediately began to negotiate with their Chinese counterparts to arrange the exit of their troops after Hideyoshi died on the eighteenth of the ninth month of 1598.

7. Kim Kwang, a relative of the Korean king, was taken captive in 1597 by Shimazu Yoshihiro, one of the Japanese field generals. Sō Yoshitoshi located Kim and brought him to Tsushima in 1603. The *daimyō* seemed to have convinced Kim of the imperative need for a full restoration of relations between the two countries, Japan and Korea, for when Kim returned to Seoul, possibly taken back to Korea by Son Munik, who went to Tsushima in 1602 with Chŏn Kyesin to attempt to assess Japanese intentions, he reasoned that need to the court.

8. See Toby, *State and Diplomacy in Early Modern Japan*, p. 33.

9. *Ibid.*, p. 34.

10. *Ibid.*, pp. 36-37; see also Eizō Bunka Kyōkai (comp.), *Edo jidai no Chōsen tsūshinshi*, Tōkyō: Mainichi Shinbunsha, 1979, p. 0 (1st chart) and *Iltong Changyu Ka*, p. 16.

11. Cf. *Edo jidai no Chōsen tsūshinshi*, p. 16.

12. See George M. McCune, "The Exchange of Envoys between Korea and Japan during the Tokugawa period", *The Far Eastern Quarterly* V (1945-1946), pp. 308-325, p. 315; *Sunjo Sillok* 12:40b (Western year 1809; Eastern 8th month, 27th day).

13. See Tashiro Kazui, "Kanei 6 nen Gojōkyō no toki mainikki", *Chōsen Gakuhō* 95 (April 1980), pp. 73-116.

14. See McCune, "The Exchange of Envoys", pp. 310-311.

15. One of these three clerks was Kim Ingyŏm, the writer of *Iltong Changyu Ka*.

16. Among the duties of a literary official was the composing and exchanging of poems with their Japanese hosts.

17. The "artist" of those days is to be compared with our present day "photographer", instead of taking pictures, he made drawings of beautiful sceneries, of important people and events, of something spectacular, of (to the Koreans) peculiar or uncommon things, in short, anything that was worth "recording".

18. The acrobatic stunts the skilled horsemen exhibited in the presence of members of the Tokugawa Family, *daimyō* and retainers were quite spectacular and were greatly admired by the Japanese spectators. See e.g. the catalogue of the exhibition "Envoys from Korea, Japan-Korean Cultural Exchange for 200 Years in Pre-Modern Period", held in the Ueno National Museum in Tōkyō from Oct. 29th-Dec. 1st 1985, pp. 34, 35 & 73 and *Edo jidai no Chōsen tsūshinshi*, 7th page of the illustrations (no page numbers).

19. See McCune "Exchange of Envoys", p. 313.

20. *Ibid.*, p. 314.

21. *Ibid.*, p. 314.

22. See Toby, *State and Diplomacy*, p. 5.

GLOSSARY

Akamagaseki	赤間関
Ashikaga	足利
Bakufu	幕府
bakuhan	幕藩
bakumatsu	幕末
Chep'o	薺浦
Cho Hyŏng	趙珩
Cho Ŏm	趙曦
Cho T'aeŏk	趙泰億
Chŏn Kyesin	全継信
Chŏng Ip	鄭岦
Chosŏn	朝鮮
Chūzan	中山
daimyō	大名
Dejima	出島
Edo	江戸
Fushimi Castle	伏見城
go-tairō	五大老
Gotō Islands	五島
Hakata	博多
Hayashi Razan	林羅山
Honda Masanobu	本多正信
Hong Ch'ijung	洪致中
Hong Kyehŭi	洪啓禧
Honshū	本州
Hyojong	孝宗
Iki Islands	壱岐島

Iltong Changyu Ka	日東壯遊歌
Im Kwang	任絖
Injo	仁祖
Kagoshima	鹿児島
kaikoku	開国
Kanghwa Islands	江華島
Kanpaku	関白
Katō Kiyomasa	加藤清正
Keitetsu Genso	景徹玄蘇
Kihaku Genpō	規伯玄方
Kim Igyo	金履喬
Kim Ingyŏm	金仁謙
Kim Kwang	金光
Konishi Yukinaga	小西行長
kuni o tozasu	国を鎖ざす
Kwanghaegun	光海君
kyorin	交隣
Kyōto	京都
Meiji Restoration	明治維新
Ming	明
Nagasaki	長崎
Nagoya	名古屋
O Ŏngnyŏng	呉億齡
O Yun'gyŏm	呉允謙
Ōsaka	大阪
Ōuchi	大内
Pak Taegŭn	朴大根
Peking	北京

Pusan	釜山
Pusanp'o	釜山浦
Ryūkyū	琉球
sadae	事大
Saishō Shōtai	西笑承兌
sakoku	鎖国
Sakokuron	鎖国論
samurai	侍
Satsuma	薩摩
Sekigahara	関ケ原
Seto Naikai	瀬戸内海
Shimazu	嶋津
Shimazu Yoshihiro	嶋津義弘
Shimonoseki	下関
Shizuki Tadao	志筑忠夫
Shizuoka	静岡
Shōgun	将軍
Sō Yoshitoshi	宗義智
Sō Yoshinari	宗義成
Son Munik	孫文彧
Song Imun	成以文
Song'un	松雲
Sŏnjo	宣祖
Sugimura Uneme Toshihiro	杉村采女智廣
Sukchong	肅宗
Sunjo	純宗
Sunjo sillok	純宗實録
Sunpu	駿府

Taemadoju	対馬島主
Toju	島主
Tokugawa Period	徳川時代
Tokugawa Hidetada	徳川秀忠
Tokugawa Ieharu	徳川家治
Tokugawa Iemitsu	徳川家光
Tokugawa Ienari	徳川家齊
Tokugawa Ienobu	徳川家宣
Tokugawa Ieshige	徳川家重
Tokugawa Ietsugu	徳川家継
Tokugawa Ietsuna	徳川家綱
Tokugawa Ieyasu	徳川家康
Tokugawa Ieyoshi	徳川家慶
Tokugawa Tsunayoshi	徳川綱吉
Tokugawa Yoshimune	徳川吉宗
t'ongsinsa	通信使
Toyotomi Hideyoshi	豊臣秀吉
tsubo	坪
Tsushima	対馬
tsūshinshi	通信使
waegwan	倭館
wakan	倭館
wakō	倭寇
Yanagawa Kagenao	柳川景直
Yanagawa Shigenobu	柳川調信
Yi Kong	李珙
Yŏ Ugil	呂祐吉
Yŏmp'o	塩浦

Yŏngjo	英祖
Yun Chiwan	尹趾完
Yun Sunji	尹順之

THE TRANSLATION OF SIJO

B.C.A. Walraven

"Übersetzen heisst zwei Herren dienen. Also kann es niemand. Also ist es wie alles, was theoretisch besehen niemand kann, jedermans Aufgabe. Jeder muss übersetzen und jeder tuts." (Franz Rosenzweig)[1]

To translate poetry is generally considered the most exacting task a translator may set himself. And yet, time and again, we try. In this article I intend to point out both the difficulties and the rewards of translating the brief Korean poem called *sijo*. The difficulties are, indeed, formidable enough to lend persuasion to the arguments of those who maintain that the translation of poetry is impossible. I myself am not convinced that failure is inevitable. But even if we do agree with these harsher critics, and assume that the translation of poetry can never be completely satisfactory - because in poetry too much depends on *how* things are said, which, again, depends to a high degree on the peculiarities of one language, perhaps not reproduceable in another - it does not follow that one should not attempt it.

Any serious effort at translation will force us to reflect on the nature of what we are translating. We read the text again and again, while our native tongue becomes a foil to the characteristics of the other language, making them stand out more clearly. Viewed in this way, translation becomes a technique for the study of poetry. Moreover, if we do not examine our own attempts at translation only, and examine those of others as well - especially of translators who lived in a more remote period of time - we realize that translation is the transference of a message expressed in one particular aesthetic code to another aesthetic code. Studied from this angle, translation helps us to understand our own literary history as well as that of others. In this respect, too, translation - or the study of translation - can be a method to reach a better understanding of literature.

Selecting those aesthetics in his own language that match the aesthetics of the language he is translating from, is the most fundamental task of the translator, even where this choice is an unconscious one. If the message of the text that is to be translated is too closely bound to the aesthetics of the original, translation will fail, as it will when the target language has no aesthetics that more or less match those of the original language. Good translation sometimes will add something to the aesthetics of the target language and change them, but no successful translation can do entirely without the foothold of already existing, more or less matching, aesthetic conceptions in that language.

What may happen when someone is confronted with aesthetic forms that are radically different from those he is accustomed to, the following example will show. In 1899 a serious and rightly famous scholar wrote about the poetry of a certain country: "Narrow in its scope and resources, it is chiefly remarkable for its limitations - for what it has not, rather than for what it has." One might conclude that such poetry - apparently of a quite inferior kind - would be the poetry of a nation that cared but little for this art, preferring to employ their intellect and emotions in a different manner. How could it be otherwise when their poetry is "chiefly remarkable for its limitations." This opinion was expressed, we are surprised to learn, by W.G. Aston in his *History of Japanese Literature*.[2] We know that, from early times on, the Japanese always valued their poetry very highly, and today Japanese poetry enjoys a great vogue in the West, there being hardly a country which has not its clubs of aficionados writing that extremely "limited" form of poetry: the *haiku*. Apparently, in Aston's days it was difficult to properly evaluate *haiku* and *tanka* because they were so unlike the Western poetry of that age. In the meantime the tradition of Western poetry has changed and there have been translators who have been able to present *haiku* in a manner that is more in tune with our conception of poetry.

Because aesthetic conceptions change, translations of the same work in different periods will vary. Richard Rutt, in an interesting article published in *Korea Journal* in 1973, has given several examples of Homer Hulbert's attempts to disguise Korean poetry as what to Hulbert was English poetry, with true English rhymes and a true English metre, attempts that were guided by the conviction that this was an absolute necessity if one were to make English readers feel what Koreans feel when enjoying poetry.[3] Basically, he cannot be said to have been wrong: English readers confronted with a completely literal translation, making no concession at all to what is considered acceptable poetic form in their own culture, will not easily be captivated by whatever native charms the translator is trying to preserve. But Hulbert went too far, as a comparison with the translations of his contemporary, James Scarth Gale, shows. Gale, too, often tried to adapt to the taste of his native culture, but in a more moderate fashion, at the same time experimenting with somewhat looser forms. An examination of some of his translations will illustrate this.

The *sijo* that appears as No. 54 in Chŏng Pyŏnguk's *Sijo munhak sajŏn*[4] ("*Sijo* Dictionary", hereafter: *SS*) was translated by Gale as follows[5]:

> My dreams last night, how fair!
> A letter from my love, so rare!
> A hundred times I read and read:
> It slept with me, it shared my bed.
> So light its weight, so fleet its part
> And yet it almost broke my heart.

For the sake of rhyme Gale had to add "so rare" and "so fleet its part", which have no counterparts at all in the Korean text. The total effect is polished and smooth; the lines of the translation are almost equal in length, obscuring the fact that this is not a "regular *sijo*" (*p'yŏng sijo*), but an *ŏs-sijo*, with an extended second line (lines 3 and 4 in the translation). Compare this with another *sijo* translated by Gale[6]:

> My home is in the White Cloud Hills
> Who knows to call on me?
> My only guest a clear soft breeze;
> My ever-constant friend, the moon.
> The crane-bird passes back and forth;
> He stands my guard.

This translation is free of the padding which the use of rhyme brought with it and produces a much more "modern" effect. This is not to say that it is much more literal than the first translation: "White Cloud Hill" sounds all right, but in no Korean text is there anything to justify the "Cloud."[7] Then, in the original text the moon is not described as my ever-constant friend, but as the drinking companion of the poet, and, as we may have guessed already, the crane in this poem is not an English guardsman stiffly marching up and down, but just a friend. The image of the guard was evidently suggested to Gale by the verb "to pass back and forth." Nothing in the translation, moreover, indicates that the diction of the original text is heavily Sino-Korean.

In these two poems we see Gale experimenting with poetic forms. Presumably his intention is to be true to the spirit of the original, but, at the same time, he has tried, for both poems, to find an aesthetic form that will satisfy the English reader. Obviously, an entirely literal translation is not his aim.

If we move closer to the present, we continue to see that translators, in their efforts to do justice to the Korean originals, employ the aesthetics and the techniques of Western poetry. Peter Lee, for example, in his translation of a poem by Songgang Chŏng Ch'ŏl, makes good use of enjambment, which in Korean traditional poetry is virtually nonexistent.[8]

> A dash of rain upon the delicate
> Lotus leaves. But the leaves
> Remain unmarked, no matter
> How hard the raindrops beat.
> Mind, be like the lotus leaves,
> Unstained by the mad world.

It is, in short, inevitable that translations will continue to change with the times. Even very successful translations are not "definitive translations". As T.S. Eliot has said in a discussion of the translations from the Chinese made by Ezra Pound (whom he praises as "the inventor of Chinese poetry for our time"): "Each generation must translate for itself."[9]

Putting more general and fundamental problems aside, we may ask what are the specific opportunities and problems which the *sijo* present to the translator? Perhaps the greatest problem lies in the fact that the *sijo* - that is, the older *sijo* of the Chosŏn dynasty (1392-1910), not the modern *sijo* written today - were traditional poems, poems that followed certain patterns and

conventions dictated by tradition, and were, first of all, meant
to be sung. But the modern translator works for a reading
public who do not know anything about the tradition of the *sijo*
and have, on top of that, difficulty grasping the fact that
tradition is not necessarily the arch-enemy of originality.
Traditionality - in the form of fixed patterns, recurrent phrases
et cetera - is in the West still accepted in songs, at least to a
certain extent. But in a printed poem - and only as such is the
sijo introduced to the West - such devices are unlikely to
impress the public favourably.

The easy way out for the translator is, in this case, to
avoid the traditional elements (not too difficult, because they
only show clearly when a large number of poems are translated
faithfully and in a consistent manner) and to leave the reader
the illusion that the whole thing is entirely original. The Korean
text of the first *sijo* translated by Gale begins with the words
kan pam-e, "the night that has passed", "last night". There is an
entire group of *sijo* beginning in this way; Chŏng Pyŏnguk's *Sijo
munhak sajŏn* presents the text of fifteen of such poems. That a
number of such *sijo* existed must have affected the appreciation
of each separate poem in the group. Some will have suffered
from the implicit comparison and have been shown to be unin-
spired clichés, but others will have been enriched by the added
layers of meaning given by the poems associated with them
through the simple traditional opening: *kan pam-e*. The reader of
Gale's translation cannot have an inkling of this, nor, for that
matter, can a modern Korean reader if he has read only a few
sijo.

Some *sijo*, as I have tried to demonstrate elsewhere, are
almost entirely made up out of traditional formulaic phrases, but
the majority are a mixture of formulaic parts and more unusual,
more original phrases.[10] It could be argued that the charm and
essence of the *sijo* lie exactly in this mixture. Of course, *sijo*
are still written and modern *sijo* writers, although they do not
employ the traditional vocabulary, stick to what they apparently
think of as the *sijo*'s essence: its metrical scheme. Not a few
literate and literature-loving Koreans, however, consider modern
sijo a little insipid. This may be because it is the very tension
between tradition and variation that constitutes the attraction
of the *sijo*. A widening of possibilities, such as the departure
from the traditional vocabulary, is not necessarily an improve-
ment. This is clearly shown in another art form: the singing in

p'ansori and *ch'angguk*. *Ch'angguk*, with its many singers, theoretically should have the edge over traditional one-man *p'ansori*, but in reality, the intensity, which makes *p'ansori* so exciting, is lost.

However this may be, the traditional nature of *sijo* does not make translation easier. Particularly the last half of the last line, which tends to be more formulaic than other lines, poses problems for the translator, who will find that in literal translation it comes out weak and colourless. In short written poems, modern Western readers expect some kind of climax at the end. In most *sijo*, certainly, the beginning of the last line contains an interesting twist, comparable to the *volta* of the sonnet, but this twist, too, may be very traditional, as traditional as many of the highly formalized hemistichs that form the end of the line. In many cases, therefore, the last line may appear to be too much of an anticlimax. Richard Rutt has noted this problem and said: "A sijo in translation may .... often seem to lack the firm clinch that the Westerner would expect in a poem whose style and length suggest an epigram."[11] We may assume, however, that this was not the way the Koreans of old judged *sijo*, or they would not have continued for such a long time to fashion poems in this way.

Is it possible to explain the appeal the form had to them? It seems that when the *sijo* is sung, entirely different values emerge. The very slow, drawn-out singing paces the poem in a way that is completely contrary to the spirit of the quick epigram. When sung, the last half line (abbreviated in singing) may be regarded as a kind of coda. It nicely rounds off the poem, often adding a wistful, melancholy note. By returning to the familiar it also serves to set off in greater contrast the preceding lines, which usually are less formalized.

In order to illustrate the blend of the familiar and the new, characteristic of *sijo*, a few examples of formulaically patterned final lines are listed below.

1. "Now she is dead and stays in the green tomb;
   infinitely sad it is." (*SS* 1438)

2. "Now he cannot cross the Wu River;
   infinitely sad it is." (*SS* 258)

3. "Now she is a fragrant spirit at Ma-wei;
    infinitely sad it is." (*SS* 1737)

4. "Now he cannot master the Art of the Sword;
    infinitely sad it is." (*SS* 1468)

5. "Now he has flown to Heaven riding a dragon from
        Cauldron Lake;
    infinitely sad it is." (*SS* 343)

6. "Now he cannot composedly go to his death;
    infinitely sad it is." (*SS* 963)

7. "Now my spirit goes to you, but my body cannot
        reach you;
    infinitely sad it is." (*SS* 208)

In these lines the part that is different is the second group of the first hemistich and in all cases this part is Sino-Korean, a traditional pattern which can be observed in many *sijo*. The parts that are different have in common not only that they are Sino-Korean phrases (of a kind that one will not find in ordinary speech), but also that, with one exception only (Example 7), they all refer to figures from Chinese history; to Wang Chao-chün, Hsiang Yü, Yang Kuei-fei, Ching K'o, the Yellow Emperor and the Sung general Wen T'ien-hsiang.[12] This is, of course, not accidental and can be regarded as proof of the fact that the old *sijo* poets consciously used such traditional patterns. Unfortunately this aspect will be appreciated by few people these days, be they Korean or non-Korean, because generally the knowledge of ancient history needed to understand these allusions is lacking. And explanations will not be much good, for an allusion explained is an allusion spoiled.

The use of allusions is, in fact, a separate, and major problem for the translator. As one can also see in the lines cited above, many *sijo* mix Sino-Korean phrases with formulaic phrases of purely Korean origin. With these poems it is, in many cases, difficult enough to bring out the traditional nature of the formulaic phrases in translation. But how to render the Sino-Korean is a more daunting problem still, what with the many allusive quotations that were meaningful to the audiences of the Chosŏn dynasty, but must, for the greater part, escape the modern Western reader. Here one of the poems of the 18th century *sijo*-singer and anthologist Kim Ch'ŏnt'aek *(SS* 2147) may serve as a striking example. Roughly translated it goes as follows: " When, as spring clothes are ready, with six or seven men and boys/ I enjoy the breeze at the Rain Altar and return home full of glee/ Oh what reason would I have to envy the visit to the Hsiu River." The greater part of the first two lines has been taken out of the *Analects* of Confucius. They are from a fragment in which four of Confucius' disciples relate what they would like to do if their abilities were recognized. Three of them say that they would like to serve the state in various capacities, but the fourth answers that he would like to go out, bathe in a river, enjoy the breeze and recite poetry. Confucius agrees with him rather than with the three others.[13] This poem contrasts the simple joys of the retired scholar with various ways to make a career in the world. Reading Kim Ch'ŏnt'aek's poem without this knowledge, one may get an inkling of what it is about, but why exactly the poet mentions spring clothes, the six or seven men and boys, or the Rain Altar will remain obscure. The last line is interesting, too. It has a familiar structure: a traditional third-line opening is followed by a Sino-Korean phrase, and then a formulaic phrase in pure Korean to conclude the line. The Sino-Korean second part of the first hemistich is again a quotation, this time from a poem by the celebrated Neo-Confucian philosopher Chu Hsi (1130-1200).[14]

With a poem like this it really becomes impossible to produce a faithful translation that will be convincing to the Western reader as literature. We have to assume that the appeal of the poem lay in the way a text from a work which enjoyed enormous cultural prestige was fitted into the typical cadence of the *sijo*. Kim Ch'ŏnt'aek has written a similar poem where he works quotations of Lao-tzu into a traditional *sijo* pattern.[15] It is not possible to carry over the charm of this in another language.

In fact, I doubt that one could find a modern Korean who really likes this kind of poem. Clearly, Korean appreciation of the *sijo* is not what it was two hundred years ago. A modern compiler of old *sijo*, Ch'oe Changsu, says in one of his comments that one particular poem cannot be rated very high, because it contains too many Sino-Korean words and classical allusions. What importance the poem has, he adds, lies in the fact that it shows modern Koreans a glimpse of the spirit and moral values of their ancestors.[16] I would say that this poem also shows us the *literary* values of the past. It is not open to question that the Koreans of the Chosŏn Period appreciated the deft use of Sino-Korean and classical allusions as their twentieth-century descendants cannot.

It goes without saying that we may not assume that literary values in one culture always remain the same. The concept of literature and its functions in the Chosŏn dynasty was quite different from that in modern times. It is this which makes literary translation so difficult. For modern Westerners, for example, it is not easy to feel a genuine liking for a poem that is a hundred percent didactic in content. Then there are the poems that deal with topics that have very little meaning for us. One example is a poem about the frustrations brought on by the impossibility to take revenge on the Manchu invaders of 1636 (*SS* 910). Feelings even more difficult to enter into if we know that the poem was written a century after the invasion. However, someone raised in a milieu where there was continuous talk of castigating the barbarous Manchu and restoring true civilization as it existed during the Ming dynasty, might well be moved by the poem's topic. And such was the atmosphere in Korea during the 18th century, if we accept the evidence of Pak Chiwŏn's story *Hŏ-saeng chŏn*.[17] For us, however, it is difficult to sympathize with the emotions behind this *sijo*.

There are other poems with subjects closer to what the Western reader is used to, that nevertheless fail to satisfy him as literature. A category that comes to mind is that of the, quite numerous, occasional poems among the old *sijo*, poems which were, for instance, sung at banquets. I want to cite one example which, as a piece of functional literature, certainly has its merits.

> *Onāl-do chyohŭn nar-io i kot-to chyohŭn kos-i*
> *chyohŭn nal chyohŭn kos-e chyohŭn saram mannaisyŏ*
> *chyohŭn sul chyohŭn anjyu-e chyohi nolmi chyohaera*

Clumsily translated this becomes something like: This is a fine day / and this place is fine, too. / On a fine day, in a fine place / We meet fine people. / Enjoying fine food and fine wine, / how fine our fine enjoyment. The wordplay, the excessive use of one word, which is the essential point of the poem, is hard to fit into the aesthetics of English literature, but not only this makes translation difficult. There is also the fact that the public for whom we usually translate will read this in cold, dead print and will not be listening to it with a cup in their hands, in the company of good friends. Of course, there are *sijo* of the kind that used to be sung on such occasions, that can stand on their own, but others will never work as translated poetry. This is because the modern western view of poetry does not recognize the function these poems have: that of enhancing the conviviality of a banquet or a drinking party.

This is but one example of the way ideas about poetry change with time and place. It will leave the average modern reader equally indifferent that some poems - according to contemporary evidence - were thought to have the power to cleanse the human heart of defilements and improve the behaviour of the people.[18] To bring about an appreciation of such aspects of the *sijo* in the West would require so much explanation that it is hardly feasible.

So far I have emphasized the difficulties of *sijo* translation, but everyone has read at least a few successful translations of this form and therefore it is obviously not impossible to achieve a creditable result. Apparently the *sijo* offers the translator opportunities as well as problems.

Imagery is often a translator's best friend. Some images translated literally are just as good as in the original. Fortunately there is a great deal of imagery in *sijo* that is easily transposed to another language. Different types of the use of imagery may be distinguished. One common technique is to present a metaphorical image (e.g., a long piece of cloth compared to the long, long nights of winter as in Hwang Chini's famous poem)[19] and then to develop this basic comparison; so Hwang Chini tells how she will fold the cloth, put it in store, and eventually use it for lengthening the shorter nights of spring, when her lover returns.

Sometimes - especially in the *sasŏl sijo* - the comparison is developed to a high degree of elaboration. A quite simple example is the following poem (*SS* 1019). Here love or thoughts of love are "imagined" to be solid objects, which you may load on a horse.

> One by one I'll gather my amorous thoughts,
> When I have a bushel I'll put them in a sack
> Lift it and load it on the back
> Of a big strong horse.
> Boy, crack your whip!
> Go to the house of my love!

In another *sijo* (*SS* 1021) love and parting are in similar fashion represented as concrete objects, which one might buy and sell. In Gale's translation this poem runs as follows:[20]

> Buy me love! Buy me love! I say,
> But who sells love?
> Buy my parting! buy my parting!
> Who will buy my tearful parting?
> No one sells and no one buys,
> My lover's gone; my spirit dies.[21]

A similar technique, by the way, is employed by the modern poet Sŏ Chŏngju in his well-known poem "Winter Sky" (translation by David McCann):[22]

> Winter Sky
>
> With a thousand nights' dream
> I have rinsed clear the gentle brow
> of my heart's love
> to transplant it
> into the heavens.
> A fierce bird
> knows, and in mimicry
> arcs through the midwinter sky.

This poem develops an image which could have been thought up by a traditional poet, although it does so in a modern way; its pattern of elaboration of one basic image is very similar to that of the *sijo* just quoted, and alerts us to the fact that we should not look only at modern *sijo* poets when examining the influence of the past on the present. Sŏ Chŏngju has used traditional elements, but he has used them freely. There is a kind of twist in the last lines, as in the *sijo* but, in contrast to most *sijo*, these lines do not describe the subjective feelings of the persona that speaks in the poem. Instead, they present a forceful objective image, which considerably adds to the impact of the poem. This is not at all like the slowly fading note of the last line of traditional *sijo*.[23]

Another use of imagery is that which we may call "parallel imagery": first one or two images are presented of things, or events, of a rather objective nature; then, in the last line, we find subjective feelings or a situation immediately affecting the persona that speaks in the poem, and the content of this line somehow forms a parallel to the earlier images, which them-selves parallel each other. This technique may give the state-ment of the final line a certain emotional or ironic colour.

An example is *SS* 738, which Richard Rutt has translated as follows:[24]

> Ride a horse through a field of flowers
>   and fragrance will spring from his hoofs.
> Enter within the Wine Springs Hall
>   and scent from untouched wine will stick.
> But why when I only looked at him
>   does word of my love spread abroad?[25]

Some of the images in *sijo* are so fresh and simple that they hardly present any problem. In a long *sasŏl sijo* (*SS* 49) an indignant girl asks a boy how he dare think that he may embrace her. The boy then reminds her that a small bird, the woodpecker which crawls around the trunks of the largest trees, "embraces" these trees. Why then, he asks, should he not be permitted to embrace a girl? Several other images are in this fanciful manner applied to the situation of the boy and the girl.

In other *sijo* the images themselves are rather worn, but still they are easy to understand and often they are so deftly combined that one cannot help liking the result. Are there bigger clichés than the pain of parting that is like fire, long sighs that are like draughts of wind, and tears that fall like rain? Presumably not, but when these three are brought together in the limited space of poem of 42 syllables, as in the *sijo* No. 1680 in *Sijo munhak sajŏn*, the clever juggling of these images may afford some pleasure.

> Our parting becomes a fire,
> Raging in my heart,
> My tears turn into rain
> Which may quench the fire.
> But the wind of my sighs fans the flames,
> so they will not die, perhaps.

Quite a few *sijo* play with these elemental images and as long as there are readers who do not necessarily want a love poem to be a straightforward emotional outburst, but who enjoy the more or less formal play of these poems, their translation deserves to be considered. In any case, owing to the elementary character of the imagery - there will be few languages which do not have similar metaphors - their translation will not pose insuperable problems. Other metaphors in the *sijo* which seem to be nearly universal are those of "flowers", beautiful women, and "butterflies", the men who are attracted to them. (E.g., *SS* 334)

Earlier it has been pointed out how difficult allusions are for the translator to cope with. Not in each case, however, do they form a serious obstacle, as when the images that are the vehicles for the allusions have a power of their own. The bright white seagull so often mentioned in *sijo* will by most readers automatically be associated with the untrammelled freedom of nature. As an example one may quote *SS* 467:

> "Where is your house?" "Over the hill,
> On the bank of the winding river.
> The brushwood gate closed, it hides
> amidst the green of a bamboo grove.
> If you see seagulls hovering in the air
> That is where you should go."

True, if the reader knows the Taoist story in the *Lieh-tzu* about the man who loved gulls and used to play with them, until one day his father asked him to lure the gulls to his house - at which point the birds immediately sensed his intention and no longer came near him - he will more readily understand that such poems are about enjoying nature with a pure heart. But the natural images of these poems will usually go a long way toward making this clear to the reader, even if he is unaware of the allusion contained in the gull-image.[26]

Because in many cultures its call is thought to be expressive of strong emotions, the image of another bird, the cuckoo, almost universally evokes an atmosphere of melancholy sadness; here there is no need to know the old Chinese story of the King of Shu who had an affair with the wife of one of his ministers, then, filled with remorse, abdicated and died, turning into a cuckoo whose call can be interpreted as meaning "better go home."[27]

Other allusions, again, pose not too much of a problem for the translator because a knowledge of exactly what they refer to is not essential. In *SS* 321, a lover says that to him his beloved is as precious as Meng Ch'ang-chün's coat made of the fur of white foxes, while he is to the beloved as the broken comb of a toothless old monk. For the understanding of this poem there is no need to know who Meng Ch'ang-chün was precisely; it is sufficient to know that the coat was of great value, which is obvious and may, moreover, be emphasized, as I have done here, by adding the word "precious." To fully appreciate this poem, it is rather more important that the reader be aware of the fact that Buddhist monks shave their heads and do not have the slightest need for a comb. In translating the poem into Dutch I found this a problem. I might, of course, have added "bald" to the description of the monk, but this seemed a little too emphatic. I also had some difficulty doing justice to the "rhyming images" of the broken, that is "toothless", comb and the toothless monk. "Broken" does not immediately evoke the image of a comb from which some teeth are missing, other possible translations were more awkward and required too many words. Nevertheless, the basic contrast between the valuable fur coat and the old comb is so strong and so easily understood, that even an imperfect translation of this poem can be appreciated. Where such simple, forthright images are wanting, however, an allusion to the same Meng Ch'ang-chün will make it almost impossible to achieve a pleasing translation. An example is *SS* 603, to understand which a greater knowledge of Meng Ch'ang-chün's life is required than the Western reader can be expected to possess. ("Rooster, don't crow! It's too early, you boaster!/It is not Meng Ch'ang-chün in the middle of the night at the gates of Ch'in/Tonight my love has come, why don't you crow a bit later?")[28]

Sijo do not have obligatory rhyme in any form (full rhyme, alliteration or assonance), but, in spite of this, the sound effect of various forms of rhyme greatly contributes to the effect of many *sijo*. A fine example is *SS* 317, a poem by Chŏng Ch'ŏl about two stone Buddha images, standing beside the road, day after day, in all kinds of weather:

> *kil uhăe tu tol put'yŏ pŏtko kumko majo syŏsyŏ*
> *păram pi nun sŏri-răl mattorok majălmanjŏng*
> *ingan-e ibyŏr-ŭl morăni kŭ-răl purwŏ hănora*[29]

The rhymes and alliterations of this poem strongly emphasize the exposure of the Buddhas to the force of the elements. It is not easy to do justice to this in translation, but in spite of that, the fact that *sijo* depend on phenomena like assonance and alliteration *does* present a happy challenge to the translator. These forms of rhyme can very well be used in European languages. Skillful handling of rhyme, alliteration and assonance is not easy and demands much from the ingenuity of the translator, but in principle the opportunity is there. These sound effects are not, as are some allusions, unsurmountable obstacles.

In conclusion we may say that *sijo* can be successfully translated, but that the translator has to face some rather serious limitations. In other words, only part of the *sijo* heritage can be so translated that it will be savoured by the modern Western reader. The translator always has to select poems that, in style and content to a certain degree suit the language and culture of those for whom he is translating. It is not that he cannot present anything unfamiliar, but he has to do it in small doses. The traditional *sijo* was composed in a society which completely different from modern Western society in its customs and thought. Also, the function of poetry was different, and so were the circumstances in which poetry was enjoyed.

To transpose literary works from the Chosŏn period to our own time is, therefore, no simple matter, but the twentieth-century translator has this advantage over his nineteenth-century colleague: the modern public are accustomed to a much greater variety of poetical forms; this allows him to stick closer to the form of the original. On the other hand, the modern translator is not favoured above his nineteenth-century colleague in all respects. In the twentieth century - in the West at least - poetry has become a highly individualistic literary art, which as such may show great variety, but as good as excludes a number of poetic forms current in earlier centuries, such as didactic poems and panegyrics. A translator who insists on translating works of this kind, will have to work hard to find in these poems certain images or a certain style that the modern reader may like, because the subject itself is not likely to appeal.

The twentieth-century translator, on the other hand, is fortunate again in that the reader nowadays may be expected to know a little more about Far-Eastern culture than his nineteenth-century counterpart, which lessens the need for explanations. Explanations are sometimes useful, but they are like scaffolding: the finished building should be able to do without it. In the same way a poem should be able to stand on its own after an explanation has made it accessible to us. The more translations from the Far East are published, the easier it becomes for at least a segment of the public to do without elaborate footnotes, to become familiar with the literary conventions of the East and to gain a perspective which will enable these readers to appreciate Oriental literature as more than something charmingly quaint and colourfully exotic. In other words, readers will no longer only know plum blossoms and orchids, but also learn to value the subtle taste of simple herbs. The translator who tries to broaden the knowledge of his public in this way, might well borrow the words of the following *sijo*, originally written as a protestation of loyalty, but equally valid as the description of the work of the translator:[30]

> A little bunch of parsley,
>> which I dug and rinsed myself.
> I did it for no one else,
>> but simply to give it to you.
> The flavor is not very pungent;
>> taste it, once more taste it, and see.

NOTES

1. Franz Rosenzweig, *Zweistromenland: Kleinere Schriften zu Glauben und Denken*, herausgegeben von Reinhold und Annemarie Mayer, Dordrecht/Boston/Lancaster: Martinus Nijhoff Publ., 1984, p. 749.
2. W.G. Aston, *A History of Japanese Literature*, Rutland, Vermont/Tokyo: Charles E. Tuttle Company, 1972 (re-edition), p. 24.
3. Richard Rutt, "Translation of Korean Poetry into English before 1950", *Korea Journal* XIII, 11 (1973), pp. 21-30.
4. Chŏng Pyŏnguk, *Sijo munhak sajŏn*, Seoul: Sin'gu munhwa-sa, 1972.
5. Richard Rutt, *James Scarth Gale and his History of the Korean People*, Seoul: Royal Asiatic Society Korea Branch/Seoul Computer Press, 1972, p. 237.
6. Rutt, *Gale and his History of the Korean People*, p. 238.
7. Sim Chaewan, *Kyobon yŏktae sijo chŏnsŏ*, Seoul: Sejong munhwasa, 1972 (2nd ed.), p. 211.
8. Peter H. Lee, *Poems from Korea*, Honolulu: The University of Hawaii Press, 1974, p. 90.
9. T.S. Eliot, in his 1928 introduction to Ezra Pound, *Selected Poems*, London: Faber and Faber, 1959, pp. 14-15.
10. B.C.A. Walraven, "Han'guk sijo munhag-ŭi p'wŏmyulla punsŏk", *Chesamhoe tonghyanghak kukche haksul hoeŭi nonmunjip*, Seoul: Sŏnggyungwan Taehakkyo Taedong Munhwa Yŏn'guwŏn, 1985, pp. 63-80. Earlier in Korea, Ch'oe Chaenam, in his 1983 Seoul National University M.A. thesis, entitled *Kubi-chŏk ch'ŭngmyŏn-esŏ pon sijo-ŭi si-jŏk kusŏng pangsik*, had independently accumulated evidence for the formulaic nature of the *sijo*.
11. Richard Rutt, *The Bamboo Grove: an introduction to sijo*, Berkeley/Los Angeles/London: University of California Press, 1972, p. 12.
12. *SS* 1504, which is about the Chinese sage, army commander and magician Chu-ko Liang, has exactly the same pattern.
13. Confucius, *The Analects (Lun yü)*, translated with an introduction by D.C. Lau, Harmondsworth: Penguin Books, 1979, pp. 110-111.
14. Chŏng Pyŏnguk, *SS*, p. 674.
15. Chŏng Pyŏnguk, *SS*, No. 1928.

16. Ch'oe Changsu, *Kosijo haesŏl*, Seoul: Seun munhwasa, 1977, p. 147.

17. Frits Vos, "Yŏn-am Pak Chiwŏn und sein Hŏ-saeng chŏn", in *Koreanica: Festschrift Professor D. Andre Eckardt zum 75. Geburtstag*, Baden-Baden: Verlag August Lutzeyer, 1960, pp. 55-56.

18. Chŏng Pyŏnguk, *SS*, pp. 563 (*Kangho yŏn'gun-ga*) and 566 (*Hunmin-ga*).

19. Chŏng Pyŏnguk, *SS*, p. 672; Dutch translation in F. Vos, *Liefde rond, liefde vierkant*, Amsterdam: Meulenhoff, 1978, p. 51.

20. Rutt, *Gale and his History of the Korean People*, p. 237.

21. This last line seems to be entirely Gale's invention. The Korean text is wittier and suggests that love and parting, because they cannot be bought and sold, are ours for ever.

22. Peter H. Lee (ed.), *The Silence of Love*, Honolulu: The University of Hawaii Press, 1980, p. 130.

23. This is not the only one of Sŏ Chŏngju's poems that might be regarded as influenced by the *sijo*; another famous poem *Mundungi* ("Leper"), too, seems to have something of the *sijo* in its ancestry.

24. Rutt, *Bamboo Grove*, No. 79.

25. A form of poetry which in some respects resembles the *sijo*, the Malay *pantun*, is to a high degree dependent on this technique of parallel imagery. One example will have to suffice: *Asal kapas menjadi benang / Asal benang menjadi kain / Sudah lepas jangan dikenang / Sudah menjadi orang lain* (What first was cotton becomes thread / What first was thread becomes cloth. / Don't think of what has passed, / Already I have become someone else); W. Braasem, *Pantuns*, Djakarta/Amsterdam/Surabaia: De Moderne Boekhandel Indonesië, 1950, p. 44.

26. For a translation of this passage see A.C. Graham (transl.), *The Book of Lieh-Tzu*, London: John Murray, 1960, pp. 45-46.

27. Some prefer to call this bird a nightjar. Ornithologically they may be right, but for literary translation "cuckoo" is to be preferred, because of the melancholy associations evoked by its call.

28. Even if the reader knows about Meng Ch'ang-chün it will do not much for the poem; the allusion is not very apt. Meng made his escape from Ch'in during the night with the

help of a man who imitated the crow of the cock, making the guards of the city gates believe that day had broken and that it was time to open the gates.

29. A Dutch translation can be found in Frits Vos, *Liefde rond, liefde vierkant*, p. 39:

> Aan de weg staan twee stenen boeddha's
> naakt en hongerig tegenover elkaar.
> Voortdurend worden zij geteisterd
> door wind, regen, sneeuw en vorst.
> Toch ben ik vol afgunst op hen,
> zij weten niet van de pijn van een scheiding...

30. The poem is by Yu Hüich'un (1513-1577), the translation by Richard Rutt, *Bamboo Grove*, No. 58.

GLOSSARY OF CHINESE CHARACTERS

ch'anggŭk	唱劇
Chesamhoe Tongyanghak kukche	第三回東洋學國際
haksul hoeŭi nonmunjip	學術會議論文集
Ch'in	秦
Ching K'o	荊軻
Ch'oe Changsu	崔長洙
Ch'oe Chaenam	崔載南
Chosŏn	朝鮮
Chŏng Ch'ŏl, see: Songgang -- --	
Chŏng Pyŏnguk	鄭炳昱
Chu Hsi	朱熹
Chu-ko Liang	諸葛亮
haiku	俳句
"Han'guk sijo munhag-ŭi	
p'wŏmyulla punsŏk"	韓國時調文學‑‑分析
Hŏ-saeng chŏn	許生傳
Hsiang Yü	項羽
Hunmin-ga	訓民歌
Hsiu River	泗江
Hwang Chini	黄真伊
Kangho yŏn'gun-ga	江湖戀君歌
Kim Ch'ŏnt'aek	金天澤
Kosijo haesŏl	古時調解説
Kubi-jŏk chŭngmyŏn-esŏ pon sijo-ŭi	口碑的 側面‑‑ ‑時調‑
si-jŏk kusŏng pangsik	詩的 構成方式
Kyobon yŏktae sijo chŏnsŏ	校本 歷代時調全書
Lieh-tzu	列子

Lun-yü	論語
Ma-wei	馬嵬
Meng Ch'ang-chün	孟嘗君
ŏs-sijo	蔥時調
Pak Chiwŏn, see: Yŏnam -- --	
p'yŏng sijo	平時調
sasŏl sijo	辭說時調
Shu	蜀
sijo	時調
Sijo munhak sajŏn	時調文學事典
Sim Chaewan	沈載完
Songgang Chŏng Ch'ŏl	松江 鄭澈
Sŏ Chŏngju	徐廷柱
tanka	短歌
Wang Chao-chün	王昭君
Wen T'ien-hsiang	文天祥
Wu River	烏江
Yang Kuei-fei	楊貴妃
Yŏnam Pak Chiwŏn	燕巖 朴趾源
Yu Hŭich'un	柳希春